FROMMER'S
1983-84 GUIDE TO PARIS

by Darwin Porter

Published by Frommer/Pasmantier Publishers
A Simon & Schuster Division of
Gulf & Western Corporation
1230 Avenue of the Americas
New York, NY 10020

ISBN 0-671-44795-5

Manufactured in the United States of America

Motif drawings by Erv Chips

*Although every effort was made to ensure the accuracy
of price information appearing in this book,
it should be kept in mind that prices
can and do fluctuate in the course of time.*

CONTENTS

MAPS

The Franc and the Dollar—and Inflation

As we go to press, the franc, like all currencies, is still fluctuating on the world market—which means that our franc-to-dollar conversions appearing in parentheses throughout these chapters may or may not be exact. At the time this edition was researched, one franc was worth approximately 18 U.S. cents (about 5.60 francs to the dollar), and the conversions were calculated on that basis. However, since there is no sure way to predict what the rate of exchange will be when you visit France, we suggest you check with a banker at home or in Paris to determine the up-to-date figure. In any case, our dollar conversions will still give you a fair idea of what you'll be spending—use them only as a gauge.

As for the prices quoted in francs throughout these pages, they are all accurate at press time, but, inflation being what it is worldwide, they cannot be guaranteed. The wise traveler will allow for increases in the prices given, particularly in the second year (1984) of this edition's lifetime.

Francs	Dollars	Francs	Dollars
0.10	$ .02	20	$ 3.57
0.50	.09	25	4.46
1	.18	30	5.36
2	.36	35	6.25
3	.54	40	7.14
4	.71	45	8.03
5	.89	50	8.93
6	1.07	75	13.39
7	1.25	100	17.85
8	1.43	110	19.64
9	1.61	120	21.42
10	1.79	130	23.21
11	1.96	140	24.99
12	2.14	150	26.78
13	2.32	175	31.24
14	2.50	200	35.70
15	2.68	250	44.60
		500	89.25

Chapter I

ÇA C'EST PARIS!

PARIS HAS BEEN CELEBRATED in such a torrent of songs, poems, stories, books, paintings, and movies that for millions of people she is an abstraction rather than a city.

Mention her name to a foreigner and you produce an instant image of sidewalk cafés and strolling lovers beneath the Eiffel Tower. Mention her women and you conjure up a vision that is part Catherine Deneuve, part Madame Defarge, part Simone de Beauvoir—a powerful combination.

To French people living in the provinces, Paris is the center of a universe, the place where laws and careers are made and broken, a giant magnet that draws the essence out of the country, a bubbling test tube eternally distilling new and alien ideas.

To North American tourists, she is still "Gay Paree," the fairytale town inviting you for a fling, the hub of everything "European," and the epitome of that nebulous attribute known as "chic." She remains the metropolis of pleasure, the picture postcard of blooming chestnut trees and young couples kissing by the Seine.

Some of these images may be very dated, some more fantasy than fact. And yet through all the clichés threads an eternal reality, that special aura of enchantment that neither technical progress nor commercialization has been able to dispel.

PARIS FOR US ALL: To Hemingway, Paris was "a moveable feast," the city to which "there is never any ending."

To us, Paris is the glamor capital of the globe, by day a stone mosaic of delicate gray and green, by night a stunning, unforgettable sea of lights—white, red, orange.

Broad, tree-lined boulevards open up before you, the mansions flanking them looming tall, ornate, and graceful. Everywhere you look are trees, squares, and monuments. Perhaps you'll come in spring when the trees lining the Esplanade are white with blossoms. In summer they turn a deep, lush green; in fall, golden russet.

Whether you see it for the first or fiftieth time, the effect always has a curiously personal note . . . this is Paris, beckoning to *me*. And the "me" is all mankind.

As novelist Romain Gary once put it: "The kid will come from Nebraska or Heidelberg, from Poland or Senegal, and Paris will be born again—new, brand-new, and unexpected, and the Arch of Triumph will rise again, and the Seine will flow for the first time, and there will be new areas, unknown, and unexplored, called Montmartre and Montparnasse—and it will all be for the first time, a completely new city, built suddenly for you and you alone."

The discovery of the city and making it your own is and has always been the most compelling reason for coming to Paris. So many have come, and so many continue to come, that France has been called *le deuxième pays de tout le monde*—"everyone's second country."

A CASE OF PREDESTINATION: Paris owes her position to a river, her status to a revolution, and her beauty to a tyrant.

More than 2000 years ago, a tribe of Gauls called the Parisii built a village on the larger of two islands rising out of the broad and navigable Seine. They couldn't have picked a better site. The island provided a stepping-stone for the communication route that ran from the cold European north to the sunny Mediterranean.

The Roman conquerors of Gaul found the place ideal for a fortified town, surrounded as it was by a natural moat of water. This island, now the Île de la Cité, was the egg from which modern Paris was hatched.

Gradually, as the city grew more populous, it spilled over onto both banks of the Seine, spreading farther and farther inland. From the air, the expansion of Paris can be seen as clearly as the age rings of a sliced tree trunk. With la Cité at the core—looking curiously like an anchored battleship—the mass of houses pushes outward in concentric circles, each ring representing a former boundary line overrun by the swelling metropolis.

Most cities become national capitals by accident. With Paris, it was predestination as soon as there was such a country as France. Standing at the meeting point of the Teutonic North and the Latin South, she was the logical seat of government for whichever faction would dominate the nation.

Nothing could alter her position as the first city of the land—not even 20 years of occupation by the English and their Burgundian allies, who held the area until driven out in 1437 by the army, spurred on by Joan of Arc.

BARRICADES AND BOULEVARDS: But until the thunderbolt year of 1789, Paris was no more than merely the brightest bauble in the crowns of her variegated monarchs, a piece of real estate to be trimmed or decorated as it pleased the royal whim.

Louis XIV, the "Sun King" and most absolute of all absolute monarchs, decided that he didn't like Paris, and he transferred his seat of government to Versailles. There he turned a hunting lodge into the most fabulous palace the world had ever seen, staffed it with 6000 officials and servants, and left Paris as a capital in name only.

The city's revenge for this slight had to wait until the Revolution, and Louis XVI. One of the first acts of the Paris mob was to march out to Versailles, slaughter the Swiss palace guards, and drag the absentee king, and thus the government, *back* to Paris.

Today, you'll find few visible traces of the Revolution in Paris. The **Bastille** was totally leveled; the square that saw the "National Razor" shave off cartloads of heads is today the dazzling **Place de la Concorde,** and the old **Hôtel de Ville,** from which Danton and Robespierre conducted the Terror, burned down more than 80 years ago.

But the spiritual heritage of the Revolution lingers on. It gives the city her jauntily independent swagger, her sardonic contempt for "provincials," the knowledge that her wishes are commands to the powers that be.

Which they are. Unlike, say, the administrations of Washington, D.C., every French government has had to cock a sharp ear to the murmurs of its capital. The stark fear of those terrible mobs and their barricades is unbroken to this day. Even the great Bonaparte never bothered to hide his concern about "What will Paris say?"

The Revolution gained Paris a power she never relinquished. All authority in France radiates from her; all roads lead to her. She houses a quarter of all the nation's civil servants and more than a third of all university students.

It took a buffoonish demagogue, however, to bestow upon Paris the beauty that made her the envy of the civilized world. He was Napoleon III, nephew of the Corsican, who made himself first president, then emperor of France. Victor Hugo dubbed him "Napoleon the Little"—and had to spend years in exile for that crack.

The "other" Bonaparte may have been a terrible general and a dismal politician, but he had an inspired touch when it came to city planning. Together with Baron Haussmann, the prefect of Paris, he gave the capital the most lavishly magnificent facelift any municipality has ever received.

Between 1860 and 1870 the maze of winding cobblestone streets in the ancient quarters of the city were penetrated by superb boulevards—wide, rule-straight, flanked by palatial buildings and shaded by some 250,000 chestnut and plum trees. Their names became architectural legends: the **Boulevards St-Michel, St-Germain, Haussmann, Malesherbes, Sébastopol, Magenta, Voltaire,** and **Strasbourg.**

Haussmann cleared the Île de la Cité of its medieval brickwork and stench, and transformed it into a showcase for **Notre-Dame Cathedral.** He created the **Avenue de l'Opéra** (as well as the **Opéra**) and the 12 avenues that radiate star-like from the **Arc de Triomphe** and give the square its name of **Place de l'Étoile** (renamed **Place Charles de Gaulle** following the general's death, although the change met with great resistance). Finally, he laid out the two wonderful parks on the western and southeastern fringes of the city: the **Bois de Boulogne** and the **Bois de Vincennes.**

When Napoleon III, his face heavily rouged to hide the agony caused by bladder stones, rode into Prussian captivity in 1871, he left behind him a defeated nation and a shattered army. But he also bequeathed to it the most stunning capital on earth.

A THREE-DIMENSIONAL BEAUTY: The beauty of Paris is more than skin deep; it goes in three layers right down to the city's bones. The first layer is thrust upon you immediately; the second permeates you slowly, like the afterglow of good cognac; the third you have to go out and discover.

The top layer consists of the breathtaking spectacles presented by, for instance, the sweep of the **Champs-Élysées** at night, with the floodlit **Arc de Triomphe** in the distance, or the fountain-sprayed **Trocadéro** by the **Eiffel Tower.**

The second stage offers less flamboyance and more intimacy, like the old stone **Seine bridges** at twilight, or the dreamy quiet of the **Place des Vosges.** The mood prevails at any one of a hundred sidewalk cafés in the early afternoon, the sun throwing patterns on the tables through the lacework of overhead leaves.

The third layer—and perhaps the finest—is reserved for explorers, those who take time to nose through narrow alleys and poke into half-hidden courtyards or climb hills instead of riding up. A sudden glimpse so utterly enchanting that one is at a loss even to snap a picture proves the explorer's reward. It may be a small Renaissance figure carved into a moss-covered church wall. Or a secret garden patch behind a Gothic archway. Or a totally unexpected view of the gleaming white dome of **Sacré-Coeur** high up on **Montmartre.** Or the jewel-box charm of the tiny, silent **Place Fürstenberg,** with its four trees and single streetlight, just one step away from the bustle of the **Boulevard St-Germain.**

Only when you've penetrated this triple layer can you appreciate the gem that is Paris. But there's danger in this knowledge . . . you may find yourself hooked on her for life, and become one of the thousands of foreigners who discover that they can't really be happy anywhere else.

MEET THE NATIVES: If the three million or so Parisians share one characteristic, it is their big-city spirit, the somewhat aggressive, novelty-addicted, extremely cynical metropolitanism that makes "provincial" the worst insult in their dictionary.

Tolerance, gentleness, and patience are not their strongest points. They don't suffer fools gladly (although they adore eccentrics), and the gravest crime a public figure can commit in their eyes is to make himself ridiculous.

Their wit has been dreaded for centuries. It is totally lacking in Cockney good humor or American folksiness, and can cut like a razor. A fairly typical sample would be the *bon mot* coined at the expense of a sadly disappointing prime minister named M. Marie. The Parisians promptly called him "The Immaculate Deception."

Foreign visitors frequently find Parisians brusque to the point of rudeness, exclusively preoccupied with their own affairs, and unwilling to go out of their way for anyone else's benefit. This, however, is not a symptom of xenophobia. They are just as tough with each other.

The Parisians' behavior pattern is produced by their environment. Paris, for all its matchless splendor, is a hard place in which to scramble for a living. Working hours are long, competition murderous, the traffic nerve-grinding, accommodations crowded and difficult to get, the pace hectic, and the cost of everything the highest in the country.

Add to this the generally low rates of pay, the mocking showcases of a thousand unattainable luxuries, and the jungle of red tape planted by an archaic bureaucracy, and you'll comprehend the reason for the Parisians' notorious astringency.

But this hard-boiled crust often protects a soft center. There is a startling contrast between the face Parisians show to passing strangers and their manner toward anyone with whom they share even the slightest personal rapport.

Compliment a surly bistro owner on her cuisine and—nine times out of ten—she'll melt before your eyes. Admire a Parisian's car or dog, or praise his window display, and you'll find you have a loquaciously knowledgeable companion for the next five minutes. Ask about the correct pronunciation of a French word (before you mispronounce it), and they'll become your language teachers.

For Parisians, some kind of personalized, individual contact seems necessary to display their best qualities: their famed charm, their savoir-faire, the delightful courtesy that marks their social life.

Which brings us to one of the most endearing Parisian attributes of all—

CHERCHEZ LA FEMME: The war between the sexes may be raging everywhere else, but the Parisians have achieved if not peace, then at least a working armistice. This is one city where men and women actually appear to *like* each other and to cooperate in making life as pleasant as humanly possible.

You'll see them nestling close to each other while shopping, holding hands between restaurant courses, going into torrid clinches on rush-hour subway trains, kissing through open car windows. And this isn't confined to the young. Middle-aged couples with grown families will stroke each other in public like honeymooners. Gallants in their 70s flirt with gray-haired matrons, portly businessmen romance their wives. Whatever else you may think of them, they leave you in no doubt that their response to sexual differences is a unanimous *Vive la Différence!*

The city's most universally acclaimed product is the female of the species—the Parisienne. Even today, with international competition red hot, she still retains the special niche carved for her by a dozen generations of enraptured troubadours.

The ingredients of the Parisienne's proverbial sex appeal are as varied and subtle as those of a delicate French gourmet sauce. The base of the concoction is her utter femininity, the constant awareness of her gender (and a male's), which lends her an air of coquetry even when she's washing windows.

At the same time she lacks the inhibited coyness of so many Spanish and Italian women, which stems from a social inferiority complex. She can hold her own conversationally with any man, and she flirts frankly, without demurely lowered lashes and titters behind a glove. In fact, men and women in Paris have an identical way of looking at each other, a kind of slow, appreciative measuring that holds pleasant promise—even if neither party is thinking of fulfillment.

If we had to choose an anthem for Mademoiselle de Paris, it would be "I Enjoy Being a Girl." It could pass as her signature tune. It might even be the key to her celebrated attractiveness.

"LES AMÉRICAINS": At 35 rue de Picpus, a few blocks from the Place de la Nation, there is a spot over which the Stars and Stripes has flown for more than 150 years. It lies in a small secluded cemetery and marks the grave of the **Marquis de Lafayette**—the man who forged the chain during the American Revolution that has linked the two countries ever since.

It was here that Col. Charles E. Stanton (*not* General Pershing) uttered the famous words, *Lafayette, nous voilà!* ("we are here!") to announce the arrival of the Doughboys on the soil of her hard-pressed old ally.

Politicians may blow hot and cold, but Paris remains studded with tokens of a deep friendship that hopefully will endure as long as this city stands. Our similar revolutions made for a strong common bond.

At the **Pont de Grenelle**, at Passy, you'll find the original model of the Statue of Liberty, which France presented to the people of the United States. One of the most impressive paintings in the **Musée de l'Armée** shows the battle of Yorktown which— however you learned it at school—was a combined Franco-American victory. And throughout the city, you'll keep coming across statues, monuments, streets, squares, and plaques commemorating George Washington, Benjamin Franklin, Presidents Wilson and Roosevelt, Generals Pershing and Eisenhower, and scores of lesser names that have carved themselves into the heart of France's capital.

Some of the carvings are invisible. They linger in the spirit of the Left Bank, the writers' and artists' quarter around **St-Germain-des-Prés.** The names are those of Ernest Hemingway and F. Scott Fitzgerald, of John Dos Passos and Gertrude Stein, of James Baldwin, Mary McCarthy, Henry Miller, and Richard Wright . . . the legion of American literary greats who worked here and left their signatures indelibly printed on the very bricks of the district.

Nobody knows the exact number of Americans still living in Paris. Not quite as many as during the Roaring Twenties perhaps, but still thousands. You'll find them studying at the Sorbonne, playing in a string of jazz clubs, working in business offices, design centers, and art studios, lecturing to students, and—yes—still toiling away in Left Bank writers' garrets or their current equivalents, the no-star hotels.

For the sheer magnetism of this town is as powerful as ever. Today, as more than 50 years ago, Paris is indeed an—

INTERNATIONAL CITY: The metropolis is so packed with minority groups that the true natives ironically refer to themselves as the "Parisians of Paris."

There are the Russians—descendants of the flood of White Russian refugees who poured into Paris after the Bolshevik Revolution—the Poles, English, Belgians, Italians, and Spaniards. Here, too, are vast colonies of Vietnamese, Algerians, Moroccans, Lebanese, and West Africans, all of them mingling with less friction than anyone who's ever heard a U.N. debate would have believed possible.

For one of the secrets of Paris's charm is the virtual absence of racial hostility. The Parisians have always been "color blind," in the best meaning of the term. Whatever their prejudices and quirks—and they have plenty—the hue of a person's skin or the slant of his or her eyes has never struck them as being of any consequence.

In return, they have gained a city that is free of ghettoes and their poisons, where you can stroll anywhere, anytime, without feeling displaced. This is a city which can absorb every alien current without losing its identity.

Cathedral of Notre-Dame

Chapter II

PARIS: GETTING TO KNOW HER

PARIS ISN'T A BIG CITY—as world capitals go. It occupies only 38 square miles of land—eight less than the "Paris of the West," San Francisco. It's far more populous, containing some three million people. But it's compact, and the majority of tourist attractions are so concentrated that it's a sheer joy to navigate.

The city is bisected by the wide arc of the **Seine.** The northern part is called the **Right Bank** (Rive Droite), and the southern part the **Left Bank** (Rive Gauche). The unusual designations make sense when you stand on a bridge facing downstream and watch the waters flow out toward the sea—to your right is the north bank; the south is on your left.

Thirty-two bridges link the Right and Left Banks—as well as the two small islands at the center of the Seine, the **Île de la Cité,** out of which contemporary Paris grew, site of the imposing Cathedral of Notre-Dame, and the **Île St-Louis,** a moat-guarded oasis of sober 17th-century mansions and country-quiet streets. These islands can cause some confusion to walkers who think they've just crossed a bridge from one bank to the other, only to find themselves caught up in an almost medieval maze of old buildings and courtyard greenery.

The best way to orient yourself to Paris is to climb to a high point on a clear day and simply look around. The best places for this—either the **Eiffel Tower** or the **Arc de Triomphe.** From the top of the Eiffel Tower, you can see all of Paris in one giant sweep. The view from the Arc de Triomphe is more detailed. From the Place de l'Étoile (renamed Place Charles de Gaulle) beneath you 12 avenues radiate, sweeping majestically across the minor city streets, linking the Arc, like giant wheel spokes, with the Place de la Concorde down the Champs-Élysées, the green lawns of the Bois de Boulogne, the stately white buildings of the Palais de Chaillot, and the honky-tonk joints of "Pig Alley." The city crowds around, condensed and intimate like a scale model, and you feel you could reach out and pick up a bridge to examine it or pluck some sugar off the birthday-cake peaks of Sacré-Coeur.

After taking in the overall view, take a boat ride up the Seine (for details, see our "Daytime" chapter). Choose a sunny day when the breeze is warm and you can sit outside on deck. Tune out the gabble around you and the recorded guide in four languages. Specific buildings aren't the point—and anyway you can hardly mistake the luminous towers of Notre-Dame. Sit and absorb Paris, letting her sights and sounds seep into you.

You'll see the shadowy quay where Voltaire worked and died. Gargoyles will gape down at you with the irritability of old age. Golden horses will take flight overhead from the stanchions of Pont Alexandre III. Barge women will be exchanging confidences over family clotheslines. Students—curled up in puppy clusters on the banks—will tease your boatload as it glides past, with hoots and guitar fanfares. Not all these, of course, are remarkable sights, but each is an essential piece of the Parisian landscape.

PARIS BY ARRONDISSEMENT: The city is divided into 20 municipal wards called "arrondissements," each with its own mayor, city hall, police station, and central post office. Some even have remnants of market squares left over from those independent days before the city burst its boundaries and engulfed the surrounding towns. Most city maps are outlined by arrondissement, and all addresses include the arrondissement number (written in Roman or Arabic numerals and followed by "e" or "er"). Paris also has its own version of a ZIP Code. And thus, the proper mailing address for a hotel or restaurant is written— say, 75014 Paris. The last two numbers, the 14, indicate that the address is in the 14th Arrondissement, in this case, Montparnasse.

Not all arrondissements concern the visitor—"tourist" Paris is only a minute proportion of the city as a whole—but a passing acquaintance with the more relevant districts can help you get your bearings.

When people speak of the Right Bank, they are usually referring to that traditionally monied area on the north side of the

Seine comprising the **First, Second,** and **Eighth** Arrondissements. Here are houses of fashion, the Stock Exchange, luxury trades such as the perfume industry, the most elegant hotels, expensive restaurants, smartest shops, and the most fashionably attired women and men. Along the river, in the First, are the classically precise **Tuileries Gardens** and the **Louvre.** The Second is a business district, with many offices and shops, but it also contains the **Opéra.** The Eighth includes the vast showplace of the Champs-Élysées, linking the mighty Arc de Triomphe with the delicate Obélisque on the Place de la Concorde.

The **Fourth** Arrondissement encompasses both small islands in the Seine. Cross the river to the south and you reach the **Fifth** Arrondissement which, along with the **Sixth,** are what people mean when they speak of the Left Bank—that part of the city dedicated to art and scholarship. The Fifth is the **Latin Quarter,** center of Paris University and site of the **Sorbonne.** Students, cafés, and cheap restaurants abound. The adjoining Sixth, heartland of the publishing industry, is the most colorful quarter of the city, an exciting, Greenwich Villagey area, where the School of Fine Arts sends out waves of earnest would-be artists. This is also the finest area for finding a good budget-priced hotel or meal, and later on we recommend many of both.

Neighboring the Seine is the **Seventh** Arrondissement which is primarily smart and residential, with embassies and government ministries operating out of what once were the fabulous mansions of French aristocracy. At the western river edge stands the **Eiffel Tower.** In the center is **Napoleon's Tomb** and the **Invalides Army Museum** (beside this is the city air terminal).

Look at a city map and you will see that these arrondissements, One to Eight (we didn't mention the Third because there's little there to interest you), form a circular core in the center of the city. Other districts have their attractions, of course. The famed **Sixteenth,** which shades out from the Seine to the vast park of the Bois de Boulogne, has the classiest living quarters, as well as the museums in the **Palais de Chaillot.**The part of the **Seventeenth** closest to l'Étoile is equally smart and riddled with executive-priced apartments. The delightful hill of Montmartre, crowned by Sacré-Coeur, is in the **Eighteenth.** But you could easily confine yourself to that magic inner circle and take in almost everything you came to Paris to see.

If you are staying more than two or three days, consider investing in one of the inexpensive pocket-size books that include the "plan de Paris" by arrondissements, available at all major newsstands and bookshops. Most of these guides provide you with a Métro map, a fold-out map of the city, and indexed maps of each arrondissement, with all streets listed and keyed.

WHEN TO COME: April in Paris is as magical as promised. Autumn is even better. In August, Parisians traditionally evacuate for their annual holiday and put the city on a skeleton staff to serve visitors. Now, too, July has become a popular vacation month, with many a restaurateur shuttering up for a month-long respite.

Paris: Average Bimonthly Temperatures			
Jan.-Feb.	44.5	July-Aug.	75.7
Mar.-Apr.	55.7	Sept.-Oct.	64.6
May-June	69.9	Nov.-Dec.	46.4

From May through September, the city is swamped with tourists, and you must write well in advance for hotel reservations. Avoid the first two weeks in October, when the annual motor show draws thousands of boy-at-heart enthusiasts.

The best time to come to Paris is off-season, in the early spring or late autumn, when the tourist trade has trickled to a manageable flow and everything is easier to come by—hotel rooms, Métro seats, even good-tempered waiters.

Paris has an uncommonly long springtime, lasting through April, May, and June, and an equally extended fall, from September through November. The climate is temperate throughout the year, without those extremes so common to New York or Chicago. The coldest months are December and January, when the average high reaches 42 degrees and the average low drops to 32. There's occasional snow during these months. The warmest months are July and August, when the daily averages range from 55 to 76 degrees. Sunshine is plentiful in summer; rainfall is moderate but heavier in winter. The city looks best in autumn leaves, but its sweetest fragrance is the soft scent of spring air.

THE CURRENCY: French currency is based on the franc (F), which consists of 100 centimes (c). Coins come in units of 1, 5, 10, 20, and 50 centimes; and 1, 5, and 10 francs. Notes come in denominations of 5, 10, 50, 100, and 500 francs. Around 1960, the French issued new coins and notes which are current today and known as "new francs."

All banks are equipped with foreign exchange prices, and you will find exchange offices in the airports and airline terminals. Banks are open from 9 a.m. to noon and 2 to 4 p.m., Monday through Friday. Major bank branches also open their exchange departments on Saturday between 9 a.m. and noon.

WHAT TO WEAR: Parisians are both stylish *and* conservative. Big-city clothes are in order here, the kind of thing you might wear to visit San Francisco or when walking along Fifth Avenue in New York. If it suits Miami Beach or Malibu, it won't look good on the rue de Rivoli. Men will feel at ease in suits or sports jackets of a weight appropriate to the season. Women will fit in wearing suits, skirts and sweaters, simple dresses, and good pants. Unlike the British, the French tend to dress down rather than up. But always with style. Parisiennes go to work, restaurants, or the theater wearing beautifully cut and tailored pants suits. You can follow their lead; you won't be turned away at the door by some disapproving manager. While ties for men are advisable in the poshest places, they are seldom required in more moderate restaurants. Even churches don't insist that women wear head coverings, although that, of course, is your option. The only special precaution is a travel umbrella to take with you on your rounds. Especially in off-season, the rains are frequent and unpredictable.

Not that you can't wear your designer jeans—you just can't wear them everywhere. In a student café on the Left Bank they're hardly out of place.

WELCOME "ÉTRANGERS": You need never be totally alone in Paris. There's always someone who speaks your language standing ready to dispense aid, give you information, and help you solve problems. Two tourist board **Welcome Offices** in the center of town will give you free maps, informative booklets, and "Paris Weekly Information," an English-language listing of all current shows, concerts, and theater. At 127 Champs-Élysées (tel. 723-61-72), you can get information regarding both Paris and the provinces.

FOR STUDENTS: Armed with a student identification card in Paris, you can enjoy many bonuses, including savings of up to

30% on transportation or meals at certain establishments. You'll need proof of full-time student status (university or high school), best obtained by requesting an **International Student Identity Card** (which costs $6 U.S.) from the **Council on International Educational Exchange**, 205 E. 42nd St., New York, NY 10017; or 49 rue Pierre-Charron, Paris 75008. Write first for the application form which, properly filled out and submitted with payment and required documentation, will expedite receiving your ISIC. Allow three to four weeks for delivery during the busiest travel seasons.

A good base for students is the **Foyer Jacques de Rufz de Lavison**, 18 rue Jean-Jacques-Rousseau, 1er (tel. 508-02-10), which receives both male and female students from April 1 to October 1, charging them 46F ($8.21) in double or single rooms, including a continental breakfast, taxes, service, and showers. Meals are generally available. Métro: Les Halles, Palais-Royal, or Louvre.

Year-round temporary housing (44 beds) for students, male and female, is available at the **Association des Étudiants Protestants de Paris**, 46 rue de Vaugirard, 6e (tel. 354-31-49), on the Left Bank. Rates, including a continental breakfast and showers, are 36F ($6.43) for dormitories, 41F ($7.32) for double rooms, and 44F ($7.85) for singles. Métro: St-Sulpice, St-Germain, or Odéon.

FOR SENIOR CITIZENS: For those who reach what the French call "the third age," there are a number of discounts. At any railway station in France, a senior citizen (that means 60 for women and 65 for men) can obtain a **Carte Vermeil** (Vermilion Card), for a cost of 48F ($8.57). With this card, a person gets a reduction of 50% on train fares in both first- and second-class compartments. Further discounts include a 10% reduction on all rail excursions and a 10% reduction on the Europabus running from Paris to Nice. The catch is that these discounts do not apply at certain peak periods of travel, including runs on express trains and on Paris commuter lines.

The French domestic airline, Air Inter, honors "third-agers" by giving them 25% to 50% reductions on its regular, nonexcursion tariffs. Again, certain flights are not included. Reductions are given on about 20 Air France flights a week to Nice. Carte Vermeil also allows reductions on certain regional bus lines, plus on theater tickets in Paris.

Finally, half-price admission to state-owned museums is yet another concession the French make to seniors. Detailed information is available at the French Government Tourist Office, 610 Fifth Ave., New York, NY 10020 (tel. 212/757-1125).

The Eiffel Tower seen from the Trocadéro Gardens

Chapter III

GETTING AROUND

PARIS IS A CITY FOR WALKERS, for strollers-about whose greatest joy in life is rambling through unexpected alleyways and squares, sniffing out a city's innermost secrets. Whatever your specific intention when you come, one long, free, exhilarating saunter will be enough to convince you that you don't *want* to spend your Parisian days charging from art-book exhibition to history-book monument. Given a choice of conveyance, make it your own two feet every possible time. Only when you're dead tired and can't walk another step, or in a roaring hurry to reach an exact destination, should you consider the following swift and prosaic means of urban transport.

LE MÉTRO: If the Paris subway system, the Métropolitain, had an English slogan, it would be: "So simple a child can work it." That would be no overstatement. The Métro is so brilliantly organized, so efficient, and so well sign posted that if you do get lost, don't mention it to your Parisian friends. They'll have too good a laugh at your expense.

One run of the course is all you need to get the details down pat. Walk to any Métro station and look at the huge map posted outside. Decide on the station you want to reach. Now put your finger on the station where you are standing (it will be encircled by red) and trace the quickest route. In some of the larger stations, such as the Opéra, there are automatic light-up maps to do this for you. You may have to change from one line to the other. Interchange stations are encircled in black.

Now run your finger to the end of the line you wish to take. The name of the last stop is the "Direction" you are going toward. Cling to this name with the tenacity of mother love. It will guide you through the station maze of ticket takers, swinging metal gates, narrow stairwells, moving platforms, even lead you from the elevated line out into the open air, and underground again, eventually to deposit you safely on the guaranteed correct coach.

Enter the station and buy a ticket. One fare covers every station on the urban lines except on some extensions, and you only have to specify first or second class. The exceptions are the following: On the extension of line #8 beyond Charenton Écoles, you have to buy one, two, three, or more tickets, according to the distance traveled. It is the same on line #13, where you buy an additional ticket for a journey beyond Carrefour Pleyel. On the Sceaux line, as well as on the Boissy-Saint-Leger and the Saint-Germain-en-Laye lines, which serve the suburbs, fares are charged according to the distance covered.

First class may be cozier, but second class is cheaper—only 3F (54¢) per ticket, in contrast to 4.50F (80¢) in first class. Your best buy is a *carnet* (a ticket book), which contains ten individual second-class tickets for only 20F ($3.57), 35F ($6.25) in first class.

Hold onto your ticket now, until you've finished your journey. There are occasional ticket checks in first-class or second-class compartments, and on the station platforms and corridors. Locate your "Direction" and start walking. Maps and station lists on the walls will reassure you as you go. Don't rush if you hear the train coming. As soon as it enters the station, large metal doors swing shut and "passage" to the platform is "interdit" (*Verboten!*).

The tickets are checked at the entrances by automated turnstiles, a labor-saving device that saves the Métro a lot of money and eliminates all that confetti. Insert your ticket in the machine and pass through the turnstile.

Don't be surprised if you have to stand even during the quiet of midday. The cars have 48 seats (24 are tip-up seats). Some are reserved by law first for: the war injured, those injured in the line of civic duty, pregnant women, and persons accompanied by children under 4—in that order of priority. If nobody of that description seems nearby, have a seat.

If you are changing trains, get out at the interchange station, determine the "Direction" of the next line you want to take, and follow the bright-orange "Correspondance" signs until you reach the proper platform. Don't be tricked out into the open by a "Sortie" sign, which means "Exit." You'll have to pay another fare and start all over again.

The Métro starts running in the morning at 5:30, and the cars pull into their barns for the night around 1:15 a.m. Unlike the

New York subway, the Métro is reasonably safe at any hour. For the newcomer it is more foolproof than the London tube. And it boasts some amazing aesthetic incongruities, such as flamboyant, bower-like art nouveau entranceways. Don't miss the Louvre station, where floodlit statues, photos, and bas-reliefs act as coming attractions to the museum's collection.

BUSES: A more slapdash, less efficient way to get where you want to go, but marvelous for seeing Paris in the close-up, ticking off famous buildings and peeking into people's windows. Use the ticket books purchased at Métro stations or else Métro tickets which can be used in buses, giving you an average ride of about two to three miles. You can also buy tickets at bus terminal kiosks, in *café-tabac* stores, and in other various retail shops bearing a red circular RATP sign. Bus journeys are divided into stages, and you are charged according to the distance you are going. Within the city limits, charges never exceed two tickets. If you stay a week or a month, you can buy a special "Go as You Please" tourist ticket valid for two, four, or seven days on all the RATP networks or a "carte orange" valid for two, three, four, or five zones in the Paris area.

If you intend to do any serious bus riding, pick up an RATP bus map at the office on the Place de la Madeleine or at the tourist offices at RATP headquarters, 53 bis quai des Grands Augustins, Paris (6e). You can also write to the RATP to obtain maps of the transportation systems operated by this authority and other information and pamphlets on the networks. When in Paris, you can also telephone the enquiry center (tel. 346-14-14) to get precise details on the fares, routes, and schedules concerning buses as well as the Métro.

Learn bus stop customs. Wait for a bus at a bus stop, and wave to the driver to stop the bus. On each stop post, the route numbers are displayed as well as the name of the place served. When waiting at a bus stop, get in line and board in order. You are entitled to defend your place in line with your life. *No* tactic is considered unmannerly. There are 55 bus lines in Paris, many running out to the near suburbs. The majority operate only between 7 a.m. and 8:30 p.m. A few run as late as 12:30 a.m. And even fewer maintain service on Sunday and holidays.

You may also want to use the bus system for excursions outside Paris. Many different trips are offered from Easter to the beginning of October during the weekends at reasonable prices to off-the-beaten-path places. You can, of course, go to such standard attractions as Chartres, Amiens, Beauvais, Chantilly, Compiègne, Épernay en Champagne, Fontainebleau, Orléans, Pierrefonds, Vaux-Le Vicomte, even Mont Saint-Michel. Also, you can visit various châteaux in the Loire Valley. To get more details on the prices and on the sightseeing tours, you can write to the RATP at its headquarters (address above). When in Paris, you can also get the details and book space by going to the office at the Place de la Madeleine. It is open from 7:30 a.m. to 6:45 p.m. weekdays (from 6:30 a.m. to 6 p.m. on Saturday, Sunday, and holidays).

TAXIS: This is not the cheapest means of propulsion, but it's nothing to get paranoiac about, either. Paris's cab drivers are decent enough chaps—with amazingly placid dispositions considering the insanity of their working conditions—and they seldom try to gouge you too much. Most of those surcharges they like to tack on are legal anyway.

To begin with, all legitimate taxis have meters. (If yours doesn't, get out and find one that does.) The flag drops at 8F ($1.43), and from that moment on it's 1.80F (32¢) per kilometer. If your trip should take you outside any of the boundaries of the 20 arrondissements, another and slightly higher tariff will go into effect. At night, expect to pay an increase of about 30% of the fare.

You're not required to pay for the driver's empty return ride between airports and the center of the city, but you are assessed 1F (18¢) extra to be delivered to railroad stations.

You are allowed several small pieces of luggage free if they're transported inside and do not weigh more than five kilograms. Any suitcases weighing more are carried in the trunk at a cost of 1.50F (27¢) per piece of luggage. On top of the fare, tip from 12% to 15%—the latter occasionally elicits a *"Merci."*

Beware of those no-meter cabs that await tipsy patrons outside nightclubs—or settle the tab in advance. Horse-drawn cabs called *fiacres* are out in summertime, ready to trot tourists up the Champs-Élysées or through the Bois de Boulogne. There is nothing budgety about their prices, however; they charge pretty much what the traffic will bear. Here, too, bargain the driver down before you set off. Fiacres can be found near the **Opéra, Madeleine, Tuileries Gardens, Bois de Boulogne, Eiffel Tower,** and at the **Rond-Point des Champs-Élysées.** Regular cabs can be hailed on the street when their signs read "Libre."

RENTED CARS: Don't even consider driving a car in Paris. Even if you trained on the "chicken" courses of adolescence, you don't have the requisite nerve, skill, and above all ruthlessness, of the humblest Parisian driver. Parking is impossible, and so many of the inner streets survive from days when the hand-carted litter was the common mode of transportation that two cars and a pedestrian are all that's needed these days for a traffic jam. Add to this the Parisian's glee in irritating his fondest neighbor, and you can see why you don't want to get involved.

If you insist on ignoring our well-meant advice, then here are a few tips: Get an excellent street map and ride with a co-pilot because there's no time to think at intersections. Wherever you see "Zone Bleue," it means that you can't park without a parking disc, which you attach to your windshield, setting the disc's clock to show the time of arrival. Between 9 a.m. and noon you may park for one hour, from noon to 2:30 p.m. you get 2½ hours, and thereafter to 5 p.m. it's back to one hour. These discs are available at garages, police stations, and hotels. The rules are suspended on Sunday and holidays.

Other Tips: Watch for the gendarmes who consistently countermand the lights and aren't patient fellows. Horn-blowing is absolutely forbidden in Paris except for dire emergencies. Parisians have a proclivity for dire emergencies, however.

On the other hand, don't even consider exploring the French countryside without a car, unless you intend to see the bigger cities only. There are few pleasures more magnificent than cruising through the back lanes of the provinces, stopping for a memorable lunch at the local widow's one-room restaurant. Car-rental arrangements can be made in Paris, where a number of firms are available to suit your needs.

Avis comes highly recommended as you can place your reservation in advance in the States and have a car waiting for you when you arrive at Orly Airport or Roissy Airport. It has several locations in Paris, with the main office at 5 rue Bixio (tel. 550-32-31).

Europcar, 137 Avenue Jean-Jaurès, Clamart (tel. 645-21-25). This company offers special advantages. First, it's European-owned and -based, with a network of more than 200 branches all over France, including 30 stations in Greater Paris and major airports. Europcar is affiliated with National Car Rental on a worldwide mutual representation agreement. Its rental fleet is divided into eight categories, ranging from a Renault 5 to the air-conditioned Mercedes 280E. You can make reservations in the U.S. via the national toll-free number: 800/328-4567.

Hertz has nine offices in Paris and depots throughout most of France, as well as booths in both airports. It offers six general groupings of cars with stickshift gears, three with automatic, and two in the luxury category. It's also possible to make arrangements to rent a car for a week on an unlimited-mileage basis. In the United States, car rentals can be arranged in advance by calling toll free 800/788-5151, or your nearest Hertz office.

The flower market

Chapter IV

WHERE TO STAY

PARIS SUPPORTS MORE THAN 1400 hotels—among which only a handful at the top are world-famous. Of course, if you're willing to pay the tab at the top hotels, you can rent some of the finest rooms in Europe. But many modestly run hotels also provide top value. Their only drawback is that they are known among shrewd travelers and are likely to be booked, especially in summer. We've surveyed some of the best of them. In these, we'd suggest reserving rooms a full month in advance at *any* time of the year and as far as six weeks ahead during the tourist-jammed months from early May through mid-October. You might send a one-night deposit just to be sure.

The majority of these hotels, in fact the majority of all Parisian hotels, also share another common problem. Noise. It's strange how Paris traffic sounds seem to magnify in the narrow streets, echoing and reechoing through the chimney-topped canyons. Add in late-night revelers and early-morning markets, and we'd heartily recommend that light sleepers request rooms at the back.

Hotel breakfasts are fairly uniform and include your choice of coffee, tea, or chocolate, a freshly baked croissant and roll, plus limited quantities of butter and jam or jelly. It's nowhere near as massive as the English or American breakfast, but it has the advantage of being quick to prepare, is at your door moments after you call down for it, and can be served at almost any hour requested.

There could be a riddle, if the French were so crude, going something like "When is a hotel not a hotel?" The answer is when it's another kind of building. The word *hôtel* in French has several meanings. It means a lodging house for transients, of course. But it also means a large mansion or town house, such as the Hôtel des Invalides, once a home for disabled soldiers, now the most important military museum in the world. Hôtel de

Ville means town hall; Hôtel des Postes refers to the general post office; and Hôtel-Dieu is a hospital. So watch that word.

Now, having cleared away the background information, let's get down to specifics on where *you* are going to be staying. The following hotels are grouped geographically, and by descending order of price. Also, right after most addresses we've included the number of the arrondissement (i.e., 8e, 1er), which you may find helpful.

Deluxe Right Bank Hotels

If you crave smartness in your surroundings, choose a Right Bank hotel. That puts you central to all the most elegant shops—Dior, Cardin, St. Laurent—and within walking distance of such important sights as the Arc de Triomphe, the Place de la Concorde, the Tuileries Gardens, and the Louvre. The Opéra is in this area, and its attendant attraction, the American Express office. And for relaxing after sightseeing during the day or for an apéritif at night, you have all the glittering cafés along the Champs-Élysées.

The Right Bank is noted for "hotel-palaces" internationally celebrated. They're also among the most expensive deluxe citadels in the world. If you book in any of the establishments described immediately below, expect to pay plenty for a double room with private bath.

Le Bristol, 112 Faubourg Saint-Honoré, 8e (tel. 266-91-45). The decoration is sumptuous, the art of museum caliber, the service impeccable. This is not only one of the top two or three hotels in Paris, but in all of Europe. Naturally, its clientele is among the international upper crust, with particular appeal to the diplomatic corps.

Founded in 1924 by Hippolyte Jammet, Le Bristol is a true palace. It's on the famous shopping street of Paris, near many of the capital's most elegant boutiques. Nearby is the Palais de l'Élysée, the official residence of the French president. The hotel is not large enough to be a monument, as is Le Ritz, but it is, instead, just the right size for a guest to receive individualized old-world attention.

The facade is in the classic 18th-century Parisian style, characterized by an entrance of glass and wrought iron. The furnishings are of the highest caliber. For example, many signed Louis XV and Louis XVI pieces abound. In the writing room and study are gilt clocks, crystal chandeliers, even an 18th-century tapestry. In

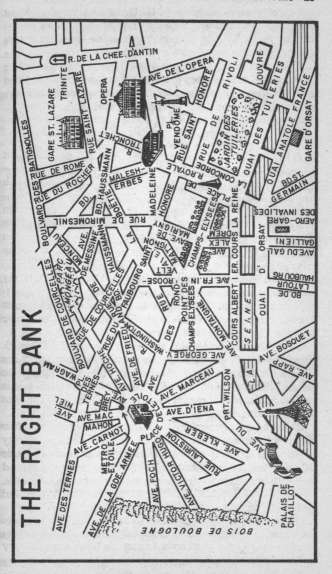

yet another salon hangs an F. H. Drouhais portrait of Marie Antoinette. Her husband, Louis XVI, is represented in a marble bust by Pajou. Some of the salons open onto a formalized patio, landscaped with potted plants and shrubbery.

The force behind this elegant style is Pierre Jammet, son of the founding father. He's seen to it that all the bedrooms and suites are furnished opulently and luxuriously. Original oil paintings, Oriental carpets, antiques or skillfully made reproductions, inlaid woods, and the mandatory bronze and crystal have been used extensively. Depending on the size of the room, its view and location, the tariffs are wide ranging. Singles start at 700F ($124.95), graduating up to 850F ($151.73). The least expensive double is priced at 820F ($146.37), although you'll pay 1300F ($232.05) for the most lavish. All rooms contain separate stall showers, and rates include a continental breakfast and tax. Service is extra.

Le Ritz, 15 Place Vendôme, 1er (tel. 260-38-30), is a legend. Many critics have called it "the greatest hotel in the world," and with its $25-million facelift it aims to keep that reputation. You're assured that you'll be in "close proximity to the most important French and foreign banks." In 1898, César Ritz, the self-proclaimed "little shepherd boy from Niederwald," converted Le Ritz into a hotel that would soon make the word "ritzy" part of the language. Here he welcomed Edward VII and lesser royalty. The luxurious suites were occupied by the Rothschilds, the Goulds, the Vanderbilts, and the Astors. In the 1920s the hotel was host to such famous stars as Mary Pickford and Charlie Chaplin. Fitzgerald loved the bar more than Hemingway did. Marcel Proust wrote of the Ritz. Everybody from Greta Garbo to Rose Kennedy to, regrettably, Herman Goering has strolled down its long shopping corridor, called "Temptation Walk," with showcases representing the wares of some of the most prestigious shops in Paris.

The Ritz startled Paris by providing a private bath with every room. When corpulent King Edward VII got stuck in a regular tub with one of his lovely young bathing companions, the king-size tub was invented. Singles range in price from 700F ($124.95); doubles, from 800F ($142.80) to 950F ($169.58); plus 15% for service, although tax is included. The bedrooms are excellent, probably the most fastidiously maintained in the entire French capital. Antique chests, bronze hardware, marble baths, mellow woods, crystal lights—everything is well chosen and tastefully coordinated both in style and color.

The hotel, actually two town houses, opens onto one of the most historic squares of Paris, the Place Vendôme. The town houses were joined together, their union creating the various courtyards and gardens. The public rooms are furnished with gilt and mirrors, Louis XV–and Louis XVI–style furniture, as well as tapestries and stately bronze torchères.

Diners have their choices of the grill room (recommended separately as a restaurant, "Espadon") or the classic dining room where the great chef Escoffier once cooked for emperors.

Crillon, 10 Place de la Concorde, 8e (tel. 265-24-10), offers the most dramatic setting in Paris: overlooking the Place de la Concorde, the square on which the guillotine claimed the lives of such celebrated victims as Louis XVI, Marie Antoinette, Mme. du Barry, Mme. Roland, and Charlotte Corday. Designed by the famed Gabriel, the building was the former home of the duke of Crillon. Although more than 200 years old, it has only been a hotel since 1909. As such, it sheltered Woodrow Wilson during his stay in Paris following World War I.

The colonnaded exterior is so discreet you won't think it's a hotel at first—rather, the headquarters of a minister of government. The hotel envelops a large formal courtyard, which is one of the ideal places in Paris for those of refined taste to order afternoon tea. Tables under parasols are placed around a reflection pool with floral borders. Statues lend further dignity.

Massively restored in 1967, the hotel still evokes the 18th century, with its parquet floors, crystal chandeliers, sculpture, scenic murals, and paneled walls. If you get a front room, you'll be treated to a view of what has been called one of the most beautiful city plazas in the world. However, you'll also hear the roar of traffic that even the thick walls of the Crillon can't seem to blot out. Tranquility seekers should ask for a chamber opening onto an inner courtyard. The rooms, for the most part, are generous in size and classically furnished. All the bathrooms are fresh and well maintained, unlike some of the creaky plumbing in many of Paris's deluxe hostelries. Singles rent for 755F ($134.77); doubles, 800F ($142.80) to 935F ($166.90); plus 15% for service.

In days of yore, we've seen everybody from Averill Harriman to Charlie Chaplin in the dining room. Even Gloria Swanson has put in an appearance, bringing her own food, of course. Our favorite main course is simple but luscious: poached salmon in a creamy mustard sauce. Also, huge ham-and-egg breakfasts are available, offering a bit of nostalgia and comfort to an American in Paris.

Raphael, 17 Avenue Kléber, 16e (tel. 502-16-00), enjoys special patronage from the Italian-American movie world, plus a host of world celebrities. Checking in at any time, you're likely to rub elbows with Anthony Quinn, Rafaele Vallone, Michael Caine, Monica Vitti, Joseph Losey, or Claudia Cardinale. Right near the Arc de Triomphe, the hotel is a tranquil oasis of stately dignity.

Paying your bill is made less painful here by an original Turner, an orange-and-gold painting to the right of the cashier. The tone of the hotel is set by the main hallway, with its dark-paneled walnut walls, oil paintings framed in gilt, and lavish bronze torchères. The rich wood-paneling theme continues into the music salon, with its opera-red carpeting and marble fireplace.

The bedrooms are impressive, furnished in a luxuriously conventional way, with brass-trimmed chests, tables of inlaid wood, armoires, and silk draperies. Tariffs depend on where the rooms face. A single with private bath rents from 435F ($77.65); a moderate double room with private bath costs from 515F ($91.93); and a medium-grade double room is priced from 690F ($123.17). All these tabs include taxes, service, and continental breakfast.

If you're staying here, you'll surely want to have a meal in the formal dining room, with its gold-and-red carpeting, its paneled walls of white, and arched windows with rich draperies. Métro: Kléber.

Plaza Athénée, 23–27 Avenue Montaigne, 8e (tel. 225-43-30), was known to Mata Hari, although now it's more popular with South American tycoons and visiting Arab oil sheiks. Between the Seine and the Champs-Élysées, it is a veritable palace. Arched windows and ornate balconies evoke the pre-World War I style. A liveried attendant stands under a glass shelter waiting to help you out of your taxi. The reception staff seats you at a Louis XVI marquetry desk that faces an antique Flemish painting, when you check in.

The style of the hotel is exemplified by the Regency Salon, with its mellow wood-grain paneling and marble fireplace. In the courtyard, tables are sheltered by parasols, and climbing vines and borders of flowers add a touch of gaiety.

The more preferred air-conditioned bedrooms overlook this courtyard. Recently renewed, most of the private bedchambers are interestingly furnished with reproductions from one of the

Louis periods. Woven carpets and bronze hardware carry out the deluxe theme. Singles range in price from 700F ($124.95) to 875F ($156.19); regular doubles, 950F ($169.58) to 1100F ($196.35); plus service. Le Régence-Plaza serves what is considered the finest lobster soufflé dinner in the world. In the brightly decorated Relais Plaza grill you can order light fare.

George V, 31 Avenue George V, 8e (tel. 723-54-00), is affectionately called "George Sank" by the bustling expense accounters who crowd its ornate lobby. Midway between the Champs-Élysées and the Seine, it is sheer luxury. (Reportedly, the management keeps a "black file" on the mysterious "whims and preferences" of its habitués, likely to include everybody from Gina Lollobrigida to Sam Spiegel.) The George V is often referred to as "the French Waldorf-Astoria." The service is excellent, beginning with registration at the Empire reception desk. From here on, just press a buzzer and servants will attend to your whim and fancy.

The public lounges, through which J. Paul Getty used to wander, are adorned with tapestries and 100- and 200-year-old paintings. Inlaid marble walls in the Pompeian style add the right touch of staid dignity. Rooms are preferred that overlook the courtyard, and those that boast terrace balconies as well are the height of perfection. Unfortunately, some of the regular chambers are furnished with lackluster furniture, although all is seemingly well maintained. A single goes for 750F ($133.88); a double, 1100F ($196.35); plus 15% service. In fair weather, you can have lunch in the courtyard.

Meurice, 228 rue de Rivoli, 1er (tel. 260-38-60), is one of the great palaces of Paris. When he's in Paris, that self-proclaimed "mad genius," Salvador Dali, makes his headquarters at the Meurice. He stays in Suite 108, which used to shelter Alfonso XIII, the former king of Spain who was forced into exile.

Massively renovated and overhauled, the Meurice has retained a decidedly 18th-century aura, with gilt-edged paneled walls, Flemish and French tapestries, Louis XVI–style furniture, and the ever-present crystal chandeliers. The bedrooms are well furnished and most comfortably equipped, although not with antiques. One person pays 770F ($137.45); two persons, from 1022F ($182.43); plus 15% for service.

Take a quick meal in the modern Copper Grill. Of course, the location's impressive—just off the rue de Rivoli and the Tuileries Gardens, a short walk from the Louvre.

Inter-Continental, 3 rue de Castiglione, 1er (tel. 260-37-80), has been called the largest and splashiest deluxe hotel in Paris. Back in the 19th century when it was known as the Continental, it was the epitome of the "grand luxe" hotel, reigning as the "queen of the rue de Rivoli." Now massively and meticulously restored, it has found new life in this century. Across from the Tuileries Gardens, it was originally opened in 1878. By 1883 it was entertaining such illustrious guests as Victor Hugo. Over the years it sheltered such tenants as Jean Giraudoux, Omar Bradley, and Lyndon Johnson. When Inter-Continental Hotels purchased it in 1968, it was completely rebuilt (except for its facade) at a cost of $8 million.

At the colonnaded front entrance note the pair of bronze candelabra—they were purchased from a palace in Leningrad. The main lounge, with its rich opera-red carpeting, is furnished with period pieces. The 500 bedrooms have been handsomely and tastefully outfitted in the classic French idiom, with many reproductions of Louis XVI pieces. Paneled walls and color-coordinated draperies and bedspreads create the effect of an intimate salon. All the rooms are air-conditioned, with direct-dial phones and radios. Naturally, there is 24-hour room service should you desire a steak at three in the morning. Single rooms range in price from 710F ($126.74) to 840F ($149.94); twins, from 840F ($149.94) to 950F ($169.58); plus tax and service.

Instead of the old-fashioned grand hotel dining room, the Inter-Continental prefers the more modern way of having several intimate "character" rooms. One of the more favored is the Rôtisserie Rivoli, offering spit-roasted specialties. Another spot, Terrasse Fleurie, is the interior courtyard landscaped to depict the four seasons. The Bistro is a fashionable Paris restaurant for cocktails and luncheons, serving regional specialties. It becomes the Bistrothèque when it's transformed every evening into a disco from 10 p.m. to 4 a.m. Café Tuileries is a typical French restaurant and bar in the belle époque style, serving breakfasts, snacks, light meals, informal suppers, cocktails, and French pastries (open till midnight).

Lancaster, 7 rue de Berri, 8e (tel. 359-90-43), is like a large private town house, just off the Champs-Élysées. Its salon has long been known among artists and writers. Movie stars, such as Elizabeth Taylor, have also shown a fondness for the place. No two rooms are alike. A single ranges in price from 500F ($89.25) to 650F ($116.03); a double, from 770F ($137.45) to 880F ($157.08). The better rooms open onto the blissful courtyard, although all are well furnished in a traditional style. That means, of course, paneled walls, gilt mirrors, Louis XVI–style furniture, and lots of brocade. In the small and intimate restaurant, you're likely to run into Gregory Peck (he met his present wife here when she came to interview him for a magazine story) or Peter Ustinov and his brood.

Royal Monceau, 37 Avenue Hoche, 8e (tel. 561-98-00), is a classic and traditional French hotel, only two minutes from the Arc de Triomphe. A sophisticated international clientele patronizes this well-known choice, guests preferring one of the bedrooms opening onto a formal courtyard, with lamps, flower urns, a lawn, even tables set under brightly colored parasols.

A note of high style is set by the tapestry on the landing of the grand staircase. Throughout the lounges a mixture of periods is evident, ranging from Empire to Directoire, with an occasional Persian carpet thrown in for emphasis.

Most of the bedchambers are generously endowed and refurnished in period style. Two sets of tariffs are charged for the standard rooms, depending on size and location. Singles range from 720F ($128.52); doubles, from 830F ($148.16) to 930F ($166.01).

Prince de Galles, 33 Avenue George V, 8e (tel. 723-55-11). Right off the Champs-Élysées, the Prince of Wales shows greater sparkle than ever with wholesale revamping of its bedchambers and some public rooms. Long a favorite of *le tout Paris,* this address has always attracted what the American composer, Ned Rorem, termed "inapproachable innermost snob-life of Paris."

It's built around an open courtyard with a fountain in the center. The public lounges are furnished in the traditional French manner. The Regency Bar is especially nice, with its dusty rose-and-blue velvet chairs. In the restaurant, Panache, guests seated in brass opera-style chairs are served fine food against a backdrop of sienna-colored marble pilasters.

The preferred bedrooms have balconies looking down on the patio in the Andalusian style. Some of the chambers are quite large, furnished in a classic manner, often with Louis XVI–style pieces. The baths are good-sized, too, with polished marble and lots of large luxurious towels. A single costs 811F ($144.76) to 866F ($154.58), and twin and doubles go from 987F ($176.18) to 1068F ($190.64). A continental breakfast, taxes, and service are included.

Majestic, 29 rue Dumont d'Urville, 16e (tel. 500-83-70), is in a class all by itself. Docteur Bayerez has installed apartment suites, often decorated in the Louis XV or Directoire styles. The high tone is set by a still life by Giovanni Trimboli in the lounge. A short distance from the Arc de Triomphe, the quiet, almost secluded hotel has a large diplomatic following and is especially favored by a well-heeled crowd who like to visit Paris for at least a month every year. Downstairs are two petit salons for receiving guests, although you can also entertain as you would in your own apartment. For one person, an apartment ranges in price from 379F ($67.65) to 417F ($74.44). Two persons pay anywhere from 402F ($71.76) to 440F ($78.54), breakfast, service, and tax included. If you rent a suite, the cost is from 620F ($110.67) to 750F ($133.88).

Lotti, 7–9 rue Castiglione, 1er (tel. 260-37-34), just off the historic Place Vendôme, is known as a "junior Ritz." Inside its doors unfolds an elegant French world of marble and gilt, tapestries and crystal. Although reproductions are used, the bedrooms turn to the 19th century for their inspiration. Rosewood and mahogany, gilt and silk damask, even tambour desks, recreate the ambience of an elegant town-house bedroom. Some of the upper-story rooms, however, were probably used at one time by servants to wealthy clients, yet they have their own peculiar garret-like style. Singles range in price from 520F ($92.82) to 590F ($105.32); doubles, 700F ($124.95) to 830F ($148.16). Breakfast is included, but service is an extra 15%.

Deluxe Left Bank Hotels

Paris Hilton, 18 Avenue de Suffren, 15e (tel. 273-92-00). When the Eiffel Tower was built, it sparked controversy all over town—many Parisians thought it had destroyed the skyline of the city. Now the Parisians have lovingly adopted it as their most characteristic landmark. At its doorstep, the Hilton opened to the same sort of hostility. Now its "Le Western" restaurant is so popular with the French that an American usually has to wait in line to sample beef flown in fresh daily from the United States.

The hotel's gleamingly modern 11 floors house a total of 492 rooms. Furnishings blend harmoniously, achieving both style and practicality. The furniture designed by the hotel's French decorator is not only aesthetically pleasing, but blends the modified period style with contemporary shapes. The rooms facing the Seine, incidentally, have been totally redecorated and refurbished. A single starts at 430F ($76.76), peaking at 560F ($99.96). Doubles are in the 490F ($87.47) to 640F ($114.24) category. To all these tariffs add tax and 15% for service. Each room is equipped with color television, and every day, from 11 a.m. to 2 a.m., you have the choice of two free push-button full-length feature films with the original soundtracks. As a special service to the vacation traveler, a documentary film on the *Great Paris Exhibition of 1900* and a guide film to the city are also featured.

The rooftop restaurant and cocktail lounge, Le Toit de Paris, offers one of the most exciting views of Paris plus French gastronomic specialties. Specialties include baked sea bass in a puff-pastry shell, duckling with apples and green pepper, and a pineapple charlotte soufflé. The Coffeeshop offers a different dish for each day of the week—either a regional specialty of France or a particular recipe from a specific country. Should you not desire the plats du jour, you can order corn which has been shipped in fresh from America, or chicken—served southern style—in a basket. It took the chef 18 months to perfect the cheesecake, and it's really good. Incidentally, the floor on which Mississippi-plantation-style furniture sits is made of stainless-steel squares. Finally, Le Bar Suffren is more traditional, evoking the gaslight era.

Paris-Sheraton, 19 rue du Commandant-Mouchotte, 14e (tel. 320-15-51), is one of the newest hotels on the Paris scene. With 1000 rooms encased in a 32-story white tower, the Paris-Sheraton is one of the largest hotels in Western Europe.

The hotel is surrounded by an acre of landscaped terraces, its restaurants and cocktail lounges opening onto sunken gardens. It's all part of a civic complex in the artists' quarter of Montparnasse. Part of the development includes a parking lot for 2500 cars, a skating rink, plus apartment buildings and a shopping center.

The Paris-Sheraton is deluxe, its spacious bedrooms having a bright, airy feeling. Each contains its own sitting area, air conditioning, and bedside buttons to control color TV, music, and radio. Accommodations are on a sliding scale, ranging from "standard" to "superior." Incidentally, there is an abundance of rooms in the less expensive "standard" classification, and many satisfied guests have found these quite good. Singles start at 495F ($88.36), ascending to 700F ($124.95), and doubles range in price from 540F ($96.39) all the way up to 740F ($132.09), service and taxes included. Breakfast is extra.

The coffeeshop, La Ruche, has a beehive theme. In bright colors, it opens onto an al fresco terrace. The specialty restaurant, Montparnasse 25, serves gourmet French cuisine. Here, the

If Oscar Wilde Could See It Now

L'Hôtel, 13 rue des Beaux-Arts, 6e (tel. 325-27-22), was a 19th-century "fleabag." It was called the Hôtel d'Alsace, and its major distinction was that Oscar Wilde, broke and down and out, died here. In one of the upstairs rooms he wrote to Frank Harris, the Victorian author, to send him "the money you owe me." However, today's clients aren't exactly on poverty row. Through the lobby of what is known only as l'Hôtel march Leopold Rothschild, Julie Christie, Ava Gardner, even Mia Farrow. Elizabeth Taylor wanted to stay here, but the rooms were too small to accommodate her trunks.

On the Left Bank, l'Hôtel is the love-hobby creation of French actor Guy-Louis Duboucheron. He's responsible for establishing this intimate atmosphere of super-sophistication, a hotel that's been called a "jewel box." A Texas architect, Robin Westbrook, was called in and he proceeded to gut the core of d'Alsace, making a circular courtyard and an interior evocative of the Tower of Pisa.

Life here is somewhat like a house party. Duboucheron told the press: "I wanted it to be like raiding the icebox at home in the middle of the night." For all this pampering, however, you must pay the piper. The least expensive chambers (and are they tiny) rent from 440F ($78.54) to 520F ($92.82). Four larger doubles, two with fireplaces, open onto the garden, costing 650F ($116.03). You'll feel like a movie star yourself when you take a bath in your tub of rosy-pink imported Italian marble. At the edge of your tub will be a delicate vase holding a single rose. Throughout the building antiques are used with discretion, an eclectic collection that includes Louis XV and Louis XVI, as well as Empire and Directoire.

For nostalgia buffs, the ideal rooms are the recreation of Wilde's original bedchamber and that of Mistinguett, the legendary star of the French stage. In the latter room, the star's original furniture—designed by Jean-Gabriel Domergue—has been installed. Enjoying these rooms has been everybody from Katharine Hepburn to Princess Grace to Mick Jagger.

Breakfast is served in a stone cellar which in the evening becomes a tavern for intimate dinners. The Winter Garden has been turned into a luxurious piano bar/restaurant.

theme is that of the glamorous Montparnasse period of 1925. Part of the decoration is formed by reproductions of paintings by artists who lived in the quarter, including Modigliani and Van Dongen. Large-scale photos of theatrical personalities of that era are also used. For drinks, the most attractive spot is Le Corail, with an oceanic theme using both coral and futuristic driftwood.

The subway stop, Montparnasse Bienvenue, is across the street, and Gaîté, exactly underground, connects directly to the Champs-Élysées (six stops).

Modern Four-Star Hotels

PLM Saint-Jacques, 17 Boulevard Saint-Jacques, 14e (tel. 589-89-80). Baron and Baronne Elie de Rothschild have come up with a vivid and splashy French-American-style, 812-room, 14-story, steel-and-glass palace on the Left Bank. Although the hotel is somewhat impersonal on the outside, inside it abounds with stylish accommodations, bright colors, and top-rate service. The streamlined rooms are provided at 518F ($92.46) for a single, 601F ($108.89) for a double, including service, tax, and a continental breakfast. The beds are large, and there's a refrigerated automatic bar in each room. The baron promises "the maximum service at the minimum price." And what does PLM stand for? One definition has been ventured—"Pleasure, Leisure, and More."

The Rothschilds have created a colorful bistro, the Café Français, a fanciful version of belle époque style, with bentwood chairs, frosted globes, potted plants, and Gay Nineties posters. A meal here would run about 160F ($28.56) for all you can eat. In addition, you can enjoy quick meals in Le Patio, and Far Eastern cuisine in Le Jun. You'll also find an American bar, Le Saint-James, a Polynesian bar, and a string of boutiques and hairdressing salons. Métro station: St-Jacques.

Hôtel Méridien, 81 Boulevard Gouvion Saint-Cyr, 17e (tel. 758-12-30), is the largest hotel in the country, boasting 1027 rooms. The hotel, at Porte Maillot, opposite the air terminal and the Paris Convention Center, is mainly geared to accommodate the vast international conventions which descend on Paris, as well as the ever-increasing tide of business people.

For those who want all the conveniences, the Méridien lives up to expectations: air conditioning in compact and streamlined bedrooms, separate toilets and baths, television and radio, direct-dial telephones, an underground garage, a superb message service, as well as English-speaking secretarial and stenographic help. You can even get the latest stock-market reports. Parties are checked in via their own separate lounge, and the hotel offers multidimensional convention facilities of outstanding level, for up to 2000 people. All the chambers have panoramic-view windows. Doubles cost from 580F ($103.53) to 645F ($115.13); singles, from 520F ($92.82) to 590F ($105.32).

A number of boutiques on the premises offer variety and convenience in shopping. Four restaurants serve an international cuisine ranging from traditional French at Le Clos Longchamp, to typical American sandwiches at Le Coffeeshop. One even offers Japanese dishes. Guests gather for cocktails at Le Patio, one of the liveliest bars in Paris, or at the Écume des Nuits, the elegant disco and nightclub.

Resort-Style Living at Neuilly

Hôtel du Club Méditerranée, 58 Boulevard Victor-Hugo (tel. 758-11-00), in Neuilly, is a resort-style hotel, set in a tranquil section of Neuilly, at the edge of Paris. Highly flavored with the sexy, friendly vitality of the world-famed Club Méditerranée, it places its emphasis on the young in spirit. Club members are allowed a discount on their room; but the big news is you don't have to be a member to anchor here.

The 340-room, U-shaped hotel is like something on a Caribbean island. You're smilingly welcomed by young men who will check you in and take your luggage; but from then on, you're on your own.

The bedrooms are colorful, with many luxurious touches, such as television, direct-dial telephones, air conditioning, a private mini-bar with drinks, and at the ring of a bell, laundry service. A double room with complete private bath costs 450F ($80.33) nightly. Taxes and service charge are included, and tips aren't allowed. Breakfast, a buffet type, costs an extra 31F ($5.53) per person.

Meals here are social functions, especially at the help-yourself buffet. And in the brilliantly colored lobby, there is an ever-changing art exhibit. The hotel is reached by bus 174, or by the Métro to the Sablons stop.

Leading First-Class Hotels

San Régis, 12 rue Jean-Goujon, 8e (tel. 359-41-90), is a charming town-house hotel in the center of embassies and boutiques, catering to the carriage trade. Between the Seine and the Champs-Élysées, it is one of the best-known addresses in Paris, although it modestly doesn't call attention to itself. A private-club atmosphere prevails. The rooms are discreetly and tastefully decorated, antiques interspersed with reproductions. Some have private salons for a quiet tête-à-tête. One person pays from 380F ($67.83); doubles go for anywhere from 450F ($80.33) to 500F ($89.25). Breakfast is extra. Métro: Alma-Marceau or F.D.R.

La Résidence du Bois, 16 rue Chalgrin, 16e (tel. 500-50-59). This is a Napoleon III mansion which has been completely renovated and elegantly equipped by Monsieur and Madame Desponts who bought the 300-year-old residence in 1964 from the comte de Bomeau. Gleaming white under a mansard roof, the charming little villa sits on a shady lane right off the chic Avenue Foch in the vicinity of the Arc de Triomphe. The Desponts have furnished it with their own personal collection of antiques, including Louis XVI pieces, original paintings, bronzes, and sculpture. Added refinement is reflected in the crystal chandeliers, the use of bronzes, and the silk draperies. The quiet, luxurious rooms are furnished in different periods and styles. Based on the plumbing, doubles range in price from 460F ($82.11) to 710F ($126.74). Those in need of more space may want to rent one of a trio of garden apartments, suitable for two or three persons, each containing a salon. The prices for these begin at 730F ($130.31) to 850F ($151.73), taxes, service, and a continental breakfast included.

Résidence Foch, 10 rue Marbeau, 16e (tel. 500-46-50), is a gracious and artistic hotel run by Mr. and Mrs. Schneider. Off the Avenue Foch, it's only a few minutes from the Arc de Triomphe and a short walk from the Bois de Boulogne. Popular with the diplomatic corps, the hotel is well decorated. All rooms contain private baths, direct-dial phone, radio, television, and clock. The regular doubles rent for 310F ($55.34) and 330F ($58.91), the singles for 250F ($44.63). Prices quoted include tax and service, although breakfast is extra at 20F ($3.57). Guests drop in for afternoon drinks in the front bar-lounge, enjoying its warm, quiet atmosphere. Métro: Porte Dauphine or Porte Maillot.

Claridge-Bellman Hôtel, 37 rue François 1er, 8e (tel. 359-62-51), stands on a street running parallel to the Champs-Élysées. It's a prestigious address in Paris and for many years was known for its theatrical clientele. French newspaper people are attracted to its bar. Bedrooms are furnished in various period styles, costing 507F ($90.50) in a double. Singles rent for 450F ($80.33). Taxes are included, but a continental breakfast costs 30F ($5.36). Classic adornments include bronze hardware, grained wooden chests, Louis XVI–style beds, and silk-paneled walls. The downstairs lounge has somewhat the aura of a men's club.

Château Frontenac, 54 rue Pierre-Charron, 8e (tel. 261-85-11), has broken imaginatively from its past. The hotel is in a classic Parisian building, but it has been totally revamped. Stylish baths have been added and the decor turned contemporary, with low, modern furniture. Neutral walls provide the right foil for splashes of color on the bedspreads. A single room with bath costs 300F ($53.55) to 350F ($62.48); doubles, 370F ($66.01) to 500F ($89.25). All rooms are equipped with self-dial telephone, mini-bar, television, and radio. Between the Champs-Élysées and Avenue George V, the 100-room "château" also shelters the unique restaurant and bar, La Salamandre, previewed under "Cafés and Bars" in a following chapter.

Hôtel Windsor, 14 rue Beaujon (tel. 563-04-04), recently renovated, is in a business and residential area, just a few yards from the Étoile, Champs-Élysées, and Parc Monceau. The warm colors and distinguished decor of the entrance hall and lounge symbolize the quiet good taste and elegance of the whole hotel. There are 135 large, airy, and beautiful bedrooms with private bath and toilet, direct-dial telephone, radio, color TV, video, and automatic private bar. A single costs 545F ($97.28); a twin, 615F ($109.78). Breakfast is 31F ($5.53). In its restaurant, Le Clovis, Pierre Larapidie will provide you with a memorable meal. Métro: Étoile (Charles de Gaulle).

Hôtel de France et Choiseul, 239–241 rue St-Honoré, 1er (tel. 261-54-60), is a remake of a gracious 1720 town house, just off the glamorous Place Vendôme. Actually, it's been a hotel since the 1870s, and became a fashionable oasis in fin-de-siècle Paris. Now, more than a century later, it has been completely remodeled. The bedrooms—most of which open onto the inner courtyard—were entirely gutted, then turned into tiny bandbox-size accommodations that are, nevertheless, attractively decorated. All sorts of conveniences are offered as compensation for the lost belle époque glamor: a refrigerator, television, radio, a dressing table, plus a decorative tiled bath with all the latest gadgets. All is color coordinated, and every room has its token Louis XVI–style chair "to set the right tone." A few mini-suites have been installed on the top floor under the mansard roof, with a rustic staircase leading up to twin beds on a balcony. Singles go for

390F ($69.62); doubles, for 490F ($87.47); including taxes and service. There is a small Pullman-style dining room for guests and a charming restaurant, La Lafayette, opening onto the inner courtyard and consisting of the historical salon where Lafayette received the subsidies to participate in the American War of Independence. Métro: Concorde, Tuileries, Opéra, Madeleine.

Le Grand Hôtel, 2 rue Scribe, 9e (tel. 260-33-50), is a good example of a successful regeneration of an old hotel. Time had passed Le Grand by, although it once had tremendous glamor. It was created by Charles Garnier, the architect of the Opéra, and was inaugurated by the Empress Eugénie. Now, with its new lease on life, it is again one of the leading first-class Parisian hotels. The lounge, with its central glass-covered courtyard, is quite beautiful. Fine contemporary furniture is arranged for conversational groupings, and the central reflection pool is traditionally correct. The color scheme is burnt orange, harmoniously blended with wood tones and contrasted with crisp white.

The bedrooms are neat in appearance, graciously designed and decorated with tasteful color schemes. All the chambers have radio and television sets, as well as bars and refrigerators. The most desirable accommodations are the quieter rooms opening onto the courtyard. Singles with bath rent for 660F ($117.81) to 720F ($128.52); double or twin-bedded rooms, also with bath, go for 760F ($135.66) to 810F ($144.59). Rates include taxes, service, and a continental breakfast. On the premises is the world-famous Café de la Paix, where every visitor sooner or later is fated to meet someone for drinks. Métro: Opéra.

California, 16 rue de Berri, 8e (tel. 359-93-00). You'd hardly expect to find such an incongruously named hotel in Paris. A bank clerk cashing a check for one of the hotel's guests said, after asking the man where he was staying, "No, monsieur . . . not where you're from! The name of your hotel in Paris." Nevertheless, the California is very French. It's only a short stroll from the Arc de Triomphe and the Champs-Élysées, and is part of the Mapotel Best Western chain.

In the center is a formal patio, complete with plants. The California is large, offering more than 187 bedrooms. Doubles with private bath rent for 565F ($100.85) to 630F ($112.46). Some of the rooms contain antiques; others, tastefully selected reproductions. All rooms are equipped with self-dial telephone, mini-bar, television, and radio.

The Golden Gate bar is fun and relaxed, and in the San Francisco restaurant you can enjoy traditional French and international cuisine. During the summer months, the restaurant goes outside into the flowered courtyard. This is a cheerful hotel where you can feel at home. Métro: F. D. Roosevelt or George V.

Regina, 2 Place des Pyramides, 192 rue de Rivoli (tel. 260-31-10). The Place Vendôme, the Opéra, the *Mona Lisa,* the Tuileries —all are virtually at your doorstep. But everything at the Regina is peaceful and relaxing, starting with the flagstone courtyard, with its dolphin fountain and urns of flowers. Antiques, some of which would have been familiar to Mme. de Pompadour and Marie Antoinette, are used wisely to create an old-fashioned, French big-city hotel. Bronze statuary, "brown gravy" oils, inlaid desks, and private salons for that cozy tête-à-tête, create the ambience. All rooms contain private baths. Singles with bath rent for 270F ($48.20); doubles with bath range in price from 310F ($55.34) to 350F ($62.48), including a continental breakfast and service. Métro: Pyramides, Tuileries, Palais Royal.

Best Western–Mapotel Pont-Royal, 7 rue de Montalembert, 7e (tel. 544-38-27), stands on a comparatively calm corner between the Boulevard St-Germain and the Seine, a handy spot that gives you quick access to the Right Bank (and the Louvre) across the bridge, the artists' quarter a few blocks to the east, and the air terminal a short walk to the west. The hotel has long been a favorite with French writers who meet in the bar with their publishers, as well as art-gallery owners from the dozens of shops nearby. They are often seen in the hotel's fine restaurant, Les Antiquaires, with a new terrace on the street, which presents a menu gastronomique. Rooms are done in a traditional style, often with beds either of ornate brass or inlaid wood, and there are gilt mirrors, Regency chests and desks, plus such conveniences as televisions, radios, and refrigerators stocked with drinks. Including a continental breakfast, with orange juice, rates in a single range from 420F ($74.97) to 480F ($85.68). In a double, the tariff is 480F ($85.68), going up to 560F ($99.96) in a twin-bedded room. Taxes and service are also included. Métro: Bac.

Other Leading Choices

Alexander, 102 Avenue Victor-Hugo, 16e (tel. 553-64-65), is a pleasant little hotel, with a fine sense of French taste and flair. The bedrooms reflect a feminine touch, with color-coordinated spreads and draperies, balanced by patterned walls. Many of them open onto balconies. Singles rent from 280F ($49.98) to 325F ($58.01); doubles, from 340F ($60.69) to 395F ($70.51). These prices include taxes, service, and a continental breakfast. An open courtyard with a small garden is an attractive feature, and the lounge invites a cozy tête-à-tête. English is spoken.

Royal-Alma, 35 rue Jean-Goujon, 8e (tel. 225-83-30), near the Seine, lies about an eight-minute walk from the Champs-Élysées. Unlike most of the hotels in the neighborhood, this one is modern and is on a fairly quiet street (Métro: Alma-Marceau). Everything's scaled down, even the lounge, opening onto a rear courtyard. Each bedroom, somewhat small, contains its own tiled bath and built-in furnishings. Everything is immaculately kept, and for this you pay 320F ($57.12) in a single, increasing to 390F ($69.62) in a double, including a continental breakfast, tax, and service.

Hôtel des Deux-Îles, 59 rue Saint-Louis-en-l'Île, 4e (tel. 326-13-35), is a restored 17th-century mansion on this most charming of Seine islands. The interior decorator, Roland Buffat, was so successful with his two other hotels on the same street (the Hôtel de Lutèce and the Hôtel Saint-Louis) that he decided to open his most elaborate hotel to date. The tropical garden of plants and flowers sets the tone, suggesting the charm and taste level provided by this most recommended hotel. Bamboo and reed are used extensively in both the public and private rooms. A single with shower costs 250F ($44.63), rising to 300F ($53.55) in a double with complete private bath. Monsieur Buffat suggests an occasional touch of whimsy by his use of a cage of white doves. The favorite meeting place is the rustic-style tavern on a lower level, where guests in cool weather gather around the open fireplace. Métro: Pont-Marie.

Hôtel de Lutèce, 65 rue Saint-Louis-en-l'Île (tel. 326-23-52), is like a drink of sparkling champagne. This winning little hotel is on the historic St. Louis island where everybody seemingly wants to live, although there just isn't enough room. You pass through the glass entrance doors into what appears to be the attractive and inviting living room of a Breton country house. All this is the creation of a French interior designer, Roland Buffat. His decorating flair is excellent. The all-purpose reception salon and lounge focuses on a stone fireplace surrounded by soft, downy couches and armchairs. Tall plants and modern paintings add the new look, while antique tables and crude tile floors pay homage to the traditional. Each of the 23 bedrooms is uniquely decorated, many with antiques interspersed with tasteful reproductions. Either singles or doubles rent for 280F ($49.98) with shower, to 300F ($53.55) with private bath, taxes and service included. Breakfast is another 20F ($3.57) per person. The duke and duchess of Bedford treat the Lutèce as if it were their Paris town house. Métro: Pont-Marie.

Résidence Lord Byron, 5 rue de Chateaubriand, 8e (tel. 359-89-98), lies just off the Champs-Élysées on a curving street of handsome buildings. Inside, the world of Madame Françoise Coisne unfolds. She's from the Île de France. To Paris she brought her special touch for running a hotel. This is reflected in her furnishings, often fine antique reproductions. Framed prints of butterflies and of scenes in France are discreetly placed throughout. The rooms are personalized, comfortable, and well kept. The most expensive suites—that is, a twin-bedded room with complete bath, petit salon, TV set, and refrigerator—cost 375F ($66.94). A room with a twin or large bed, suitable for two, with complete bath, goes for 285F ($50.87). Breakfast, at 18F ($3.21), is served in an inner garden, although you may prefer it in a petit salon.

Schweizerhof, 11 rue Balzac, 8e (tel. 563-54-22), is in the vicinity of the Champs-Élysées and the Arc de Triomphe, yet for many it evokes a small hotel in a quiet Swiss town. This former private residence with a garden in front has been converted into a well-run and friendly hotel. The owners have added antiques wherever possible. Each room is different, particularly as regards size, and all have TV, radio, and private bars. A single rents for 420F ($74.97); a double, for 500F ($89.25).

Hôtel de Castille, 37 rue Cambon, 1er (tel. 261-55-20). The address is certainly good—between the Chase Manhattan Bank and the Paris headquarters of Chanel. Le Ritz is across the street. Foreigners usually find this one appealing. Its finest feature is an open-air terrace, with potted flowers, climbing vines, and tables set under parasols. The rooms, some quite large, are furnished with typical French flair. All contain private baths. There are no singles, but doubles cost from 250F ($44.63) to 340F ($60.69), the latter rate for the better positioned accommodations. The dining room is provincial in style, with ivory-paneled walls and an open brick fireplace. A tiny salon with Louis XVI–style chairs is suitable for a cozy get-together.

Lutetia-Concorde, 43 Boulevard Raspail, 6e (tel. 544-38-10), is one of the largest hotels on the Left Bank. With 300 rooms, it always seems to tuck you in somewhere—even when every hotel accommodation in the city is seemingly occupied. Business people are especially fond of the Lutetia, as it has facilities appropriate to a large city hotel. Amenities include a brasserie, a bar, ten large reception lounges and ten small ones, and that indispensable porter who produces theater tickets.

Most of the bedrooms are fully renovated. Some guests, however, preferring the untouched vintage accommodations, choose the old-fashioned but very comfortable rooms of traditional style. Each room, modern or ancient, has its own radio, television, direct-dial telephone, and most have mini-bars. The cost for a double room with a private bath is 640F ($114.24); 540F ($96.39) for a single with bath. Breakfast, service charge, and taxes are included.

Victoria Palace Hôtel, 6 rue Blaise Desgoffes, 6e (tel. 544-38-16), is a fine old Montparnasse hotel which has survived the past century through an outpouring of a mountain of francs and a desire to create a setting for those who covet comfort and quiet living. It lies off a busy artery leading to the Boulevard St-Germain. As an aid to tranquility, an inner courtyard with greenery beckons.

The ornate century-old facade remains the same, but the interior has been streamlined considerably. The bedrooms are traditional, with white-paneled walls, Louis XVI–style beds and chairs, and finely grained chests with marble tops and brass hardware. Most of the baths are in Italian marble, with a hand shower in addition to the tub.

The rate in a single begins at 170F ($30.35), from 355F ($63.37) to 380F ($67.83) in a double with bath. These tabs include a continental breakfast, service, and taxes. A generous-size dining room opening onto the courtyard offers à la carte meals. There's a reception lounge as well as an American bar, plus a garage on the premises. Métro: St-Placide.

Louvre-Concorde, Place André-Malraux, 1er (tel. 261-56-01). What a location! A 240-room island of comfort where your window may overlook the Louvre across the street from one side, the Palais Royal on the other, or even the Opéra at the end of the avenue. Singles with shower or bath rent for 580F ($103.53); doubles with shower or bath, 690F ($123.17); plus service and taxes.

The bedrooms have been totally renovated and furnished in modern style, with several built-in pieces, including indirect lighting over the beds and sliding mirrored doors on the wardrobes. Double sinks are found in many of the large bathrooms, too. In addition to direct-dial phones, all the outside

Offbeat: Where Monks of Old Used to Wander

Hôtel de l'Abbaye, 10 rue Cassette, 6e (tel. 544-38-11), is the most alluring of the "new/old" hotels to open in Paris. Before the enlightened restoration by its owners, Monsieur and Madame Lafortune, the building was a 17th-century abbey and later a school. During the restoration, skeletons and artifacts were discovered under stone arches.

Now, everything is luxurious and tasteful. You pass through heavy, 15-foot street doors into a large stone-paved courtyard, with huge pots of greenery and flowers. The entry lounge is formal, with marble floors, a proper background for the 18th-century antiques. A central living room has soft, low sofas around a marble fireplace. Behind this is a winter or garden room with green-and-white floral paper, white wicker furniture, and, naturally, plants. Beyond this is a patio with garden furniture set against flowers and shrubbery. Off the living room is an attractively intimate little drinking bar.

A tiny elevator was installed to take you up to one of the 45 bedrooms with private baths. Madame Lafortune used "blasts of my intuition" in her design concepts. All the bedrooms are medium size, with many built-in features. Beds, chairs, and tables are attractive, with an effective use made of simulated bamboo. The colors are imaginative, the accessories appropriate, and the fabrics unusual. Doubles range from 320F ($57.12) to 400F ($71.40). Taxes, service, and a continental breakfast included.

Most important, the manners and attitude of the staff are impeccable, beginning with the English-speaking woman who checks you in. Métro: St-Sulpice.

rooms are equipped with color television and have double windows to protect them from street sounds.

The main lounge and adjoining bar are still graciously old-fashioned, with columns, walls, and carpets of Pompeian red. One mirrored wall has a room-wide planter of greenery. Nearby are underground public garages. Métro: Palais-Royal.

Hôtel Mont-Thabor, 4 rue du Mont-Thabor, 1er (tel. 260-32-77). No matter which way you walk from this Right Bank hotel, you're within minutes of some of the major attractions of Paris: the Louvre, the Tuileries, the Place de la Concorde, the Place Vendôme, the Opéra. The facilities are excellent, and every room —more than 100 in all—has a private bath.

The character of most of the bedrooms suggests the 19th

century, each one in a "salon" mood, with color-coordinated fabrics on the bed and at the windows. All is comfortable and traditional. Tiled to the ceiling, the bathrooms feature separate circular or square stall showers. In a single room, the tariff is 170F ($30.35), 270F ($48.20) in a double, and 330F ($58.91) in a triple. There's a glass-domed circular reception lounge with intricately patterned marble on the floor and walls. This classic effect is softened by the use of fruitwood provincial furnishings arranged on a circular red-and-white hand-loomed rug. The other salons are more formal, with Louis XV reproductions in red and gold, complete with a grand piano. Métro: Concorde.

Farnése, 32 rue Hamelin, 16e (tel. 720-56-66), looks comfortably lived in. The warmly paneled lounge resembles the library of a men's club, sprawling with books and magazines and deep, cushy leather armchairs. The rooms, all with private bath, toilet, mini-bar, color TV, direct-dial telephone, and treated water for drinking, are distinguished by intimate touches. Singles cost 160F ($28.56); doubles, 250F ($44.63); and triples, 350F ($62.48). Taxes, service, and a continental breakfast are included. Magnifying mirrors with built-in lights aid madame in making up.

The building is in its 77th year and has such extravagant turn-of-the-century flourishes as gleaming terrazzo floors and stained-glass windows in the hallways. All the rooms are spacious and well maintained; some have beds set into alcoves, others, marble fireplaces. The hotel sits about midway between the Arc de Triomphe and the Palais de Chaillot, on a quiet residential street off the broad Avenue Kléber. On your left as you exit from the hotel, you can see the spire of the Eiffel Tower, only a ten-minute walk away. Métro: Iéna or Boissière.

Grand Hôtel Littré, 9 rue Littré, 6e (tel. 544-38-68), is a total remake of an old hotel. Some of the accommodations are done in a stylized Italian marble. Its location in the heart of Montparnasse on a quiet street makes it ideal for those requiring peace in noisy Paris. The hotel is only two Métro stops from the Boulevard St-Germain-des-Prés.

All the furnishings are reproductions of traditional French pieces—some 120 bedrooms employing adaptations of Louis XVI items, using a liberal dose of bold colors. The rates are kept simple: 320F ($57.12) in a single, 360F ($64.26) in a double. If you're traveling with a child, an extra bed will be put in your room for 85F ($15.17). These tariffs include breakfast, service, and taxes. Every room now contains a private bath, telephone,

A 300-Year-Old Town House

Hôtel de l'Université, 22 rue de l'Université, 7e (tel. 261-09-39), has rapidly become the favorite little hotel for those who want to stay in a St-Germain-des-Prés atmosphere. Unusually fine antiques are lavishly used to furnish this 300-year-old, 28-room converted town house. It's the love child of Madame Bergmann, who has a flair for restoring old places and a collector's nose for assembling antiques. She's renovated l'Université completely, giving each bedroom a skillfully designed private bath. The prices depend on the plumbing, with singles in the 200F ($35.70) to 250F ($44.63) bracket; doubles, in the 260F ($46.41) to 390F ($69.62) range (tariffs include tax and service). It's not terribly cheap, but it's well worth the money if you desire a glamorous setting. A favorite room is No. 54, all in shades of Gainsborough blue, with a rattan bed and period pieces, as well as a marble bath. No. 35, opening onto the courtyard, is another charmer—like a living room, with a fireplace and a large provincial armoire decorated in shades of orange. A small breakfast room, in the bistro style, opens onto a tiny courtyard with a fountain. Everything is personal—and reservations are imperative. Métro: Bac or St-Germain.

and radio.

You can dine in the lower-level restaurant, neatly designed in red and white, with a glassed-in ceiling. The Scottish bar, with a decor of green "plaid" and wood paneling, is a popular gathering place. Two salons for entertaining guests are moderately formal, one with wood paneling, white Doric columns, and antique chests.

The Middle Bracket

Odéon Hôtel, 3 rue de l'Odéon 6e (tel. 325-90-67), where some now-famous American artists stayed in the 1930s and 1940s, has been transformed to resemble a colorful Normandy inn. The renovation uncovered old beams, rough stone walls, and high, crooked ceilings. After new plumbing was installed, rooms were designed and furnished, each with a character of its own. Furnishings have successfully blended the old with the modern, ranging from oak and bookbinder wallpaper to bright contemporary fabrics. All accommodations are doubles, renting anywhere from 220F ($39.27) to 300F ($53.55), breakfast, tax, and service included. Rooms are equipped with either private baths or showers. The guest lounge is dominated by an old Parisian tapestry, an amusingly beamed and mirrored ceiling, and white plastic furnishings. The hotel is one minute from the Odéon Théâtre and Boulevard St-Germain. Métro: Odéon.

Hôtel de Fleurie, 32 rue Grégoire-de-Tours, 6e (tel. 329-59-81), is at a select little address on the Left Bank, a relatively unknown choice for most visitors, because the Parisians secretly guard the address. It is an old building that has been beautifully restored with a healthy respect shown for its past life. The facade contains stone statuary in niches which are spotlit at night, giving a 17th-century elegance to the building. Inside, guests are welcomed by a manager who sits at a refectory desk. The old walls have been exposed, revealing their natural stone. A spiral staircase leads down to a room where you can either watch TV or else order a continental breakfast. Placed about are old paintings and 19th-century antiques. The rooms, however, are reached by elevator, and they are well maintained and furnished in a modern idiom. In a twin-bedded chamber with bath, the tariff is 300F ($53.55), although this is lowered to 235F ($41.95) in a double with bath. Breakfast is an additional 20F ($3.57). Métro: Odéon.

Saint-Thomas-d'Aquin, 3 rue du Pré-aux-Clercs, 7e (tel. 261-01-22), is one of the more tranquil choices in the St-Germain-des-Prés area. The entirely renovated hotel lies on a small street between the bustling Boulevard Saint-Germain and the rue de l'Université. A small lounge and reception hall suggest the refined and tasteful tone of the hotel with their flocked paper, paneled woodwork and ceiling, and bronze chandeliers. An elevator takes guests to the private bedrooms with rent for 240F ($42.84) in a twin with a complete private bath. The rooms often contain reproductions of provincial pieces, and some have tester beds in oaken alcoves, everything set against a backdrop of paisley or floral wallpaper. The management and staff are courteous and helpful. Métro: Bac or St-Germain-des-Prés.

Étoile-Maillot, 10 rue de Bois-de-Boulogne, 16e (tel. 500-42-60). You pay a moderate price for prestigious living in this small hotel which is on a quiet shady street halfway between the Arc de Triomphe and the Bois de Boulogne. Although it offers only a minimum of public rooms, its bedrooms are decorated with an unusually fine collection of antiques: bulging bombé chests with marble tops, Louis XV and Louis XVI tapestry-covered chairs, Oriental rugs, gilt and inlaid marquetry beds. A single or a double room with a private bath and toilet costs 240F ($42.84), increasing to 300F ($53.55) if a salon is included. English is spoken. Métro: Argentine.

Grand Hôtel de l'Univers, 6 rue Grégoire-de-Tours, 6e (tel. 033-52-31), is the restoration of a 15th-century inn, just a minute off the Boulevard St-Germain. It's an attractive hotel, the creation of Monsieur Beck, who saw to it that the architectural features were preserved, including the time-aged beams and the whitewashed, rugged stone walls. The combined reception lounge and adjoining bar has style, with overscale black-plastic tufted sofas and armchairs and many green plants. Even the bedrooms have dash, and each is unique. One, for example, is furnished with white wicker furniture evocative of *Suddenly, Last Summer.* Another comes with Danish modern, effectively set off by burnt-orange coordinated fabrics and carpet. Yet another is in the provincial style with color-coordinated fabrics and an entry balcony. All rooms have private tiled baths, television, piped-in music, and a small bar stocked with drinks. The price of the rooms depends on size and decoration. Singles or doubles range from 260F ($46.41) to 350F ($62.48). Métro: Odéon or Mabillon.

Montpensier, 12 rue de Richelieu, 1er (tel. 742-54-34), was built three centuries ago as a private home for the duchess of Montpensier. Nowadays, it's a charming 45-room hotel that has retained its noble facade and elaborate staircase while fitting out 30 of its rooms with 20th-century baths or showers.

The hotel lies on a street of historic buildings, two blocks up from the Louvre, one block over from the sequestered gardens of the Palais-Royal. The rooms and hallways are excellently maintained, the furnishings an attractive mixture of modern functional and antique decorative. Big double doors open into the rooms, which are high-ceilinged and red-carpeted. The majority of the rooms open on the inner court and therefore are quiet. The English-speaking staff is friendly and helpful.

Doubles with private baths, some with showers, rent for 170F ($30.35) to 190F ($33.92). In a single with toilet (no bath), the tariff drops to 56F ($10). Three can be accommodated in a room with bath for 198F ($35.34). Tariffs include a continental breakfast, service, and taxes. Métro: Palais-Royal.

La Régence Étoile, 24 Avenue Carnot, 17e (tel. 380-75-60), is an especially good buy in the district surrounding the Arc de Triomphe. Many of its rooms are particularly well furnished, some with reproductions of French antiques. And most important, almost all rooms come equipped with a tile bath as well as direct-dial phones and, in some, color TV. They rent for 250F ($44.63) to 270F ($48.20), the former with twin beds, the latter with double beds. Single rooms with complete baths range in price from 180F ($32.13) to 214F ($38.20). Tariffs include continental breakfasts, service, and taxes. Métro: Charles de Gaulle (Étoile).

Tivoli-Étoile, 7 rue Brey, 17e (tel. 380-31-22), is the best and most up-to-date hotel on this street of budget accommodations, right near the Étoile. Lying right off the Champs-Élysées, the hotel is only 150 feet from the Étoile subway station. It has been completely redecorated, the small rooms color-coordinated, often using a soothing olive. Each of the rooms contains a bath with radio and TV. But for all this midtown convenience, you pay—295F ($52.66) for two persons, and this tariff includes a continental breakfast. The hotel opens onto an inner patio. If you're a motorist, you'll find a parking lot nearby.

Madeleine-Plaza, 33 Place de la Madeleine, 8e (tel. 265-20-63), is a delight. It has a prime Right Bank position, at the center of all the best shopping districts and within equal walking distance of both the Tuileries and the Opéra, a striking view from its front windows of the Madeleine Church, and a staff that remembers the names of every second-time visitor.

The rooms are contemporary enough to please the most motel-jaded. Headboards and breakfast tables are of shiny brown formica. Black-leather easy chairs provide comfortable resting places. The bedrooms are not overly spacious. For those who don't want their breakfast in bed (at whom the manager can only express wonder), there is a sunlit breakfast room overlooking the church, serving a continental breakfast for 18F ($3.21).

Doubles with shower range in price from 190F ($33.92), going up to 250F ($44.63) with bath. All tariffs include service and tax. Métro: Madeleine.

Hôtel du Pas-de-Calais, 59 rue des Saints-Pères, 6e (tel. 548-78-74), is a historic building with literary connections that has been smartly updated. The five-story structure was built in the 17th century by the Lavalette family and inhabited by Chateaubriand from 1811 to 1814. Possibly its most famous guest was Jean-Paul Sartre, who struggled away with the novel *Dirty Hands* in Room 41 during the hotel's prerestoration days.

Today, although the hotel retains its elegant facade—complete to the massive wooden doors—it offers 40 modern rooms. The baths are generously sized, the rooms brightly appointed with chenille bedspreads in autumnal colors. The inner rooms surround a modest courtyard, with two garden tables and several green trellises. Off the somewhat sterile lobby is a comfortable, carpeted sitting room with TV.

The Pas-de-Calais is an antique-laden street, a half block off Boulevard St-Germain, two blocks from St-Germain-des-Prés. Two guests in a room with private bath pay 280F ($49.98); singles in similar accommodations are charged 240F ($42.84). A continental breakfast is included in these tariffs. Métro: St-Germain-des-Prés.

Trianon Palace, 3 rue de Vaugirard, 6e (tel. 329-88-10), offers a good location, quite adequate amenities, and reasonable prices. The eight-story, 120-room building blends smoothly with the adjoining apartment houses, sitting back a half block from the café-crammed student thoroughfare of Boulevard St-Michel, a slightly removed situation that cuts the noise level considerably. The Trianon is just a short block from the Place de la Sorbonne.

The hotel is more functional than personable. The lobby is large and simple. At the rear is a small, plain dining room where breakfast is served. The rooms are spacious and comfortably furnished in various vintage pieces. Loners with romantic natures should request the single rooms "under the eaves" on the eighth floor, each of which has a dormer-window view of the Latin Quarter.

Doubles with bath rent for 250F ($44.63); with a shower but no toilet, they cost 210F ($37.49). These rates include a continental breakfast, service, and tax. Métro: St-Michel, Odéon.

Aviatic, 105 rue de Vaugirard, 6e (tel. 544-38-21), is a bit of old Paris, with a modest inner courtyard and vine-covered lattice on the walls. The reception lounge, with its overscale marble columns, brass chandeliers, antiques, and petit salon, attractively provides a traditional setting. Completely remodeled, the hotel lies in an interesting center of Montparnasse, with its cafés frequented by artists, writers, and jazz musicians. Each comfortably furnished bedroom is treated differently. In rooms with complete bath, singles rent for 250F ($44.63); doubles, for 290F ($51.77); including tax, service, and a continental breakfast. Métro: Montparnasse-Bienvenue.

Hôtel du Quai Voltaire, 19 Quai Voltaire, 7e (tel. 261-50-91), is an inn with a past and one of the most magnificent views in all Paris. The hotel occupies a prime site on the Left Bank quays of the Seine, halfway between the Pont Royal and the gracefully arched Pont du Carrousel. Twenty-nine of its 33 rooms gaze directly out across the tree-shaded river at the Louvre.

Nor can the Voltaire be easily matched in famed guests. Living here down through the years have been: Charles Baudelaire, Jean Sibelius, Richard Wagner, and Oscar Wilde. Photos of Wagner and Baudelaire are enshrined in the small plush-and-tapestry sitting room inside the main door.

The rooms are pleasantly appointed. But the focal point of every front room is that view—seen through floor-to-ceiling, double French windows.

Twenty-three of the rooms are equipped with good-size modern bathrooms. The Voltaire doesn't have a restaurant, but it does have a bar for drinks and snacks, and an outdoor café on the quay.

Double rooms with private bath rent for 270F ($48.20) to 320F ($57.12). Bathless singles go for 120F ($21.42), increasing to 220F ($39.27) with bath, taxes, service, and a continental breakfast included. Métro: Bac, St-Germain-des-Prés.

Hôtel de Bourgogne et Montana, 3 rue de Bourgogne, 7e (tel. 551-20-22), is the perfect selection for those who want a central hotel with a quiet, almost sedate ambience. A six-story, 35-room, middle-aged structure, the Bourgogne fits inconspicuously into the aristocratic Place du Palais-Bourbon, opposite the mansion that houses the president of the National Assembly. Two blocks equidistant from the Seine and the air terminal, it is directly across the river from the Place de la Concorde.

Everything about this hotel is relaxing and intimate. The staff is a personable lot, quick with helpful attentions. The guest rooms are provided with deep-cushioned easy chairs. A tiny, two-person elevator carries you up to your room. On the ground floor is a circular writing room with columned walls and a cozy lounge. In the homelike dining room, daily meals are served. Doubles begin at 275F ($49.09) and go up to 450F ($80.33). Singles cost from 220F ($39.27) to 420F ($74.97), breakfast, service, and taxes included. Métro: Invalides or Chambre des Députés.

Hôtel Opéra-Lafayette, 80 rue Lafayette, 9e (tel. 824-41-50), is a friendly, three-star hotel where each room has a bath or shower, and quiet elegance describes the decor. An added bonus is the hotel's own fine French restaurant, plus a comfortable lounge and bar offering quick-service food. Both the hotel and restaurant have ambience par excellence. Depending on the plumbing, singles cost 122F ($21.78) to 200F ($35.70); doubles, 130F ($23.21) to 220F ($39.27). Métro: Cadet-Poissonière.

Some Budget Hotels

Hôtel Saint-Louis, 75 rue Saint-Louis-en-l'Île, 4e (tel. 634-04-80), is that rarity, an intimate, charming little hotel (25 rooms), right in the center of historic Île St-Louis. It's the creation of talented Roland Buffat, who has a decorator's flair and a quiet personal style which makes his establishment a true oasis. Single rooms range in price from 150F ($26.78) to 180F ($32.13). Doubles with shower and toilet cost 230F ($41.06). Métro: Pont-Marie.

Regent's Hôtel, 44 rue Madame, 6e (tel. 548-02-81), near the Luxembourg Gardens, is owned by the Jacque and Cretey families, who provide comfortably furnished double- and twin-bedded rooms with private bath for 210F ($37.49); 130F ($23.21) with basin and bidet only. These tariffs include a continental breakfast, taxes, and service. Métro: St-Sulpice.

Lindberg, 5 rue Chomel, 7e (tel. 548-35-53), proves that tiny, formerly unstylish hotels can be given a new lease on life. Off Boulevard Raspail, this hotel has had a major facelift, emerging as a fine, moderately priced address on the Left Bank. The minuscule reception lounge has turned to a most contemporary decor to give it chic. The rooms are pleasantly and comfortably furnished as well, containing direct-dial phones and TVs. A single with shower rents for 155F ($27.67), and doubles with the same plumbing go for 190F ($33.92). However, for the doubles with complete baths or showers the charge ranges from 205F ($36.59) to 230F ($41.06). A telephone-booth-size elevator takes guests to their rooms. Métro: Sèvres-Babylone.

Prince Albert, 5 rue St-Hyacinthe, 1er (tel. 261-58-36), is directly across the street from the Hôtel des Tuileries, and is heralded by a striped awning and green marble front. The 36-room hotel looks as if it were transplanted panel by panel from some English country town. The wood-walled lobby and lounge set the atmosphere here, with more paneling leading back to a miniature bar with a pleasant mixture of English and French furniture.

But there the similarity to an English inn ends for, despite the fact that the Prince Albert does a seam-bursting business in British clients, it is a distinctly French hotel when it comes to comfort. Meaning that the central heating is turned up full-blast in winter, and the drafts are programmed *out,* not in.

Five stories tall, with pin-plain corridors, the Albert dates back to Victorian days and provides some ballroom-size bedrooms, handsomely—albeit somewhat eccentrically—tricked out in splashy wallpaper and brightly hued spreads. Twenty-two private baths have been installed. Doubles with bath are 212F ($37.84); singles with bath, 196F ($34.99). The economical specials are the bathless doubles at 132F ($23.56), the bathless singles at 116F ($20.71). All rates include a continental breakfast, taxes, and service. Métro: Tuileries.

Saint-Roch Hôtel, 25 rue Saint-Roch, 1er (tel. 260-17-91), is your best choice if you're seeking a charming little French provincial-style hotel, right off the Tuileries. The gracious hostess-owner has decorated the hotel with attractive touches, and has carpeted the bedrooms and installed quite a bit of plumbing. Her costliest doubles, with a full private bath, rent for 220F ($39.27), but most North Americans may prefer a double with shower at only 195F ($34.81). A single with shower or toilet rents from 155F ($27.67). The hotel stands behind a glass-and-marble facade. As you enter you'll see a small spiral staircase. However, the well-cared-for bedrooms are reached by a tiny elevator. Only breakfast is served and it is included in the tariffs quoted. Métro: Opéra or Pyramides.

Deux-Continents, 25 rue Jacob, 6e (tel. 326-72-46), is breezily run by Madame Chresteil who has connected two continents—that is, two adjoining buildings. When the sun pours into a little courtyard, you'll feel the essence of the Left Bank. Rooms are tidily furnished, and doubles with twin beds and private bath or shower range from 165F ($29.45) to 230F ($41.06); singles with showers and toilets go for 150F ($26.78) to 210F ($37.49). A continental breakfast, taxes, and service are included. Métro: St-Germain-des-Prés.

Hôtel de Sèze, 16 rue de Sèze, 9e (tel. 742-69-12). Off the Avenue de l'Opéra, this hotel is small, but exceptional in the atmosphere of its public rooms, which sport some Louis XVI–type furnishings. The actual bedrooms provide pot luck: some are graceful with antiques, others somewhat sterile with contemporary pieces. The cheapest doubles go for 140F ($24.99), including hot and cold running water and a bidet, plus use of the corridor baths and toilets. For a room with basin, bidet, and shower, two persons pay 190F ($33.92). For a room with private bath and toilet, the tariff is 210F ($37.49) for two. Bathless singles cost 125F ($22.31), going up to 195F ($34.81) with private bath. A continental breakfast, service, and taxes are included. Métro: Madeleine.

Hôtel Opéra d'Antin-L'Horset, 18–20 rue d'Antin, 2e (tel. 073-13-01), near the American Express and the Opéra, is run by L'Horset chain. Antiques and reproductions give it a traditional look. The service is polite and friendly, and the price is right: 350F ($62.48) for a double with private bath or shower. Economy tip: Book a double with hot and cold running water only at 190F ($33.92) nightly. Singles range in price from 190F ($33.92) bathless to 290F ($51.77) with a private bath or shower. Tariffs include a continental breakfast, service, and tax. Métro: Opéra.

Hôtels de France, 22 rue d'Antin, 2e (tel. 742-19-12), are two side-by-side hotels in the vicinity of the "Grands Boulevards," off the Avenue de l'Opéra. Some of the bedrooms have been modernized, and contain rather impersonal contemporary furnishings; others are made more inviting through the use of reproductions of antiques. For a double room with private bath or shower, the rate ranges from 170F ($30.35) to 230F ($41.05) nightly. A single with toilet only goes for 80F ($14.28). A continental breakfast, taxes, and service are included. Métro: Opéra.

Hôtel du Grande Turenne, 6 rue de Turenne, 4e (tel. 278-43-25), is for those who want to live in what was once the heart of aristocratic Paris, an increasingly chic thing to do these days. Le Marais is still a bastion of inexpensive hotels. If you go now, you can take full advantage of the low tariffs. The entrance of du Grand Turenne has a canopy with potted plants placed about. Inside this little two-star hotel you'll find unqualified respectability. It's one of the more expensive hotels in the Marais, as it has been considerably upgraded in recent years, with many comforts and modern conveniences added. The breakfast room and reception area are quite attractive. A well-furnished double with complete bath or shower goes for 159F ($28.39), but only 95F ($16.96) with less plumbing. The management speaks English. Métro: St-Paul-le-Marais.

Another more modest choice in the same area, **Stella,** 14 rue Neuve St-Pierre, 4e (tel. 272-23-66), is perhaps one of the least known hotels of Paris, lying deep in the Marais off the Place des Vosges, near the Métro stop at the Place de la Bastille. The government grants it only one star, and it's admittedly a very modest selection, but it is clean, friendly, and provides routine comfort. A corner building, it offers mainly bathless accommodations. Depending on the plumbing, singles range from 53F

($9.46) to 64F ($11.42); doubles, from 83F ($14.82) to 143F ($25.53). Breakfast is another 14F ($2.50) per person. The lounge is in the provincial style, with comfortable armchairs where guests sit watching TV.

Airport Charles de Gaulle

Sofitel Paris Roissy, Aéroport Charles de Gaulle—Zone Centrale, Roissy-en-France (tel. 862-23-23), is a 352-room hotel a few minutes from the airport, from which there is free bus service. All its rooms are air-conditioned and soundproofed, and there are enough bars and restaurants to save you from making a difficult trip into Paris. Double-bedded rooms and twins are offered, and all of them contain TV sets, phones, radios, and harmoniously attractive furnishings. One person pays from 300F ($53.55) to 370F ($66.01), and doubles rent for from 330F ($58.91) to 450F ($80.33). Guests who use the room only for the day pay 150F ($26.78) in a single, 170F ($30.35) in a double.

Soaking Up Atmosphere

Hôtel du Lys, 23 rue Serpente, 6e (tel. 326-97-57), is a renovated 17th-century town house in the Latin Quarter. Its creator, Monsieur Steffen, has exposed the old-world beams and added a discreet assortment of antiques. The bedrooms may be either spacious or cramped, depending on your luck. For a double room with a shower, the cost is from 130F ($23.21) to 155F ($27.67). Singles with shower rent for 105F ($18.74) to 125F ($22.31). Reservations are imperative if you wish to stay here in summer. Métro: St-Michel or Odéon.

Mont-Blanc, 28 rue de la Huchette, 5e (tel. 033-49-44). On one of the most famous small streets in Paris, the Mont Blanc extravagantly bills itself as a "grand hotel." Actually, it's a rather small but celebrated Left Bank inn, just off the Place St-Michel; and it's also the place where Elliot Paul wrote *The Last Time I Saw Paris.* A double room with a complete bath is 200F ($35.70), only 125F ($22.31) without bath. Métro: St-Michel.

Saint-André-des-Arts, 66 rue Saint-André-des-Arts, 6e (tel. 326-96-16), is a popular St-Germain-des-Prés hotel, in the midst of several galleries and shops selling paintings and sculpture. No singles are available, but doubles, depending on the plumbing, range from 90F ($16.06) to 135F ($24.10). Triples go from 135F ($24.10) to 150F ($26.78). Included in these tariffs are a continental breakfast, taxes, and service. Métro: Odéon.

At Orly Airport

Hilton International Orly, 276 Orly Sud (tel. 687-33-88), one of the biggest and most modern airport hotels on the continent. Across from the main terminal, it is about 25 minutes outside the center of Paris on the Great Southern Expressway. The hotel has surprising style and flourish. It's a long, "sawtooth," soundproofed structure which has added 120 rooms. The hotel provides free shuttle bus service to and from the airport.

Your room may have chalkwhite walls accented by lemonyellow furniture. Air conditioning and heating are individually controlled. In a newer extension, guest rooms have a self-service refrigerator/bar which dispenses snacks and drinks at the touch of a button. The nicest part of the hotel is its rates. You get the same service and facilities as the Left Bank Hilton, previewed earlier, but the tariffs are as much as one-third lower. Singles cost 210F ($37.49) to 330F ($58.91); doubles, 275F ($49.09) to 390F ($69.62). Special rates for day use of the rooms—that is, between 7 a.m. and 8 p.m.—are granted at 180F ($32.13), an ideal arrangement if you're between planes. In addition, up-to-date flight information is provided by direct guest-room telephone connections to the airport information center.

There's a wide choice for dining as well. The main restaurant, La Louisiane, features Créole and international specialties (also good American steaks and chops) in a Mississippi-riverboat setting. Overlooking the garden is Le Café du Marché, good for snack or a quick meal. Finally, l'Atelier, next to La Louisiane, is a recreation of a bohemian artist's studio in Montmartre.

Chapter V

DINING IN PARIS

EVERYTHING YOU'VE EVER HEARD about French cooking is true—it's absolutely superb. And Paris is where you'll find French cuisine at its best. So if fine dining, at any price level, is what you enjoy, then you've come to the right place. All of the world's large cities boast a certain number of fine restaurants, but only in Paris can you turn onto the nearest side street, enter the first ramshackle hostelry you see, sit down at a bare and wobbly table, glance at an illegibly hand-scrawled menu—and get a memorable meal.

But what about the cost? Paris has gained a reputation as being damnably expensive in the food department. True, her star-studded, internationally famous establishments are very expensive indeed. Places like **Tour d'Argent, Maxim's, Grand Véfour,** and **Lasserre** are not so much restaurants as temples of gastronomy, living memorials to the glory of French cuisine. The Grand Véfour, in fact, is officially classed as a local monument and may be altered only under penalty of law. Maxim's was immortalized by Franz Lehar in his *Merry Widow,* and La Tour d'Argent boasts what is widely regarded as the finest wine cellar in the world.

In these culinary cathedrals you pay not only for superb decor and regal service, but also for the art of celebrated chefs on ministerial salaries.

There is also a vast array of expensive dineries existing almost exclusively on the tourist trade. Their food may be indifferent or downright bad, but they'll have ice water and ketchup to anesthetize your tastebuds, trilingual waiters and quadrilingual menus. It's these places which are largely responsible for Paris's high-cost reputation, and if you insist on frequenting them you'll find it only too true.

Luckily there are others. Hundreds of others. For Paris has not only more restaurants than any other city on earth, it also has more good, reasonably priced ones. And they don't take much finding. We've counted 18 of them in a single, narrow Left Bank street.

DINING TIPS: Most Paris restaurants automatically add a service charge of around 12% to 15% to your bill (*service compris*), which means you don't have to leave a tip. But you have to watch your bill for that. If service is not included, it is customary to tip about 15%.

Some restaurants include beverage in their menu rates (*boisson compris*). And do try wine with meals. French cooking only achieves palate perfection when lubricated by wine, which is not considered a luxury or even an addition, but an integral part of every meal.

Don't—unless you're a real connoisseur—worry about bottle labels and vintages. Some of the most satisfying wines we've drunk here came from unlabeled house bottles. Don't be overly concerned with that red-wine-with-red-meat, white-with-white routine. It's merely a rough guide. When in doubt order a rosé, which fits almost everything.

French beer, on the other hand, is so anemic that it can't be regarded as an alcoholic beverage. Look on it as a thirst quencher only, like Vichy water.

In many of the less expensive places we'll be taking you to the menu will be printed or handwritten in French only. Don't let that intimidate you. You needn't be timid either about ordering dishes without knowing precisely what they are. You'll get some delightful surprises. We know a woman who wouldn't have dreamed of asking for *escargots* if she'd realized they were snails cooked in garlic sauce. As it was, she ate this appetizer in a spirit of thrift rather than adventure—and has been addicted to it ever since.

Finally, a word on vegetables. The French regard them as separate courses and eat them apart from the meat dishes. But we wouldn't advise you to order them specially, unless you're an exceptionally hearty eater. Most main courses come with a small helping or *garni* of vegetables, anyway.

You'll find a large number of specific dishes explained in our restaurant descriptions. No one, however, can explain the subtle nuances of flavor that distinguish them. Those you have to taste for yourself.

Coffee, in France, is served *after* the meal and charged extra.

The French consider it absolutely barbaric to drink coffee along with the courses. Unless you specifically order it with milk (*au lait*), the coffee will be black. In the more conscientious establishments, it is still served as the traditional *filtre*, a rather slow but rewarding filter style that takes a bit of manipulating.

The Great Restaurants

Lasserre, 17 Avenue Franklin D. Roosevelt, 8e (tel. 359-53-43), is probably the finest restaurant in Paris today, dispensing the haute cuisine. What is now this elegant and deluxe restaurant was a simple bistro before the war, a "rendezvous for chauffeurs." Then along came Monsieur Lasserre, who bought the dilapidated building and set out to create his dream. His dream turned into a culinary paradise, attracting gourmets from around the world.

Two white-painted front doors lead to the dining rooms on the ground level, including a reception lounge with Louis XVI–style furnishings and brocaded walls . . . most chic. Even the small elevator that takes you to the main dining room upstairs is beautifully lined with brocaded silk. The main salon is two stories high. On each side is a mezzanine. Draped with silk, tall arched windows open onto the street. At a table set with fine porcelain, crystal glasses edged in gold, a silver candelabrum, even a silver bird and a ceramic dove, you sit on a Louis XV–style salon chair and carefully study the menu.

Overhead the ceiling is painted with lamb-white clouds and a cerulean sky. The trick here is that in fair weather the staff slides back the roof to let in the real sky, either moonlight or sunshine, depending. From time to time, Monsieur Lasserre brings in a flock of white doves from his home in the country. Then he releases them in the room. Before that, however, raffle numbers have been attached to their feet.

The food is a combination of French classicism and originality. The presentation of dishes is one of the most winning and imaginative aspects of Lasserre. Always count on high drama. For example, the garni vegetables so often neglected in most restaurants are presented here with flourish. In the hands of some artist back there in the kitchen, vegetables become flowers.

To begin, we'd suggest pâté d'anguille aux fines herbes at 98F ($17.49), a tempting dish made with eels. The chef specializes in canard (duck) à l'orange, 105F ($18.74); another favorite is the ris de veau braisé Grand Palais (sweetbreads, the finest we've tasted anywhere), 105F also. A dozen truly great desserts are presented; try the pannequet soufflé flambé, 52F ($9.28), and discover why the proprietor is often called "king of the casseroles." In honor of this distinction, the Club de la Casserole dines here—and its members are hard to please.

Reservations are a must. Closed Sunday, Monday, and in August.

La Tour d'Argent, 15 Quai de la Tournelle, 5e (tel. 354-23-31), is a national institution. The view over the Seine and the apse of Notre-Dame is superb. At night, incidentally, Notre-Dame is floodlit, partly at the expense of La Tour d'Argent. Sometimes the lights go off in this penthouse restaurant so that you may enjoy the special illumination of Paris by night.

On the Left Bank, La Tour d'Argent traces its history back a long way. A restaurant of some sort has stood on this ground since 1582. The fame of the establishment was spread during its ownership by Frédéric Delair, who bought out the fabled wine cellar of the Café Anglais. He was the one who started the practice of issuing certificates to diners ordering the house specialty, pressed duckling (caneton). The birds, incidentally, are numbered.

Under the sharp eye of its owner, Claude Terrail, the cooking is superb, the service impeccable. Dresden china adorns each table. Although a quarter of the menu is taken up with various ways you can order duck, we assure you the kitchen *does* know how to prepare other dishes. Especially recommendable are quenelles de brochet homard Lagardère and noisettes de Tournelles. To open your meal, we recommend potage Claudius Burdel, made with egg yolks, fresh cream, chicken broth, sorrel, and butter, whipped together. Expect to pay from 375F ($66.94) to 600F ($107.10) for a complete meal. The restaurant is closed on Monday, but otherwise orders are taken until 10 p.m.

Whatever your repast, you'll fare better than those attending the 1870 Christmas dinner during the war with Prussia. Raiding the Paris zoo, the chef offered such delicacies as elephant soup, antelope chops, bear steaks, camel hump, even side dishes of wolves, cats, and rats!

"Le Véfour," 17 rue de Beaujolais, 1er (tel. 296-56-27), was founded during the reign of Louis XV. Then it was known as the Café de Chartres. Habitués included Danton and Napoleon. In a splendid setting of the Palais-Royal, Le Grand Véfour later in its career attracted such artists as Cocteau and Colette who were in residence nearby. The late Cocteau is responsible for the menu cover, dating from 1953.

Officially classified as a national monument, the restaurant is run by its proprietor Raymond Oliver, who hails from Bordeaux. Monsieur Oliver is the author of many gourmet cookbooks, including *La Cuisine*. This elegant edition, incidentally, sold 100,000 copies in the U.S. alone at a cost of $30 a volume. He also makes frequent appearances on TV, lecturing on the subtle art of the French haute cuisine. And, although it may sound incongruous for a man in his position, Monsieur Oliver was also a pioneer in the frozen-food industry in France.

From April to July (usually) a special feature of the kitchen is a dish of lampreys. When you eat them with the magnificent touch they're given here, you'll forget they are merely river eels. The cost is 110F ($19.64). Another good dish is rognon de veau, 100F ($17.85). It is served aux trois moutardes, that is, veal kidneys with three mustards. For a divine beginning, ask for the salade quimperloise, made with pieces of lobster laced with cognac, 100F ($17.85). On our most recent rounds, we discovered another specialty, côtes d'agneau Albarine, costing 90F ($16.06). This is a lamb chop stuffed with slices of veal kidney and braised with a sauce of white wine, shallots, and cream. It's served with a potato pancake and a purée of seasonal vegetables. Reservations are imperative. The restaurant is closed Saturday night, all day Sunday, and in August.

Taillevent, 15 rue Lamennais, 8e (tel. 563-39-94), takes its name from a famous chef of the 14th century. Born in 1326, he was the author of one of the oldest books on cookery. The setting for this citadel of haute cuisine is a town house off the Champs-Élysées. The decoration is in the style of Louis XVI. The owner, Monsieur J. C. Vrinat, greets guests as if he were welcoming them to a private dinner party.

If you go for either lunch or dinner, know that you'll be served some of the finest food in France. A good opener to your gourmet repast might be cervelas de fruits de mer aux truffes et aux pistaches, 158F ($28.20) for two persons. For a main course, we'd suggest a house specialty, poularde de Bresse à la bousse de cresson, 78F ($13.92). The canette de Barbarie de cassis is another house specialty at 172F ($30.70) for two persons. To conclude, fromages de nos provinces, at 35F ($6.25), are always reliable. It's necessary to reserve. At lunch, business people, many on expense accounts, seem to dominate. However, the room contains more foreign visitors in the evenings. Closed Saturday, Sunday, and in August.

Lucas-Carton, 9 Place de la Madeleine, 8e (tel. 265-22-90), is a belle époque restaurant created by an Englishman, Lucas, and a supremely talented French chef, François Carton. The trappings are plush, as befitted the era. High ceilings, red-velvet banquettes, large mirrors placed in the paneling, art-nouveau bronze decorations, tasteful stemware, and bowls of fresh flowers on each table provide the aristocratic setting for some of the fine haute cuisine of Paris.

Ambassadors and cabinet members, among others, flock here to enjoy such house specialties as salle d'agneau (lamb) Madeleine and duckling in the style of Rouen. Other main-course dishes that are house specialties include délices de sole Lucas, followed by a thrilling dessert, crêpes flambées au Grand Marnier. A full dinner will cost about 320F ($57.12). The wine cellar is among the better stocked in Paris, particularly in its collection of burgundies. Lucas-Carton is open all year, serving dinner until 10:30 p.m. Always reserve in advance, although at night we've never had any trouble securing a seat.

Maxim's, 3 rue Royale, 8e (tel. 265-27-94), is the world's most legendary restaurant. It carefully preserves the era of belle époque. It's not hard to imagine the Gay Nineties when "cocottes," replete with ostrich feathers, perched in their boxes, letting their diamonds sparkle, and casting flirtatious glances at handsome, almond-eyed young men.

Maxim's was a favorite of Edward VII, then the prince of Wales. He enjoyed the slightly decadent atmosphere, far removed in spirit from the rigid London ruled by his stern mother, Victoria.

The restaurant is already known to many North American movie-goers who have never been to Paris. It was the setting for *The Merry Widow,* where John Gilbert "dipped and swayed" with Mae Murray. That memory is kept alive today. You can always be sure the orchestra will play that tune at least once a night. Much later in film history, Louis Jourdan—at that time called "the handsomest man in the world"—took Leslie Caron to the restaurant "the night they invented champagne" in the musical *Gigi.*

Over the years, the restaurant has continued to attract and has maintained its high standards. Any night in season you're likely to see a world legend dining at a table near you. Some of its present and former patrons are captured in caricature on one of the walls.

Former owners Monsieur and Madame Louis Vaudable inherited this showcase of fin de siècle from his father, Monsieur Vaudable, who obtained the restaurant in the 1930s. If he were here today, he might even recognize it—certainly the paneled walls, the leafy cut-out overlays, the stained-glass ceiling. Continuing their high standards, Pierre Cardin took over the restaurant in the spring of 1981.

The chef has a staff of some of the finest and most talented young cooks in France. Many of them train at Maxim's before going on to open up an operation of their own. One of the finest soups we've had anywhere—and it's a great opener to a repast at Maxim's—is Billi-By soup. It's made with mussels, white wine, cream (of course), chopped onions, celery, and parsley, as well as coarsely ground pepper. Another favorite, the sole Albert, named after the late famous maître d'hôtel, is flavored with chopped herbs and bread crumbs, plus a large glass of vermouth. Also highly recommendable are coquilles St-Jacques (scallops) au safran and poularde aux concombres (pullet with cucumbers). For dessert, try either the tarte tatin or the crêpes Veuve Joyeuse. The tart, incidentally, is made with thick slices of Reinette apples and a pâté brisée dough.

As for drinks, everybody at Maxim's orders champagne, or used to in the old days. After making your reservation, arrive slightly early so you can have a drink in the Imperial Bar upstairs. Formal dress is de rigueur on Friday. Maxim's is open all year except Sunday. It's most fashionable to have an after-the-ater supper here, listening or dancing to the music. The kitchen takes orders until midnight. Expect to pay from 450F ($80.33) to 550F ($89.25) per person.

Le Vivarois, 192 Avenue Victor-Hugo, 16e (tel. 504-04-31), has been called a revelation by food critics. This restaurant opened in 1966 with a modern decor (including chairs by Knoll), and it was initially popular with the American colony. Now, however, it's been fully discovered by the French themselves, perhaps belatedly. The American magazine *Gourmet* hailed it as "a restaurant of our time . . . the most exciting, audacious, and important restaurant in Paris today."

The restaurant is the personal statement of its supremely talented owner-chef, Claude Peyrot. His menu is constantly changing. Someone once said, and quite accurately, "the menu changes with the marketing and his genius." He does a most recommendable coquilles St-Jacques (scallops) en crème, and a pourpre de turbot Vivarois. His most winning dish to many is rognons de veau (veal kidneys). Expect to pay from 280F ($49.98) to 350F ($62.48) for a memorable meal.

Madame Peyrot is one of the finest maîtres d'hotel in Paris. She'll guide you beautifully through the wine selections so that you'll end up with the perfect complement to her husband's superlative cuisine. It is necessary to reserve in advance. Closed Saturday, Sunday, and in August.

Haute Cuisine

At least once in your lifetime you should forget about the budget and splurge on a great classical French meal. If you can't afford Maxim's or Tour d'Argent, know that there are many other fine establishments serving remarkable food at prices that are slightly lower than those already previewed.

Escargot-Montorgueil, 38 rue Montorgueil, 1er (tel. 236-83-51). The "golden snail" of Les Halles is as golden as ever, even if the famous market has moved elsewhere. And the Escargot-Montorgueil is firmly entrenched, the building supposedly dating from the days of Catherine di Medici. The restaurant opened its doors back in the 1830s, and inside it looks it. (The decor has been described as "authentic Louis Philippe.") The greats, such as Sarah Bernhardt, have paraded through here. The food—in the grand bistro tradition—remains consistently good, but expensive. However, you won't mind paying extra to enjoy the food, the setting of genuine antiquity, and the café society of Paris.

Everybody but the regulars appears to order escargots, although this dish doesn't seem to get much attention from the chef. We'd recommend the pieds de porcs and the feather turbot soufflé. For dessert, the specialty is strawberry beignets. Your complete meal is likely to run from 200F ($35.70) to 350F ($62.48) per person with wine, but not the 15% service charge. The restaurant is run by Mme. Saladin-Terrail, sister of Claude Terrail, the guiding hand behind La Tour d'Argent. It is open every day, and reservations are imperative. Métro: Les Halles.

Drouant, Place Gaillon, 2e (tel. 742-56-61), is, along with the Grand Véfour, the most classic restaurant in the French capital, dispensing haute cuisine for more than a century. You have two places to dine—at the grill on your left as you enter (where the menu is slightly cheaper), or in the main room, with its restrained, conventional elegance. If you're really being very French, you may prefer to reserve one of the private dining salons.

The best dishes are seafood, although the chef certainly knows how to prepare game and meat dishes with finesse. Nearly anything will be good, including the plateau de fruits de mer, 120F ($21.42); rognons d'agneau (lamb kidneys), 65F ($11.60); and the filets de sole Drouant, 80F ($14.28). In the grill, the loup (sea bass) with fennel is the specialty, costing 120F ($21.42). Other selections include escalope de bar gratinée at 95F ($16.96); blanc de turbot à la crème d'oseille, 120F ($21.42); and steake de canard au poivre vert, 80F ($14.28). The Académie Goncourt, the celebrated literary society of France, meets here once a month, by the way. The restaurant is open daily from noon to 2 a.m. (last orders at 1 a.m.). Métro: 4 Septembre.

Chez Les Anges, 54 Boulevard de Latour-Maubourg, 7e (tel. 705-89-86). This one gets better all the time. From Burgundy, land of great wine and great food, comes François Benoist, who operates one of the best restaurants in Paris. The decor has been considerably improved over the years, the ambience enhanced by a collection of contemporary paintings. All this is probably a direct result of the increasing attention and publicity this restaurant is receiving. Monsieur Benoist apparently doesn't welcome all the fanfare spinning around his restaurant, preferring to keep his own standards . . . but quietly!

Many of the celebrated Burgundian dishes are offered, including, as a starter, les oeufs en meurette (eggs in red-wine sauce). The most classic main dish is sauté de boeuf bourguignon, as well as entrecôte au vin de Rully. Other main dishes include suprême de barbue au beurre de poivrons rouges, cassolette de St-Jacques aux oursins, rognon de veau à l'aigre doux, and tranche épaisse de foie de veau. The goat-cheese selection is varied. Desserts are rich, including a sorbet made with fresh strawberries and Cassis. The average bill is about 250F ($44.63) per person. The good choice of burgundy wines will leave your head spinning.

Closed Sunday nights and Monday and from August 15 to September 15. Reservations are necessary, especially at lunch when French business people will do you out of a seat. Near the Invalides, the closest Métro stop is Latour-Maubourg.

Prunier, 9 rue Duphot, 1er (tel. 260-36-04), is the most classic seafood restaurant of Paris. The owner, Monsieur Funaro, has used the help of Gilbert and Maguy Le Coze to give this former fin-de-siècle landmark a new lease on life. They have renewed the downstairs bar and widened the small first-floor salon, turning it into a large dining room with faded blue tapestry on the walls and round tables. Monsieur Funaro's care and concern begins not just in the kitchen, but with the fishermen who catch his produce.

Most diners begin their meals with oysters, although you may prefer the palourdes (clams) of Brittany. Count yourself fortunate if you arrive on a Wednesday or Friday. On those special occasions, you can order marmite Dieppoise, Prunier's own special bouillabaisse. Other specialties include filets de sole Prunier, a civet de canard (duckling), côte de veau au citron, and poularde au curry (chicken curry). In addition to the already celebrated seafood dishes, the chef has added a zest of the nouvelle cuisine, as reflected in the preparation of vegetables and in the lighter sauces. After the richness of the sea, try a bowl of fresh fruit, chopped and sprinkled with almonds. Expect to pay some 250F ($44.63) to 350F ($62.48) per person. Prunier is closed on Monday and in August. Métro: Madeleine.

Espadon ("Swordfish"), Ritz Hotel, 38 rue Cambon, 1er (tel. 260-38-30). This is not just a mere grill attached to a deluxe hotel, it offers one of the finest kitchens in Paris. Before the war, the grill refused to admit women and was, therefore, a bastion of male supremacy with a gentlemen's club aura. And though that practice has long since been abandoned, the spirit still lingers. Classical dishes are impeccably served here, including such plats du jour as noisette d'agneau (lamb) Vendôme and filet de barbue (brill) au Porto. Framboises (raspberries) des bois make a nice finish. Ordering à la carte, expect to pay from 275F ($49.09) to 350F ($62.48) for a complete meal. Add 15% for service.

The grill room faces a courtyard garden of the Ritz. When the weather is fair, meals are served there. While listening to a bubbling fountain on the terrace, guests enjoy the seafood cuisine on the à la carte menu. Inside, the grill is decorated in a marine theme, as trompe-l'oeil vines creep and crawl. Orders are taken nightly all year until 10:30 p.m.

Ledoyen, Carré des Champs-Élysées, 8e (tel. 266-54-77), in a classic building, is considered the most glamorous garden restaurant in Paris. In gardens right off the Champs-Élysées, it is surrounded by willows, fountains, flowery borders, and chestnut trees. Your taxi pulls up, a doorman opens the car door, and you're ushered into a foyer decorated with Louis XVI–style and Directoire pieces. The interior has been aptly compared to a stage setting for *La Dame aux Camélias*. Silver tablewear, pink cloths, armchairs covered in brocaded silk, bowls of fresh flowers . . . such a romantic setting you almost forget the food.

But the director, Monsieur LeJeune, sees to it that you will be fed—and very well. He personally recommends le foie gras de canard aux quatre épices. Main courses include such dishes as marmite Dieppoise, sole soufflé à l'Armoricaine, and rognons (kidneys) flambés. Personally we prefer the *grande spécialité*, canard (duck) or pintadeaux (guinea hen) aux pêches. Special attention is paid to desserts, la surprise Ledoyen and the crêpe soufflée flambée au Cointreau. Expect to pay around 275F ($49.09) per person. The restaurant is closed Sunday and for most of August. Métro: Concorde.

La Grande Cascade, Bois de Boulogne, 16e (tel. 772-66-00), is a garden house—a belle époque shrine for lunch, afternoon tea, or dinner in the heart of Paris's celebrated and fashionable park. Originally, this indoor-outdoor restaurant was built by Baron Haussmann and was used as a hunting lodge for Napoleon III. At the turn of the century, it was converted into a restaurant, and drew the chic of its day. Picture such a theatrical personality as Mistinguett arriving in a grand carriage, complete with super-wide hat, parasol, and entourage. That was La Grande Cascade that was.

Today's humbler guest can select a table, choosing the more formal interior with its gilt, crystal, and glass roof, or the more popular front terrace. At the latter, under either parasols or portico shelter, you can order a meal, a drink, or an old-fashioned afternoon tea with a generous helping of the chef's favorite cake. Soft lights at night from the tall frosted lamps and the sound of the nearby cascade enhance the romantic feeling of the place.

The restaurant features such à la carte selections as foie gras de canard (duckling) at 93F ($16.60), panache de poisson à la vapeur au pistou at 84F ($14.99), and a côte de boeuf grillée aux trois sauces at 190F ($33.92) for two persons. A spectacular finish is provided by crêpes soufflées à l'orange, 40F ($7.14). The place is reached by car or taxi only. Service is extra. The restaurant serves dinner only from October 15 to May 15 and is closed from mid-December to mid-January.

La Nouvelle Cuisine

Many visitors to Paris today are eager to sample La Nouvelle Cuisine or Cuisine Minceur, which has been so widely publicized, including a cover story in *Time* magazine. Cuisine Minceur, which has been called the "cuisine of slimness," was launched by Michel Guérard when his girlfriend told him he'd look great if he lost some weight. Now, his fame has spread throughout the world, and chic visitors flock to his restaurant at Eugénie-les-Bains, in the Landes, just east of the Basque country.

La Nouvelle Cuisine is different from Cuisine Minceur, although they share similarities. La Nouvelle Cuisine is not a diet cuisine, and is based on classic principles of French cookery. However, rich sauces are eliminated, and cooking times which can destroy the best of fresh ingredients, particularly vegetables, are considerably shortened. The aim of both cuisines is to release the natural flavor of food, without covering it with heavy layers of cream and butter, so preferred by all the students of Escoffier over the past decades.

The new school (not so new by now) is widely growing, and restaurants featuring La Nouvelle Cuisine are opening up in Paris almost monthly. Some of the new flavor combinations are inspired, and you may want to have at least one "new cuisine" meal during your Paris sojourn. What follows is a random sampling of some of the leading centers where this original, imaginative cookery is practiced with skill and talent.

L'Archestrate, 84 rue de Varenne, 7e (tel. 551-47-33). Alain Senderens is probably the finest creative chef in Paris. At a location across from the Rodin Museum, against a backdrop of Oriental elegance, Monsieur Senderens dispenses his meticulously prepared viands. Although still young, he has had years of training at such prestigious establishments as Lucas-Carton and La Tour d'Argent. However, after leaving those classic establishments, he gave free rein to his imagination. He immediately set a high standard when it came to selecting a name for his restaurant, l'Archestrate, after the Greek poet and gastronome who has been called "the Brillat-Savarin of the time of Pericles."

In season, M. Senderens offers navets farcis (stuffed turnips) braisés au cidre. Another specialty is turbot in fennel sauce. Incidentally, Mme. Senderens shows you to your table and takes your order. For a superb beginning, try a terrine of sole and crayfish. Senderens has broken more and more from his teachers in classic French cookery, and is now one of the leading exponents of La Nouvelle Cuisine. Among the dishes he has added to this rapidly expanding repertoire are aiguillettes de canard (duck) au vinaigre, a sweetbread and asparagus salad, a meltingly tender boned and cut-up pigeon (with a thick conserve of leeks), lobster and cucumber, scallops marinated with a corn salad, and a tarte bonne femme baked to order for two persons. There are two set menus offered at 270F ($48.20) and 350F ($62.48), plus 15% for service. However, if you order à la carte, expect to pay about 500F ($89.25), depending on your selection of wine. It is necessary to reserve three to six days in advance. Closed Saturday and Sunday, and in August. Métro: Varenne-Bac.

Dodin Bouffant, 25 rue Frédéric-Sauton, 5e (tel. 325-25-14). Jacques Manière, the chef, always comes up with a surprise. He made the nearby Le Pactole into one of the most celebrated restaurants of Paris, before turning over the operation to one of his chefs. For himself, he selected a former rehabilitation center on the Place Maubert, flippantly naming it after the fictional character in 19th-century French gastronomic lore. There, in a modern setting, he has dedicated a temple to La Nouvelle Cuisine.

Try for one of his shellfish dishes. They are superb, especially the savory mussel soup. Main dishes reflect an imaginative, personalized touch—canard (duck) poêle au bitter, ris de veau (sweetbreads) à ma façon, filets de sole courtine, even something that sounds ordinary but isn't—haddock de lotte beurre à la vierge. His desserts are elaborate preparations, as exemplified by his soufflé glacé à l'orange or his simpler but still superb selections, such as a tart made with the fresh fruits of the season. Expect to pay from 180F ($32.13) to 250F ($44.63) for a complete meal, and always call far in advance for a reservation. Closed weekends. Métro: Maubert-Mutualité.

La Ciboulette, 60 rue Rambuteau, 4e (tel. 271-72-34), is your best choice for dining if you're visiting the Pompidou Museum. Because the museum is usually open late, you can ask for a table for dinner, as orders are taken up to 11 p.m. Originally, this was a 1930s-style restaurant, but it went bankrupt. The present owner, Jean-Pierre Coffe, has respected the tradition, hanging lace curtains at the windows and having a decorator make judicious use of overscale prints balanced against the wood paneling. Long ago Monsieur Coffe was adopted by Paris society, who followed him from his little bistro at Les Halles to this new place, where he tempts their palates with a combination of La Nouvelle Cuisine wisely balanced with some good dishes of the French regional school of cookery. Try, for example, his ham from Landes. He has hired a superb chef, Francis Poitevin, who offers, as a beginning, a raw foie gras de canard (duck). Among the main dishes we'd recommend are his pot-au-feu de poissons au corail d'oursins and his lapin (rabbit) confit à l'oseille à la purée d'echalotes (a shallot purée). His masterpiece is a watercress salad made with five different types of fish. For dessert, we'd suggest a stuffed pear with pistachio ice cream, covered with a chocolate sauce. The dishes we've cited are those that we've personally enjoyed on visits to the restaurant and may not be featured at the time of your visit. There is no menu; the cuisine of the day depends on the chef's inspiration. Monsieur Coffe provides a nice welcome and doesn't hesitate to make a bit of a show. Your bill is likely to run about 200F ($35.70) to 250F ($44.63) per person. The restaurant shuts down on weekends. Métro: Rambuteau.

Faugeron, 52 rue de Longchamp, 16e (tel. 704-24-53). Once horrible school meals were served at this site when it was a private school in the Trocadéro district. Nowadays, it is one of the liveliest restaurants in Paris, serving La Nouvelle Cuisine. A young, handsome chef, Henri Faugeron, has taken it over and runs it along with his lovely Austrian wife, Gerlindé. We first encountered him on the Left Bank at Les Belles Gourmandes where he established his mastery of classic French cookery, and was even disparaging about the new cuisine. Now he is one of its principal advocates.

He has already built up a faithful following, who know of his specialties such as eggs stuffed with a truffle purée and l'escalope de foie gras aux oignons. A costly, but superb, specialty is a ragoût de truffes au foie gras, a memorable dish. He also does an excellent lamb curry for two at 200F ($35.70), with just the right amount of spicing. Filet of wild duck in lemon sauce, poached turbot in a cream of leek, and a soufflé aux oranges Grand Marnier will bring the bill up to about 500F ($89.25) or more for two persons. The wine steward, M. Jambon, will guide you wisely. The restaurant is closed for Saturday lunch and all day on Sunday. Métro: Iéna.

Le Relais Louis XIII, 8 rue des Grands Augustins, 6e (tel. 326-75-96). Just a short walk from the Seine on the Left Bank will lead you to this corner restaurant on a narrow street. As a one-time convent, Le Relais Louis XIII has a historical claim to fame: Marie di Medici, mother of Louis XIII, was named regent of France here after Henri IV was assassinated.

The site has gone through many changes, and by the time the

building was discovered by Odette Delanoy, it had deteriorated badly. But behind the latter-day trappings her shrewd eye discovered an inn rich in beauty. She set out to restore it, having a healthy respect for the past.

Traveling to auctions, visiting private châteaux, even shopping through the flea markets, she sought furnishings and decorative bric-a-brac from the time. Carpenters uncovered rough stone walls and exposed the beams. Rescued from the Île de France, a 16th-century stairway added the right touch. Finally, she discovered portraits of Anne of Austria, Marie di Medici, and Louis XIII himself.

In a major shift of policy, the restaurant hired a new chef, Didier Housseau, who devotes his kitchen to La Nouvelle Cuisine. You might select such dishes as turbotin farci with crayfish or duck liver in grapes, perhaps followed by a soup of fresh fruit for dessert. Expect to pay 135F ($24.10) to 190F ($33.92) per person with wine and service. The restaurant is closed Sunday and in August. Métro: Odéon.

Île de France, Quai Debilly, 16e (tel. 723-60-21), is a reconstructed barge, given riverboat glamor. Anchored on the Right Bank of the Seine, it sits seemingly at the foot of the Eiffel Tower. It's a romantic place for drinks, and especially for dining. Try to "book passage" for that special treat.

The decor is all gleaming white, gold, and brass, with a drinking lounge on the upper entrance level, and tables set on lower decks. The lounge is a wicker world, pure Gauguin. You sink into white cane or wicker chairs, and watch the boats and barges glide by through the large portholes.

The well-known restaurateur François Benoist is now the captain of the Île de France. He has turned it into one of the most unusual settings in the French capital where diners can go to enjoy the new cuisine. A repast might begin with a cream of watercress soup or else a terrine de ris de veau (sweetbreads). Especially recommendable is the côte de veau à la crème de Ciboulette. Dishes that we've found show special zest include mignon de veau au citron vert and suprême de barbue (brill) braisé aux perles de légumes. For dessert, try the Colisée au Cointreau. Expect to pay around 250F ($44.63) per person, including a good bottle of average wine. A 15% service charge is added. The restaurant is closed on Sunday and for Saturday lunch. Métro: Iéna.

Some Famous Bistros

André Allard, 41 rue Saint-André-des-Arts, 6e (tel. 326-48-23), is the leading bistro in Paris. The setting is romantic, too—the street outside was used as the background for George du Maurier's *Trilby.* Inside, the restaurant is the special culinary world of André Allard and his wife Fernande, who inherited this chicly popular Left Bank institution from Allard's father. It was well known back in the 1930s; today, Madame Allard, considered by some as the finest female *chef de cuisine* in Paris, carries on and even surpasses the tradition.

The corner building housing Allard traces its origins back to the days of Marie di Medici and Cardinal Richelieu. In the front room is a zinc bar, a haven preferred by many a celebrated *personnalité,* such as Alain Delon or Madame Pompidou, either one of whom might be seen blazing a trail through the sawdust to one of the marble-topped tables. Others, however, prefer the quieter back room.

The menu isn't large, as the madame likes to give her individual attention to the dishes. The offering on which she stakes her reputation is canard aux olives (duck), at 120F ($21.42) for two persons. The filet of turbot in beurre blanc (delectable white butter) goes for 85F ($15.17). If strawberries are in season, order one of the tarts for 35F ($6.25). For a complete meal, expect to spend from 160F ($28.56) to 250F ($44.63) per person.

As it's a Burgundian restaurant, Allard stocks its ancient cellar with wines from that region (the family bottles it themselves). Closed Saturday, Sunday, and in August. Métro: St-Michel.

Lyonnais, 32 rue Saint-Marc, 2e (tel. 742-65-59). "À Lyon le cochon est Roi . . . !" proclaims the sign. Pig may be king at this excellent Lyonnais restaurant, but Madame Schoulder, supported by a competent staff, seems to do everything well here. If you're successful in getting a seat, you can settle back for what may be your finest regional meal in all of Paris.

Among the suggestions that invariably meet with favor is a bowl of salad greens with crunchy bits of bacon and sausage. Recommended with gusto are the main-dish specialties: tender chicken in a smooth cream sauce flavored with tarragon and served with mushrooms and roast carré d'agneau (loin of lamb), with shelled beans. Your best bet for dessert is the tarte maison. There is a set menu proposed at 100F ($17.85), but expect to pay anywhere between 175F ($31.24) and 250F ($44.63), depending on your choice of wine, if you order à la carte.

A Turn-of-the-Century Brasserie

Brasserie Flo, 7 Cour Petites-Ecuries, 10e (tel. 770-13-59). A remembrance of things past. You walk through an area of passageways, stumbling over garbage littering the streets. Then you come upon this sepia world of turn-of-the-century Paris: time-aged mahogany, leather banquettes, brass-studded chairs. Some of the chicest people come here (it's the principal rival of the more celebrated Lipp in St-Germain-des-Prés)—and it isn't even expensive.

The thing to order, of course, is "la formidable choucroûte" (sauerkraut). Don't expect just a heap of sauerkraut; rather, the mound is surrounded by ham, bacon, and sausages. It's bountiful in the best tradition of Alsace. The onion soup is always good, as is guinea hen with lentils. The average dinner will cost about 125F ($22.31) to 160F ($28.56) per person, although a set menu is offered for 97F ($17.31), plus 15% for service. Everything tastes better when washed down with a carafe of Riesling wine. If you have to wait for a table, you can always enjoy a beer from Alsace at the old mahogany bar. Closed from July 17 to September 1. Métro: Château d'Eau.

After a meal here, you'll know why Lyon is called "the gastronomic capital of France." The patron stocks the cellar well with beaujolais. Off the Boulevard des Italiens, Lyonnais is closed from mid-July to September. Métro: Richelieu-Drouot.

Le Louis XIV, 1 bis Place des Victoires, 1er (tel. 261-39-44). This restaurant is named after the monarch whose statue graces one of the most famous squares on the Right Bank. Although not as harmonious or fashionable as it was in the 18th century, the square does boast two excellent restaurants, of which the Louis XIV is preferred.

Members of the French Stock Exchange as well as the "fourth estate" flock here, knowing they'll get some of the best Lyonnais cooking in town (ever had dandelion leaves covered with a hot bacon dressing?). The atmosphere is another century, as reflected by the wrought-iron staircase carrying you to the upstairs restaurant, the bar that only time could have mellowed, and the fan revolving madly overhead. Roger Delory is the talented owner and the inspiration for the cuisine.

One of the most characteristic—and one of the best—dishes to order here is escargots (snails) pur beurre, 42F ($7.49). Gastronomes come here for onglet, 48F ($8.57), one of the choicest

Émile Zola at the Next Table

Bofinger, 5–7 rue de la Bastille, 4e (tel. 272-87-82). The popular columnist of the *International Tribune,* Naomi Barry, wrote that whenever she eats her trout with almonds "in the large mirrored dining room under the stained-glass dome, I keep looking over my shoulder for Émile Zola." Bofinger was founded back in the 1860s, and is thus the oldest Alsatian brasserie in town—and certainly one of the best. It's actually a dining palace, resplendent with shiny brass.

The fashionable make their way at night through the Marais district, right off the Place de la Bastille, to this bustling, popular brasserie. In their floor-length white aprons, the waiters bring you dish after dish of satisfying fare at reasonable prices.

"Choucroûte" (sauerkraut) is the preferred dish, accompanied by a vast array of bacon, sausages, and a pork chop. *Tip:* Look for the chef's specials. He features a different one every day, including a superb stew the French call "le cassoulet." Count on spending about 180F ($32.13) per person and up for a supper here. Take the Métro to the site of the old Bastille.

parts of beef. The chef bakes his cakes and pastries fresh daily, utilizing especially good fruit. The average cost of a tarte maison is 18F ($3.21). A meal, not including wine, goes for 120F ($21.42) and up. The restaurant is closed all day Saturday and Sunday, as well as in August. It is likely to be crowded so go in the evenings if possible. Métro: Palais-Royal.

Moderately Priced Dining

Deluxe restaurants aside, you'll find any number of less expensive restaurants in Paris whose offerings are among the world's finest. Even so, you should be prepared to pay from $25 to $40 per person for a top-notch meal, providing you stick to a good, average wine. Should that be more than you intend to spend, refer to the large selection of budget restaurants and bistros at the end of this chapter.

In the limited space available to us, we've tried to provide a fairly broad sampling of restaurants in the moderately priced category. There are many more, of course. And if you're going to be in Paris for a prolonged stay, one of the joys of such a trip will be to discover others on your own.

Le Pactole, 44 Boulevard St-Germain, 5e (tel. 633-31-31).

You never know what you're going to get when you visit this popular Left Bank restaurant, but you can be sure you'll like it.

One section of Le Pactole is glass-fronted, facing the busy boulevard; the other is farther inside, paneled in oak and decorated with oils and antlers. We'll outline some of the dishes the chef does well. For a beginning, you might prefer a terrine of avocado with kiwi fruit, followed by, say, filet of duck in a raspberry vinegar sauce. An average à la carte meal will run around 185F ($33.02) to 250F ($44.63), including wine, per person. If you select the 120F ($21.42) menu, we'd suggest, if featured, the fricassée of kid in mint sauce.

Several sorbets, depending on the fresh berries or fruits available that day, will tempt you after your main meal. Reservations are necessary. Closed Sunday and in August. Métro: Maubert-Mutualité.

Le Bistrot de Paris, 33 rue de Lille, 7e (tel. 261-16-83). His father is one of the greatest restaurateurs of France, the owner of the world-famous Grand Véfour, but Michel Oliver decided to strike out on his own. He had built up quite a following when he worked for his father Raymond, and his loyal diners pursued him when he opened his new "bistrot" on the Left Bank.

His restaurant suggests turn-of-the-century Paris, with its frosted globes and brass. In contrast to his father's concentration on the haute cuisine, Michel Oliver prefers to create his own specialties—including oeufs pochés en feuilleté, crépinettes of duck, or sauté of lamb in ginger. An average meal (in cost, not in quality) goes for about 185F ($33.02) per person. Orders are taken until 11 p.m. Le Bistrot de Paris is closed at noon on Saturday, Sunday, and in August. Métro: Chambre des Députés.

Au Quai d'Orsay, 49 Quai d'Orsay, 7e (tel. 551-58-58), couldn't be more French. It's one of those establishments that presents the badly scrawled menus that even French people have trouble reading in the dim light. However, if you can see your way through, select for a beginning the stuffed duck's neck. The skin covers a crude pâté-like blend of duck which has been chopped with pork and well flavored (we think there is a touch of pistachio nuts as well). This concoction is served with aspic and toast. Perhaps you'll order pleurotes de peupliers for your beginning. These are mushrooms, meaty in texture, that grow wild. They're served with a cream sauce.

Hold onto your appetite. The meal is just beginning. For a main course, we'd recommend veal chop à l'orange. The orange sauce is dark and savory, not overly sweet. For the more daring, the chef does a calf's head ravigote. This dish evokes for some the old days in Les Halles. Expect to pay around 180F ($32.13) to 200F ($35.70) per person, including wine. On the banks of the Seine, this restaurant is old world in every way. It's most often crowded, and it's hard to get a table, especially on Friday nights. Phone the day before for a table. Closed Saturday, Sunday, and in August. Métro: Invalides.

La Méditerranée, 2 Place de l'Odéon, 6e (tel. 326-46-75), was acknowledged by Paris's *Métro* magazine as one of the most romantic restaurants in Paris. To quote the magazine, "The outdoor terrace and small upstairs salon have witnessed many a chablis-love inspired proposal. Only Jean-Yves, one of the most conscientious young maîtres d'hôtel in Paris, knows for certain how many of these loves have been requited, and, wisely, he's not saying. Jean Cocteau and his entourage did much to publicize this restaurant and make it famous. In fact, the late Cocteau designed the menu and reportedly helped with some of the decorations, as did the stage designer Christian Bérard, and Vertès.

From the kitchen come some of the most characteristic dishes of seaside Provence. The restaurant, to our knowledge, is unique among those in Paris in that it sends a truck daily to the Normandy coast to buy the freshest seafood products. A rich-tasting fish soup will get you started, but you may prefer to go all the way and order a savory Mediterranean bouillabaisse. Specialties include frog legs in the Provençal style and coquilles St-Jacques (scallops). The crêpes suzettes make an exceptional finish. One person will pay around 165F ($29.45) to 200F ($35.70), plus 10%, with wine. Métro: Odéon.

Auberge de France, 1 rue du Mont-Thabor, 1er (tel. 073-60-16). Ever since the 16th century when it was a coachman's inn, travelers have been stopping here for food, warmth, and shelter. And the rustic, homey atmosphere—complete with wood-beamed ceilings, an ancient ceramic stove, and stained-glass windows—is still intact for 20th-century voyagers. Near the Place Vendôme, the Auberge de France offers traditional French regional dishes. The food is meticulously prepared, many of the dishes so elegant that you'd never attempt them at home. The present owners, Monsieur and Madame Martin, offer the following specialties: filet Limousin (filet mignon in a red-wine sauce), canard à l'orange (duck with orange sauce), Swiss "smoked meat" snails baked in a garlic sauce, and canard au poivre vert (duck with a green-pepper sauce). By all means, try a side order of purée de haricots verts (mashed green beans with cream).

Expect to pay at least 145F ($25.88) for a complete meal. The restaurant is open daily until 11:30 p.m. Métro: Place de la Concorde, Tuileries.

Chez la Mère Michel, 5 rue Rennequin, 17e (tel. 763-59-80), is one of those "secret addresses" so beloved by Parisians. It's famous for its "spécialité de beurre blanc Nantais," a "white butter" from Nantes. In essence, white butter is made with wine vinegar, fish stock, shallots finely chopped, and other ingredients delightfully whipped into a frothy mixture and put over such dishes as brochet (pike), bar (sea bass), and turbot. One of these fish dishes costs 68F ($12.14). Also highly recommendable is poulet Mère Michel at 48F ($8.57). The chicken has a tarragon-flavored stuffing and is flamed in Armagnac. Madeira is also poured on it. For a fine beginning, why not the terrine aux foies de volailles at 32F ($5.71)? A dessert specialty is la coupe glacée Mère Michel. The restaurant is tiny, so it's necessary to book one of the tables in advance. Closed Saturday, Sunday, and in August. Métro: Ternes.

Au Gourmet de l'Isle, 42 rue Saint-Louis-en-l'Île, 4e (tel. 326-79-27). On the Île St-Louis, in the heart of Paris, is this special restaurant, savored by its loyal habitués. It should be better known, especially among foreigners. The setting, almost medieval, is beautiful: a beamed ceiling, candlelit tables. Many Parisian restaurants approach this in decor, but where other establishments on this popular tourist island fall short (in the food department), this little "Gourmet Island" succeeds.

The set meal is 65F ($11.60), and you can order inexpensively from the à la carte menu as well. In the window, you'll see a sign, "A.A.A.A.A.," which, roughly translated, stands for the Amiable Association of Amateurs of the Authentic Andouillette. Costing 40F ($7.14), these chitterling sausages are soul food to the French. Popular and good tasting too is la charbonnée de l'Isle, at 40F also, a savory pork with onions. An excellent appetizer is the stuffed mussels in shallot butter at 15F ($2.68), and desserts begin at 14F ($2.50). Closed Thursday, Monday for lunch, and in August. Métro: Pont-Marie.

Marc Annibal de Coconnas, 2 bis Place des Vosges, 4e (tel. 278-58-16). You walk along the arcades of the oldest square in Paris, in the footsteps of Victor Hugo. It is a grand siècle atmosphere of red-brick town houses. Suddenly, you come upon Coconnas, right off the square, on the rue de Birague.

In a historic old building, near the Hugo Museum (his former apartment), you can get an introduction to French cooking that will be memorable.

The fixed-price meal for 125F ($22.31) may include a tartare of salmon with lemon juice, followed by pot-au-feu and a sherbet to finish with. This long-established favorite is a very good bargain, and because of that it can get quite crowded. It's best to phone for a reservation. The restaurant is closed Monday and Tuesday. Métro: Bastille, St-Paul, or Chemin-Vert.

L'Ambassade d'Auvergne et du Rouergue, 22–24 rue de Grenier Saint-Lazare, 3e (tel. 272-34-90). The cuisine of the ancient heartland province of Auvergne is set before you in this off-the-beaten-track restaurant near the Pompidou art center. Although not known for any great number of culinary specialties, the region does provide some rich-tasting cookery.

The chef's wares are best reflected in his typical soupe aux choux gratinées (a hearty cabbage-based soup with cheese). A personal favorite of ours is the saucisse (sausage) with aligot. Whipped in a copper pot, aligot blends the Cantal cheese with cream, garlic, and potatoes. Gastronomes go for the boned breast of veal which is stuffed and delicately cooked with herbs. It appears on the menu as la fallette. The chef, Emmanuel Moulier, has introduced among the more classical dishes some Nouvelle Cuisine plates, including kidneys with spinach and a compote of volaille (poultry) with garden vegetables. A complete meal with regional wine will cost from 130F ($23.21) to 180F ($32.13) per person. The tavern is in the rustic style, with oak beams and chandeliers of wrought iron. You have a choice of rooms for dining. Closed Sunday. Métro: Arts et Métiers.

Moulin de Village, 25 rue Royale in the Cité Berryer, 8e (tel. 265-08-47), might be an ideal choice, if you're strolling along the rue Royale toward the Madeleine district at lunch- or dinnertime, and you can't afford Maxim's. Although not on the rue Royale with Maxim's, the "moulin" is just around the corner, in a little alleyway which is the scene of a typical street market on Tuesday and Friday. In fact, the chef at the moulin, Gérard Coustal, got his training at Maxim's.

Owner Chuck Scupham, an American, has created a charming little place, with a few outside tables, serving original, creative, and well-prepared food at reasonable prices. He is aided by his partner, Steven Spurrier, an Englishman and wine expert who offers some well-selected wines.

Daily, the chef features a different plat du jour. Among his specialties are mussel soup, heart of lettuce stuffed with crayfish, and a salad of firm, fresh artichokes, and fricassée of sole. His tart he makes himself. A meal will cost about 150F ($26.78) to 175F ($31.24), including a carafe of the house wine. You don't have a chance for a table unless you make a reservation. Métro: Concorde.

Le Soufflé, 36 rue du Mont-Thabor, 1er (tel. 260-27-19). First-timers to Paris are often disappointed at how difficult it is to order a soufflé at most French restaurants. However, this maison, in a chic area near the Place Vendôme and the Tuileries, has remedied that oversight. The master of the soufflé is André Faure, who comes from a region of France known as Cahors. (The legendary wine of his region—considered by experts to be "the most deeply colored of the red wines of France"—is available from his cellar.)

To open your repast, you might try ordering the fond d'artichaut gourmande at 16F ($2.86), a delicious concoction with fresh mushrooms and mayonnaise. Others prefer to begin with a cheese soufflé at 26F ($4.64). Frankly, we find one of the house specialties, le soufflé aux crustaces, disappointing; but the chef quickly redeems himself with his raspberry soufflé at 25F ($4.46) —one of the finest we've ever had. You can also order a hazelnut or a chocolate soufflé for the same price. A highly recommendable main dish is poule sautée à l'estragon (sauteed chicken in a sauce of white wine laced with cream and sprinkled with fresh tarragon), 38F ($6.78). Closed Sunday. Métro: Tuileries or Concorde.

Chez Tante Louise, 41 rue Boissy-d'Anglas, 8e (tel. 265-06-85). Aunt Louise, who reigned here from 1924 to 1955, long ago retired to her petit château in the Loire Valley. But Monsieur and Madame Salles carry on in her worthy tradition. They've inherited her secrets, and the menu reflects numerous specialties from Landes, such as the confit d'oie (slices of goose meat kept in a goose fat), served with sauteed potatoes. Other featured dishes include turbotin au champagne, magret de canard (duck), or coq à la Juraissienne. A good dessert is the strawberry tart. Expect to pay around 180F ($32.13) to 240F ($42.84) per person, including wine.

The restaurant is open for both lunch and dinner, the last orders being taken at 10 p.m. Closed Sunday and in August. It's likely to be crowded at lunch. Add 15% to all tabs for service. Métro: Madeleine.

Les Trois Moutons, 63 Avenue Franklin D. Roosevelt, 8e (tel. 225-26-95), is a very special restaurant, featuring lamb or mutton from Le Limousin. Actually, it is a Parisian showcase of that region. The so-called mutton is really from baby lambs only four months old. The lambs, incidentally, have been raised on flour and milk which is said to make the meat extremely tender. The flavor of the meat comes from the grazing habits, and the grasses and herbs. Against a contemporary decor, you make your lamb selections, this main course determining the price of your meal. For your main dish, we'd suggest the épigramme at 174F ($31.06). This is breast of lamb, boned, roasted with onions, mushrooms, and a sauce. An amusing choice is the clou, joined with a piece of guidon. This is one hefty chop attached to the main bone, the whole thing resembling the handlebars of a bicycle. Another piece of loin is sliced and grilled with kidney and slices of roast leg of lamb. Beans and gratin dauphinois are served as an accompaniment. A wine from the south of France, Corbières, salad, cheese, and dessert, are included in the main-dish price. The restaurant is open seven days a week. Métro F. D. Roosevelt.

Les Trois Limousins, 8 rue Berri, 8e (tel. 562-35-97), is a successful Paris showcase sponsored by the landowners of Le Limousin to call attention to their region. The province of Limousin, of course, enjoys a fine gastronomic reputation. A magnificent meat comes from the cattle raised in the region. So, with the blessings of Baron Hubert de Blomac, this restaurant was opened.

Soon the grand meat-eaters of the 8th Arrondissement, usually successful business people and account executives, spread the reputation that Les Trois Limousins serves the finest beef dishes in Paris. The claim is not exaggerated.

Behind a window display of mounted cowheads, the modern restaurant holds forth. The price of your main dish determines the cost of your meal. This includes an appetizer, salads, cheese, pastries or sorbets, coffee, even wine in a carafe, as well as the 15% service charge. All meat dishes are accompanied by a potato baked in its jacket served with heavy cream and fines herbes. The T-bone is priced at 186F ($33.20), and the rib of beef at 350F ($62.48) for two persons. Many prefer the steak tartare (which one Frenchman labeled *"cannibale maison"*) at 162F ($28.92). The restaurant is open daily. Métro: George-V.

La Taverne du Sergent Recruteur, 41 rue St-Louis-en-l'Île, 4e (tel. 356-75-42), occupies a 17th-century setting on the historic Île St-Louis. But many buildings on this Seine island do that. What makes La Taverne so popular is that it offers an all-you-can-eat meal for 92F ($16.42), plus service. You more or less make your own salad with the items placed before you, including black radishes, fennel, celery, cucumbers, green pepper, hard-boiled eggs, and carrots. After that, a huge basket of sausages is brought around, and you can slice as you wish, sampling one or all. The carafe of wine, either red, white, or rosé, is bottomless. Plats du jour, ranging from beef to veal, are changed daily. You usually select from three different items. Next, a large cheese board makes the rounds; and, if you're still upright, you can take your pick from a basket of fresh fruit. The narrow dining room is beamed, with leaded glass windows and ladderback chairs. Garlic pigtails and oil lamps give it a rustic air. The restaurant is open from 7:30 p.m. to 2 a.m. Métro: Pont-Marie.

Au Beaujolais, also called "Chez Charles," 19 Quai Tournelle, 5e (tel. 033-67-74), stands in the shadow of the august Tour d'Argent across the street. But there the resemblance ends. This Seine-bordering restaurant features specialties "du Beaujolais et du Mâconnais." Incidentally "à la Mâconnaise" is a name given to various meat dishes flavored with red wine. Standard hearty fare is the rule of the day. We'd recommend the cochonnailles du Beaujolais et beurre. These are a selection of cold cuts of pork, the same as a charcuterie, served with bread and butter. For a main course, you might try coq au vin. Another good selection is an entrecôte Bercy. The bill can go from a reasonable 110F ($19.64) to a higher 140F ($24.99), depending on the plates ordered and the wines selected. Closed Monday and in August. Métro: Pont-Marie.

Relais de la Butte, 12 rue Ravignan, 18e (tel. 606-16-18). Finding a really good restaurant in Montmartre is, surprisingly, almost impossible—but this "relais" is an exception to that rule. Climbing a steep street from Pigalle, weary would-be diners follow in the footsteps of Picasso, Rousseau, Modigliani, and Max Jacob, all of whom once lived in the area. And right near the Place Émile-Goudeau, not too far from what was the legendary Bateau Lavoir, you'll come to the place run by Michel and Rose.

The restaurant is small and unpretentious, the cooking good. Lobster Newburg is the house specialty. The price depends on the season. A really superb offering is the roast duckling, followed by oranges flambées Grand Marnier, which is usually featured on the set menu, service included. If you choose not to splurge on the à la carte menu, ordering lobster and the like, you'll find two very reasonably priced and most adequate set menus, costing from 58F ($10.35) to 87F ($15.53). The bistro is open only in the evenings. Closed Thursday and in August. Métro: Abbesses.

Au Pied de Cochon, 6 rue Coquillière, 1er (tel. 236-11-75). The onion soup of Les Halles still lures the visitors. Although the great market has moved to Rungis, near Orly Airport, traditions are long in dying. Besides, where in Paris can you be assured of getting a good meal at 3 a.m. if not at the famous "Pig's Foot"?

The house specialty is the namesake: pig's feet grilled and served with béarnaise sauce, as well as the classic onion soup. Of course, you can sample any of the other tempting fares as well; try the suckling pig St-Eustache. There is a set menu for about 115F ($20.53), or else you can order à la carte, an average meal costing 150F ($26.78). The restaurant is open day and night year round.

Outside on the street, you can buy some of the freshest-tasting oysters in town. The attendants will even give you slices of lemons to accompany them, and you can down these oysters right on the spot. Métro: Les Halles.

La Tour d'Argent, 4–6 Place de la Bastille, 12e (tel. 344-32-19), is not to be confused with the world-famous Tour d'Argent already described. This one is in the Marais district, overlooking the historic Place de la Bastille. However, it provides a chance to tell people back home that you dined nightly at La Tour d'Argent during your stay in Paris. Lest they think you've suddenly inherited an oil well, you can inform them there is yet another restaurant of the same name. In its belle époque upstairs room, overlooking the square, you can order a set meal for 95F ($16.96), considerably less than you'd pay at the other establishment. Meals are served from 11:30 a.m. to 1:15 a.m. Specialties include various kinds of oysters, shellfish cooked on a skewer, trout with cream and toasted almonds, sole belle meunière, chateaubriand with pepper and raisin sauce, and onion soup. Closed in August. Metro: Bastille.

Les Chevaliers de la Table Ronde, 5 rue Suger, 6e (tel. 633-74-90). In the feudal cellar of the Chevaliers, you can, as the song says, "taste to see if the wine is good." All you can drink is served with the fine French cuisine in this Left Bank establishment. The cellar-like decor is warm, and the inlaid ceiling depicts the story of the legendary knights. A copious set meal costs 110F ($19.64), wine and service included. Call after 5 p.m. for reservations. Métro: St-Michel.

Best for the Budget

L'Assiette au Boeuf, 9 Boulevard des Italiens, 2e (tel. 742-74-35), is a second-floor restaurant, the creation of that culinary artist Michel Oliver, the enterprising son of the celebrated Raymond Oliver of the three-star Grand Véfour. The younger Oliver's concept in restaurants is exciting and innovative. He offers simple set menus of his own creation in stunning art nouveau interiors.

(At the moment he has three Assiettes au Boeuf. The other two are at Place St-Germain-des-Prés and at 123 Avenue Champs-Élysées. In addition, he offers two similar Bistros de la Gare, one at 73 Avenue Champs-Élysées, another at 59 Boulevard du Montparnasse. The younger Oliver's own higher priced specialty restaurant is called Bistrot de Paris and is recommended separately in this section. It's at 33 rue de Lille.)

At one of Les Assiettes au Boeuf, for 40F ($7.14), plus service, you are offered a meal that might begin with a plate of tender lettuce, topped by a creamy dressing, and laced with pine nuts. This course might be followed by tender sliced beef (served rare if you wish), with sauce on the side, along with a mound of slender pommes frites. Desserts are extra, a choice of 13 offered, beginning at 12.50F ($2.23) for the sorbets. There are four sizes of wine presented, including some especially bottled for Oliver. A small carafe costs 10F ($1.79); a full bottle 33F ($5.89). Coffee is an extra 6F ($1.07).

At the Boulevard des Italiens address, the setting is a white Victorian one, of the garden variety. Each of the two large dining rooms has a white piano for soft background music. You enter via an impressive winding staircase. Formally attired waiters will find you a table, but probably after a short wait (reservations aren't accepted). The ceilings are white paneled, with revolving fans and chandeliers with fringed shades. The walls are mostly mirrored, the street windows draped with long strands of ivy. Sweet-mannered waitresses in calico pinafores serve you, and hours are from noon to 3 p.m. and from 6 to 11 p.m. Métro: Opéra.

La Cigale, 11 bis rue Chomel, 7e (tel. 548-87-87), is where Monsieur and Madame Pierre Grocat welcome you. Their cicada chirps nightly, except Sunday. The small restaurant is simple and unpretentious, but it's recommended for serving truly fine meals. Such reliable dishes are featured as pâté aux morilles, l'escalope Normande, and filets de sole à la crème. If you order à la carte, your bill is likely to run between 65F ($11.60) and 90F

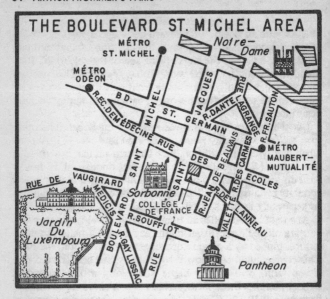

THE BOULEVARD ST. MICHEL AREA

($16.06). Because of its good food and low prices, the restaurant is usually crowded—and you'll often have to wait for a table. Closed Saturday and Sunday. Métro: Sèvres Babylone.

Restaurant Lescure, 7 rue de Mondovi, 1er (tel. 260-18-91), is a small, independently run, inexpensive restaurant serving good food in the high-priced Place de la Concorde district. Right off the rue de Rivoli, the restaurant is in a historic district (Talleyrand, for example, died in an 18th-century mansion around the corner). In fair weather, a few sidewalk tables are placed outside and these, naturally, are grabbed up quickly. The decor inside is rustic with an exposed kitchen. The cuisine (and this is no put-down, but the self-styled description of the chef) is bourgeoise. Simple, hearty cooking is the rule. For example, you might begin with a pâte en croûte at 18F ($3.21). Main-course house specialties include le confit de canard at 35F ($6.25) and that select onglet cut of beef in a béarnaise sauce at 42F ($7.49). Try also the filet of turbot with sorrel, 38F ($6.78). Our favorite dessert is one of the chef's fruit tarts, costing 16F ($2.86). Closed Sunday and in August. Métro: Concorde.

André Faure, 40 rue du Mont-Thabor, 1er (tel. 260-74-28), is a special little Right Bank establishment that needs to be better known. The owner features a special five-course dinner nightly, except Sunday, for just 50F ($8.93). The food is simple but in the classic French tradition, presenting such dishes as coq au vin, lapin (rabbit) sauté, and le poulet en cocotte Grand' Mère. Incidentally, the place is a good luncheon bet as well, offering a set dinner for 35F ($6.25). You can sit either at the bar where there's counter service, or at one of the tables. Paintings hot off the easel decorate the place. Métro: Concorde or Tuileries.

Restaurant Paul, 15 Place Dauphine, 1er. (tel. 354-21-48). This address used to be given out to first-time visitors by in-the-know Parisians who wanted to tell them about that out-of-the-way bistro where no foreigner ever sets foot. Don't you believe it! Chez Paul, on this historic square on the Île de la Cité, is too good a secret to keep. (Originally, the triangular Place Dauphine was shaped by incorporating two "islets" with the main one during the reign of Henri IV.) The food expert, Waverley Root, wrote of Chez Paul's "resistance to degeneration." And so it remains. The effect inside is much like a cold-water flat. The main-dish specialty is escalope papillotte. Another good order, for a beginning, is quenelles de brochet à la Nantua. An exciting dessert is baba à la confiture flambée au rhum. Your bill will run from 65F ($11.60) to 100F ($17.85) per person for a complete meal. Incidentally, when you see the madame at the cash register, your dreams of an old Parisian bistro will come true. May she live forever! Closed Monday and in August. Métro: Pont-Neuf.

Front Page, 56–58 rue St-Denis, 1er (tel. 236-98-69), is a challenge not only to the usual bistros of Les Halles, but to Joe Allen's nearby. The Front Page is a large-scale restaurant where you can order the specialities that America has made famous, including barbecued spare ribs, chili, cheeseburgers, and lemon pie. The walls are covered with press photos. Over the bar hang klieg lights, and tables have red-and-white-checked cloths, New York saloon style, as well as bentwood chairs. The atmosphere is most intimate. From the à la carte menu, you can order a New York–cut steak with a baked potato at 42F ($7.49), or else coleslaw at 7F ($1.25), accompanied by a jumbo hamburger at 26F ($4.64). The Front Page is open from noon to 2 a.m. Métro: Les Halles.

Also in Les Halles, **Crêperie Pommier–La Prugne,** 5 rue Berger, 1er, is the best place to go for crêpes. It's an old-fashioned place, with art deco posters and a painted dado. Collette Maraquinsky is the chef, and she invites you for some tasty cookery in her tiny restaurant which she runs along with her partner, Dimitri Maraquinsky. For 7.50F ($1.34) you can order a green salad, and if you're feeling luxurious you can ask for the smoked salmon at 25F ($4.46). But most people come here for her crêpes, costing around 18F ($3.21). A specialty is the crêpe printanière, a garden salad wrapped in a delicately thin crêpe. You can order wine, of course, but for a change we'd suggest the Normandy cider. For dessert you have a wide choice. Especially good are the banana crêpe at 9.50F ($1.70) and the chocolate crêpe at 9.50F also. Service is friendly and polite in this homey atmosphere. Métro: Les Halles.

For Vegetarians

L'Epidaure, 78 rue Labat (at the corner of rue Bachelet), 18e (tel. 259-06-63), is a favorite little Parisian oasis among devotees of the vegetarian cuisine. The restaurant at first looks as if it were transported intact from some country setting, with its light yellow painted facade and its green plants. Once inside, however, the dining room is strictly bistro style, with round tables covered with individual straw placemats. The management has carefully placed fresh flowers in vases on each table, providing a special welcome. Salad dishes are among the most popular items here, costing from a low of 7F ($1.25), ranging upward to 15F ($2.68). There is also a set menu offered at 24F ($4.28). Two exceptional choices of vegetable plates, called assiette Épidaure or assiette spéciale, cost 30F ($5.36). For your libations, you can select either a fresh fruit or a fresh vegetable juice, perhaps one of the large choices of tea or herb concoctions, ranging in price from 5.50F (98¢) to 7F ($1.25). Service is an extra 15%. The vegetarian restaurant lies at the bottom of Montmartre. Métro: Marcadet-Poissonniers

---

Crémerie-Restaurant Polidor, 41 rue Monsieur-le-Prince, 6e (tel. 326-95-34), is the most characteristic bistro in the Odéon area, serving the "cuisine familiale." You might call it a "vieille maison très sympathique." It still uses the word *crémerie* in its title, an appellation dating back to the early part of this century when it specialized in frosted cream desserts.

In time it became one of the Left Bank's oldest and most established literary bistros. In fact, it was André Gide's favorite. But many famous people have dined here, including Hemingway, Paul Valéry, Artaud, Charles Boyer, even Jack Kerouac.

The atmosphere is one of lace curtains, polished-brass hat racks, and drawers in the back where repeat customers lock up their cloth napkins. Frequented largely by students and artists, who always seem to head for the rear, the present restaurant was founded in 1930 and it's been little changed since then. The art deco ceiling fixtures are still there, and pottery pitchers of water are placed on the tables, which are most often shared.

Overworked but smiling waitresses serve such dishes as a plate of crudités at 12F ($2.14) or Greek-style mushrooms at 12F also for an appetizer. Main dishes include such hearty fare as canard (duck) Barbarie at 25F ($4.46) or côtes d'agneau (lamb) at 28F ($5). You might finish with a fruit tart at 10F ($1.79). The restaurant is closed on Sunday. Métro: Odéon.

L'Auberge Basque, 51 rue de Verneuil, 7e (tel. 548-51-98). If forced to name the best-bargain-but-high-quality meal in Paris, this restaurant would easily win. It is the tavern domain of Monsieur Rourre, who is from the Basque country of France. Basque men, on both the French and Spanish sides, are considered cooks of merit and flair.

For 95F ($16.96) to 110F ($19.64), plus a 15% service charge, you can order an excellent meal. A typical dinner might begin with pipérade, fluffy purée of eggs, cooked tomatoes, and peppers. Perhaps the chef will decide to prepare a duck in orange sauce, with potatoes, a green salad, then a selection of cheese from the board, plus dessert. The only catch is, you pay extra for the wine, but if you select a vin ordinaire the price will be reasonable.

In the evening, guitarists entertain you. The paintings on the wall, by the way, include drawings by Max Ernst, and came from a restaurant frequented by artists which the chef formerly owned in Cannes. Because of its exceptional popularity and small size, you can never get a seat unless you reserve, so phone ahead. Closed in August. Métro: Bac.

Beaux-Arts, 11 rue Bonaparte, 6e (tel. 326-92-64), is another great, discovered, alas, by a multitude before us. Classic French bourgeois cuisine is served in attractive surroundings at low prices. The Beaux-Arts caters in equal parts to immense numbers of students, local artists, authors and journalists, and visiting Anglo-Americans. The fittings and murals are almost as tasteful as the food.

The menu is 35F ($6.25), including wine and service. Try either the potage of the day or the salade de museon. Follow with the sauté de boeuf garni, a well-prepared beef stew. End with the bleu de Bresse cheese, served just at the early melting stage. With it, a carafe of vin rouge will go well. If you want more freedom in your selection, you'll probably spend from 50F ($8.93) to 70F ($12.50) ordering à la carte. You may have to share a table here, regardless of when you arrive, but the company is congenial. Closed Monday and in August. Métro: St-Germain-des-Prés.

La Cabane d'Aubergne, 44 rue Grégoire-de-Tours, 6e (tel. 325-14-75). This self-proclaimed "rabbit hutch" is like a rustic Breton tavern, where under beamed ceilings typical regional meals are served on bare plank tables with provincial stools. The stone and wood-paneled walls are decorated with farm and country implements: wooden shoes, a hayfork, copper bed-warming pans, coach lanterns, a tall grandfather's clock. A cozy entrance bar is so crowded that friendships are instant.

One waitress handles the always-filled eight tables. The owner, Gilbert Guibert, wears a wide-brimmed black hat and red sash, and hovers between the bar and dining room, keeping bright, breezy chitchat going.

The chef specializes in terrines. One is made from marcassin (young boar), another from fricandeau (larded veal loin), yet another from caneton (duckling). You can enjoy a complete meal here for as little as 50F ($8.93), although many tabs climb beyond the 80F ($14.28) mark. Métro: Odéon.

Les Balkans, 3 rue de la Harpe, 5e (tel. 326-20-96). On this teeming street in the heart of the Latin Quarter, Les Balkans has long enjoyed a reputation among budgeteers for its exotic cuisine and low prices. Directed by Monsieur Diamantis, it entices with its kebabs, its Hungarian goulash, and its couscous in five different flavors. The à la carte menu is priced inexpensively. The chef's specialties include choice kebab maison, stuffed vine leaves, and Hungarian goulash. A Hungarian-style repast will cost around 70F ($12.50) to 100F ($17.85). The atmosphere evokes what used to be called Paris bohemia, but with a distinctly 1980s accent, as young couples make their way from table to table hawking their handmade jewelry, or a group of Americans stroll by, singing folk music for a handout. Closed Wednesday. Métro: St-Michel.

Zera de Conduite, 64 rue Monsieur-le-Prince, 6e (tel. 033-50-79), is a charmer of a place, titled after a French movie classic. Rising above the street on a series of steps, it has a large, rambling, rustic dining room, with bare rock walls, wooden partitions, and a chef working in front of an open charcoal pit.

Incongruously, the walls sport photographs of Laurel and Hardy, Buster Keaton, and W. C. Fields. The cuisine is French, with a Greek flavor, and a set menu is offered at 35F ($6.25), including service. As a starter on the à la carte menu, we suggest the oeufs à la Russe (Russian eggs), 7F ($1.25). For the centerpiece, try a brochette paysanne (skewered cubes of meat with rice, roasted over the open pit), 30F ($5.36). Finally, the tarte bonne femme, 14F ($2.50), is as luscious as its name suggests. A small carafe of rosé is an extra 7F ($1.25). Métro: Odéon.

Who Wouldn't Be Curious?

Café Curieux, 14 rue Saint-Merri, 4e (tel. 272-75-97). You may think you're in the antique store of some eccentric collector. This restaurant, just three blocks from the Seine and Hôtel de Ville, will hold you transfixed. Who could collect such fascinating objects? The crusty old walls are literally covered with junk and discards from the Flea Market. Nothing on its own is worth much, but the sum total is worth the trek over. Staring at you is gargoyle-style black oak carved furniture, along with crystal chandeliers, dozens of ceramic plates and platters, art nouveau bronze figures, even a six-foot-high carved wooden bear standing under an open spiral staircase.

During regular lunch and dinner hours you can order à la carte meals here for 80F ($14.28) to 100F ($17.85). Métro: Hôtel de Ville.

La Boutique à Sandwichs, 12 rue du Colisée, 8e (tel. 359-56-69), is run by two brothers from Alsace, Hubert and Claude Schick. If you're in the Champs-Élysées area, it's a good place to drop in for sandwiches in many types and shapes. You can dine downstairs at the counter, or try to crowd into the tiny upstairs room, which is extremely active at lunch. Here they offer an unusual specialty, raclette valaisanne à gogo. To make this fondue dish, a wheel of cheese is taken, part of it is melted, then it is scraped right onto your plate. It is served with pickles and boiled potatoes, the latter resting in a pot with a crocheted hat. The other house specialty is pickelfleisch garni (Alsatian corned beef). Naturally, the apple strudel is the dessert everybody orders. Sandwiches begin at 6.50F ($1.16) and go up, and there's also a set meal offered for 34F ($6.07). However, if you prefer to order the specialties of the house on the à la carte menu, expect to pay from 60F ($10.71) to 80F ($14.28). It's closed Sunday and in August. Métro: Franklin D. Roosevelt.

The World's Oldest Restaurant

Procope, 13 rue de l'Ancienne Comédie, 6e (tel. 326-99-20), is one of the most enthralling hostelries in Paris. Allegedly the world's oldest still-functioning restaurant, Procope began its career as a café in 1686. The list of men who have dined here reads like a roster of historical greats: La Fontaine, Voltaire, Benjamin Franklin, Danton, Marat, Robespierre, Napoléon, Balzac, Victor Hugo, Anatole France.

The downstairs dining room is long and narrow, decorated in red and gold with inlaid tile floors and cut-glass chandeliers. Upstairs it's even more sumptuous. Yet despite the mirrors, gilt, and oil paintings, the place somehow manages to be as cozy as a corner saloon and to attract a mixed grouping of writers and journalists, university professors, long-haired girls and their escorts, models, business people, and assorted tourists, all relaxed and friendly.

The prices happily don't reflect the decor. A 40F ($7.14) bargain dinner includes a main course and dessert, although the regular dinner can cost 80F ($14.28) or a lot more. We'd select the assortment of charcuterie (a plate of mixed cold meats and sausages), then the rich and fragrant boeuf bourguignon (beef stew in red wine). Finally, a random selection from the cheese tray rounds out the meal nicely. You stand a better chance of catching an empty table at night (it's open till 1:30 a.m.), but even then it's a matter of luck. It's open daily, although closed in July. Métro: Odéon.

Au Caveau Montpensier, 15 rue de Montpensier, 1er (tel. 297-53-81), is run by a family. In Papa Maurice, the cuisine reflects Lyons, called the gastronomic capital of France. In his wife, Evonne, a native of Anjou, the specialties of the Loire Valley are in evidence. In their informal "cave," good, homelike meals are served. You might begin with a soup of the day, depending on what went into the big pot at the back of the stove. Specialties include foie gras de canard (duckling) with champagne, lapin (rabbit) Palais-Royal, a chicken liver dish with cognac and port wine, and tournedos Rossini with truffles and foie gras. You might finish with a cheese from a heavily laden tray or a pastry made with fresh fruit. If you wish to dine here and enjoy the house dishes, expect to spend from 200F ($35.70) per person. However, a set menu with less elaborate fare is offered for just 80F ($14.28). The building dates from 1640. Once it was a stable for Philippe-Égalité who resided in the nearby

Palais-Royal. Closed Saturday lunch and Monday. Métro: Palais-Royal.

Dining "Oddities"

Taverne Nicolas Flamel, 51 rue de Montmorency, 3e (tel. 272-07-11). Go here mainly for the atmosphere. Although the food you're served is good, its major sin is that it's more than any human being can possibly eat! The restaurant is housed in a national monument, the second-oldest building still standing in Paris, dating from 1407. The name comes from its past owner, one of the famous characters of the Middle Ages (legend has it that he was an alchemist). Flamel donated the house on the rue de Montmorency—in the Marais section of Paris—to the poor as a soup kitchen.

A set meal is offered, at 100F ($17.85) and another at 110F ($19.64). So much for the poor. But your meal does include both your wine, usually beaujolais in a carafe, and the service charge. To get you started, a glass of champagne, a container of pâté, and a terrine are placed on your table along with crusty bread. Don't eat too much of it, as there is more—lots more—to emerge out of the kitchen in the rear. Duck with orange sauce is regularly featured as a main course.

The atmosphere can't be faulted: everything, from rusty lanterns to dark beams, bears a patina that only time can give it. Métro: Rambuteau.

La Colombe, 4 rue de la Colombe, 4e (tel. 633-37-08), stands on the historic Île de la Cité. The rue de la Colombe, one of the smallest in Paris, runs into the Quai aux Fleurs behind Notre-Dame. The house of la Colombe (the dove), dating from 1275, is an idyllic setting for a meal, owned from 1924 by the Valette family. Ludwig Bemelmans painted the walls of one dining room.

Michel Valette, a movie actor, often receives customers. While drinking your coffee, you might ask him to tell you the old legend of the doves and the story of the tavern during seven centuries.

His wife, Beleine, is the chef de cuisine. She prepares for you a copious *menu touristique* at 90F ($16.06), service included. Wine is extra. Also offered is a superb *menu gastronomique* at 160F ($28.56), that price also including service but not wine. Among à la carte items, she offers such dishes as duckling with peaches, 58F ($10.35); quails stuffed with nuts, 42F ($7.49); tournedos en croûte sauce Périgueux, 66F ($11.78); filet mignon

---

The Good Things of Life Aren't Necessarily Free

Caviar Kaspia, 17 Place de la Madeleine, 8e (tel. 265-33-52). How chic can you get, sitting on the second floor of this caviar center, enjoying a view of the columns of the stately Madeleine, while casually tasting Russian caviar and sipping Russian vodka? You're welcomed by the genial, English-speaking manager, Elvino Barili, who will explain the selections to you and seat you at a tiny table to begin your life of decadence. Should you not prefer a taste of caviar, you'll also find smoked salmon, foie gras, even a more modest hot borscht at 18F ($3.21) and blinis at 15F ($2.68) a pair. The more elaborate, such as the smoked salmon and caviar, are priced by the gram, and the tabs on these delicacies fluctuate from week to week —so we won't cite them here, except to say they are always super-expensive. However, for a "taste," expect to pay 200F ($35.70). A carry-out shop is on the ground floor. The place is closed Sunday, but open otherwise from 9 a.m. to 2 a.m., perfect for a late-night snack if you're flush.

---

of pork on mushroom toast with cherries, 46F ($8.21); and other delights. The wine list presents a prestigious choice of French products beginning at 32F ($5.71).

Meals are served in the barroom, in the Bemelmans room, or in the first-floor room where a wood fire blazes in winter. In summer, guests dine in a Virginia creeper–covered terrace, unusual in the heart of Paris. The restaurant closes Monday at lunchtime, all day Sunday, for ten days in mid-August, and three weeks in February. Otherwise, it offers lunch from 12:30 to 2:30 p.m. and dinners and late suppers from 7:30 p.m. to midnight. Métro: Cité or Hôtel de Ville.

Androuët, 41 rue d'Amsterdam, 8e (tel. 874-26-93). Cheese is king here. Time was when to get invited down to taste the cheese in Monsieur Androuët's cellars was a badge of honor. Now half of Paris and three-quarters of all visiting foreigners who love cheese have probably made their way to this unique restaurant up from the railway station of St-Lazare. "Le fromage" has never been given such attention, or come in such a wide variety, ranging from the mild to what one diner called "a piece laden with enough penicillin to have sufficed for medical supplies for the Allied invasion of Normandy."

On the lower level is a luscious shop selling every conceivable variety of cheese from all regions of France. Reached by elevator, the dining room is on the second landing. It's a faithful reproduction of an ancient tavern, with high-backed wooden booths, thick stone arches, a rugged stone fireplace, as well as country-style trestle tables, and ladderback and reed chairs. To reach your table, you pass a vast array of cheese, the scent of which will activate your tastebuds.

The attractive atmosphere isn't a cover-up for good cooking. You may get your best quiche Lorraine in Paris here, at 20F ($3.57). A good main dish is the côte de veau savoyarde, 70F ($12.50). Cheese fanciers go here to order *la degustation unique de tours des fromages,* at 90F ($16.06), which allows you to sample as many of the 120 varieties as you want. Especially recommendable is the cloudlike Parmesan orange soufflé.

Incidentally, Monsieur Androuët in *Le Guide du Fromage,* a letter to his teenage daughter, has written what may be the all-time classic guide to cheese.

The restaurant is open from noon to 2:30 p.m. and from 7 to 10 p.m. Closed Sunday. It's best to reserve for both lunch and dinner. Métro: St-Lazare.

Roger à la Grenouille, 26–28 rue des Grand Augustins, 6e (tel. 326-10-55), is the lily pad for the "king of the frogs," Roger, and his wife, "Madame Frog." In this tuckaway oddity restaurant, reached by a side entrance through a courtyard, you'll find a friendly mixture of longtime patrons. The atmosphere is almost bawdily Elizabethan, and the food is deliciously edible.

A tiny display case on the street gives the clue: it's jam-packed with miniature frogs of every make, ceramic, cloth, porcelain, wood, and so forth. But it's only a suggestion of what you'll find on the walls and ceilings of the three narrow dining rooms. Monsieur and Madame Frog greet you and show you to a table (you'll probably share, but that doesn't seem to matter here). Instant friendship is the lifestyle.

The rooms with bistro trestle tables have walls papered with old banknotes from most countries. Hanging from the ceiling and walls is a forest of copper and brass soup pots, belle époque light fixtures, old candlesticks, oil lamps, Paris street signs ("the rue Jacob"), even an airplane propeller. Waitresses are in the hearty tavern tradition—genial, smiling. If one of them can't understand your French, she'll yell to one of the bilingual guests.

You're given a pair of binoculars to examine the blackboard at the end of the wall; a basket with four different breads is set before you. For a main dish, try the beef bourguignon, or duckling in orange sauce. Other dishes include frog legs and snails. A good dessert is the peach melba, specially created by Monsieur Frog himself. It's a phallic-shaped coffee ice cream standing upright on a dish with two halved peaches and crushed raspberries, all smothered in thick cream. Enjoy! A meal here will average around 120F ($21.42) per person.

When you get your bill, you'll be given either a little frog or a folding card which, when opened, becomes a butterfly. But when held up to the light . . .!!! Closed Sunday. Métro: St-Michel.

"Foreign" Food

Joe Allen, 30 rue Pierre Lescot, 1er (tel. 236-70-13). About the last place in the world you'd expect to find Joe Allen is Les Halles, that once-legendary Paris market. But here the New York restaurateur has long ago invaded Paris with the American hamburger. It easily wins as the finest burger in the city, as Joe originally set out to match those served at P. J. Clarke's in New York.

Joe Allen's "little bit of New York"—complete with imported red-checked tablecloths and a green awning over the entrance—was made possible by "grants" from such fans as Lauren Bacall, whose poster adorns one of the walls. The decor is in the New York saloon style, complete with brick walls, pine floors, movie stills, and a blackboard menu listing such items as black bean soup, chili, and apple pie. A spinach salad makes a good beginning. The barbecued ribs are succulent as well.

Joe Allen's also makes the claim that it is the only place in Paris where you can have a real New York cheesecake or pecan pie. The pecans are imported from the United States. Likewise, the English muffins for the eggs Benedict have to be shipped in. Joe also claims that (thanks to French chocolate) "we make the best brownies in the States." The bill will range from 120F ($21.42) to 150F ($26.78) per person. Hours are daily from noon to 2 a.m. Unless you want to wait 30 minutes at the New York bar, you'd better make a reservation for dinner. The managers are both Americans, and their waiters speak English. Joe Allen's has become quite well known for its nonstop jukebox, which has all the latest hits as well as the golden oldies of American music. Métro: Les Halles.

Restaurant Copenhague and Flora Danica, 142 Avenue Champs-Élysées, 8e (tel. 359-20-42), is the "Maison du Danemark," one of the finest dining establishments along the

Champs-Elysées. The good-tasting food of Denmark is served with considerable style and flair. In summer, you can dine outside on the rear terrace, an idyllic spot.

If you want to go Danish all the way, you'll order an apértif of aquavit and ignore the wine list in favor of Carlsberg or Tuborg, the two best-known beers of Denmark. For an appetizer, you might prefer nage de poisson à la crème de fenovil at 58F ($10.35) or the even better terrine de canard (duckling) Copenhague at 48F ($8.57). If you want to order the house specialty, it's called délices Scandinaves, costing 280F ($49.98) for two persons—"a platter of joy" of foods the Danes do exceptionally well. The feuilleté Cercle Polaire at 38F ($6.78) is a fine finish. The restaurant is open seven days a week.

At the Boutique Flora Danica facing the Champs-Élysées, you can have a small snack from noon until midnight. Open-faced sandwiches, Danish smörrebrod, with beer, go for around 75F ($13.39). Sandwiches, pastries, aquavit, and beer are available in the small delicatessen. Métro: George-V.

Dominique, 19 rue Bréa, 6e (tel. 327-08-80), is the finest Russian restaurant in Montparnasse, preserving a fin-de-siècle atmosphere, St. Petersburg style, in its upstairs room. Warning: Don't be tempted to order the Iranian caviar today ... it's about the same price as sterling silver. The kitchen turns out really superb food. For example, try the familiar borscht and pirozhki at 26F ($4.64), or the blinis with cream at 27F ($4.82). Even the Russian salad at 18F ($3.21) makes an interesting beginning. Recommendable main courses include côtellette de volaille (poultry) Dominique, 65F ($11.60). Of course, everything tastes better when washed down with a glass of Zubrovka vodka. It is imported from Poland and is made with a special herb. Occasional gypsy music is heard. If you're watching your budget, you can order these specialties downstairs where there is a counter and bar service, and the prices are not as expensive. The restaurant is open daily but closed during July. Métro: Vavin.

Mignonnette du Caviar, 13 rue du Colisée, 8e (tel. 225-30-35), is as small as Russia is big. This petite restaurant, with its blood-red facade, is just a minute or so from the Champs-Élysées. The madame presides behind her glistening brass samovar. The atmosphere is *très intime.* Caviar tasting begins at 75F ($13.39) per serving. Blinis with cream may tempt, or you can order borscht, herring, beef Stroganoff, even a fruit salad with vodka. You can select a Russian dinner here for about 140F ($24.99) per person.

Chitterlings and Sweet Potato Pie

Haynes, 3 rue Clauzel, 9e (tel. 878-40-63). Soul food long ago arrived in Paris. And many French people have discovered what "Kentucky oysters" really are. A good walk down from the Place Pigalle, in a section of Paris rarely visited by tourists, Haynes holds forth nightly, dispensing his own special southern viands.

Movie stars, by the way (Warren Beatty, Elizabeth Taylor, Peter O'Toole), and "names" have made their way here, as autographed photographs on the walls reveal. Even the rich and famous tire of caviar and foie gras at some point, preferring barbecued chicken, Mexican chili con carne, barbecued spare ribs, or corn on the cob. If someone gets fancy and wants hors d'oeuvres, Haynes will serve them fried gizzards. Depending on your appetite, you can dine here for as little as 40F ($7.14). Tabs rarely run higher than 80F ($14.28) per person. To judge the man from his size, he obviously enjoys good food, but eats a great deal of it as well. His place is open till 1 a.m., but not for lunch or on Sunday. Métro: St-Georges.

The restaurant is closed at Saturday lunch, all day Sunday, but open otherwise from noon to 2:30 and from 7 to 11 p.m. Métro: F. D. Roosevelt.

Goldenberg's, 69 Avenue de Wagram, 8e (tel. 227-34-79), is a Jewish-delicatessen restaurant in the Champs-Élysées area. Its owner, Albert Goldenberg, is known as "the doyen of Jewish restaurateurs in Paris." And rightly so, since he opened his first delicatessen in Montmartre in 1936.

The deli, like many of its New York counterparts, has the front half reserved as the specialty take-out section and the back half for in-house dining.

The menu features such specialties as carpe farcie (stuffed carp) at 35F ($6.25); blinis at 14F ($2.50) for two; cabbage borscht at 16F ($2.86); and pastrami, 36F ($6.43), one of the most popular items. Naturally, everything tastes better if accompanied by Jewish rye bread. For those who want to be really patriotic, the menu offers Israeli wines as well as French ones. Métro: Place Charles-de-Gaulle (Étoile) or Ternes.

Au Vieux Berlin, 32 Avenue George V, 8e (tel. 720-88-96), serves the best German food in town.

In fine surroundings, at this prestigious address (across the street from the George V hotel), you are served such classic à la carte dishes as wienerschnitzel at 52F ($9.28), followed by the typical apfelstrudel at 19F ($3.39). Another interesting specialty the chef does well is filet de porc cooked in beer, 52F ($9.28). Closed Saturday and Sunday. Métro: George-V.

A GASTRONOMIC STROLL THROUGH THE OLD NEIGHBORHOOD:

If the idea of corned beef, pastrami, schmaltz herring, and dill pickles excites you, then strike out for one of the most colorful old neighborhoods in Paris, the **rue des Rosiers** in the 4th Arrondissement (Métro: St-Paul). There is something of the air of a little village town about the place. The blue-and-white Star of David is prominently displayed. Increasingly, North African overtones, reflecting the arrival of Jews from Morocco, Tunisia, and especially Algeria, have appeared.

John Russell wrote that the rue des Rosiers is "the last sanctuary of certain ways of life; what you see there, in miniature, is Warsaw before the ghetto was razed . . . Samarkand before the Soviet authorities brought it into line."

The best time to go is Sunday morning when many parts of Paris are sleeping. You can actually wander up and down the street, eating as you go—perhaps selecting an apple strudel, a slice of pastrami on Jewish rye bread, even pickled lemons, smoked salmon, and merguez, the typical smoked sausages of Algeria.

If you want to have a proper sit-down meal, you'll find many spots. The most famous is **Goldenberg,** 4 rue des Rosiers, 4e (tel. 887-20-16). Albert Goldenberg has moved to fancier quarters off the Champs-Élysées (see above). However, his brother Joseph runs this place.

Here you can have stuffed carp or beef goulash. The Goldenbergs were born in Constantinople (Russian Jewish father). This background is reflected in such dishes as eggplant moussaka. Naturally, the traditional opener to any repast is borscht. A complete meal here will range in price from 42F ($7.49) to 60F ($10.71). Israeli wines begin at 25F ($4.46) per bottle. Dining is on two levels. Look for the collection of samovars and the white fantail pigeon in a wicker cage.

Or you might want to try the **Restaurant Tunisien,** 5 bis rue des Rosiers, 4e. It offers five different versions of that semolina-based North Africa specialty, couscous. The brochette of lamb is served as an hors d'oeuvre. You'll want to finish with mint tea, of course. You can enjoy lunch here for as little as 50F ($8.93) to 70F ($12.50).

A strictly kosher establishment is **À la Bonne Bouchée**, 1 rues des Hospitalières St-Gervais, 4e (tel. 278-79-47), right off the rue des Rosiers. It features two set meals, one costing 42F ($7.49), another 58F ($10.35). Two specialties on the à la carte menu are stuffed kiszke and roast duck. If you order from the à la carte menu, your tab is likely to be no more than 75F ($13.39).

At Bougival

Le Coq Hardi, 16 Quai Rennequin-Sualem (tel. 969-01-43), lies in the suburb of Bougival, 13 miles from Paris. Parisians are fond of coming here for special celebrations. On the banks of the Seine, the restaurant features a remarkable flower garden, forming the perfect setting for meals. Preferred are the tables on the terrace in the rear. There, shaded by a canopy, you have a view of the garden with its thousands of hydrangea. In the hillside is a cave holding more than 40,000 bottles of wine, ranging from simple to vintage.

The dining rooms inside are furnished with antiques, but before wandering through them, you might stop off first in the drinking lounge, if not for a drink then to see the collection of more than 1500 coqs (roosters), honoring the restaurant's name. The food is extremely good, especially croûte Landaise gratinée and filets de saumon (salmon). We also prefer poulet de Bresse rôti aux herbes. For dessert, nothing beats the chocolate cake. A 15% service charge is added to your bill, which is likely to be in the neighborhood of 300F ($53.55). Closed Wednesday and from mid-January to mid-February and in August. Dinners are served from 7 p.m. until 10 p.m.

This concludes our culinary roundup of Paris, the greatest of all food capitals. If we omitted your pet hostelry, we offer our sincere apologies.

But before departing to other subjects, we'd like to include a few lines about the humblest of Parisian gastronomic pleasures: the **street stalls.** You'll see them at most intersections offering wares such as marrons (roasted chestnuts), crêpes (pancakes), and gaufres (waffles). Do yourself a favor and try them.

Chapter VI

PARIS IN THE DAYTIME

THE MAIN ATTRACTION OF PARIS . . . is Paris. You'll make that discovery yourself the moment you start sightseeing. For unless you're taking an organized tour, you are liable to become so ensnared by the vistas you find en route to a particular sight that you run the risk of never getting there.

No single palace, museum, church, or monument is as captivating as any of a dozen street settings of this city. They work like sirens' songs on a visitor's senses, luring you into hours of aimless rambling when you should be steering resolutely toward some three-star edifice.

We know—it has happened to us more times than we want to remember. And knowing this, we've divided our sightseeing discussion into the following sections:

The first section deals with entire streets, squares, and islands, which are best viewed as a whole, preferably in good weather.

The second gets down to individual structures and takes you inside such tourist meccas as Notre-Dame and the Invalides.

The third and fourth discuss the famous gardens and parks of the city and special sightseeing tours that are available.

The fifth, which occupies all the next chapter, deals with museums, exhibitions, and galleries, which make ideal rainy-day fare.

All Around Paris

PLACE DE LA CONCORDE: Regarded by many as the most beautiful urban square in the world, this immense 85,000-square-yard expanse is so vast that your eye can't take it in at one glance. The center of the oval is swarming with cars, a motorist's nightmare, but the hugeness of the place seems to swallow them up.

In the middle, looking pencil-small, rises a 33-centuries-old obelisk from Egypt, flanked by cascading fountains. Grouped around the outer edges are eight statues representing eight French cities. Near the statue of Brest was the spot where the guillotine stood during the Revolution. On Sunday morning of January 21, 1793, King Louis XVI lost his royal head there, and was followed by 1343 other victims, including Marie Antoinette and, subsequently, Danton and Robespierre, the very men who had launched the Terror.

The place borders the Tuileries Gardens on the east, and on the west the second great showpiece of Paris, the . . .

CHAMPS-ÉLYSÉES: You get a bit tired of repeating "the most in the world," but, of course, this *is* the world's most famous promenade. Pointing from the Place de la Concorde like a broad, straight arrow at the Arc de Triomphe at the far end, it presents its grandest spectacle at night.

For the first third, the avenue is hedged by chestnut trees. Then it changes into a double row of palatial hotels and shops, movie houses, office buildings, and block after block of sidewalk cafés. The automobile showrooms and gift stores have marred the once-impeccable elegance of this stretch, but this is still the greatest vantage point from which to watch Paris roll and stroll by, preferably while sipping a cold drink.

TROCADÉRO: This is actually a series of adjoining sights, which a master touch of city planning has telescoped into one (a characteristic Parisian knack).

From the Place du Trocadéro, you can step between the two curved wings of the **Palais de Chaillot** and gaze out on a view that is nothing short of breathtaking. At your feet lie the **Jardins du Trocadéro,** centered by fountains. Directly in front, the Pont d'Iéna spans the Seine. Then, on the opposite bank, rises the iron immensity of the **Tour Eiffel.** And beyond, stretching as far as your eye can see, the **Champ de Mars,** once a military parade ground but now a garden landscape with arches and grottoes, lakes and cascades.

THE SEINE ISLANDS: The **Ile de la Cité,** the "egg from which Paris was hatched," lies quietly in the shadow of Notre-Dame. The home of French kings until the 14th century, the island still has a curiously medieval air, with massive gray walls rising up all around you, relieved by tiny patches of parkland. We'll visit a part of the glowering Palais de Justice and the cathedral later

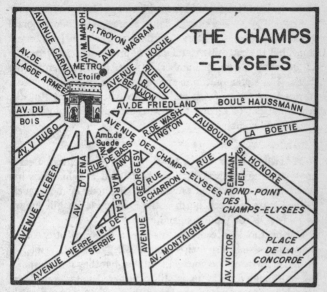

THE CHAMPS-ELYSEES

in this chapter. Now we'll make our way to the extreme eastern tip of the island, just behind Notre-Dame.

There, sunken almost to the level of the river, is the **Memorial de la Déportation,** the monument to the thousands of French men, women, and children who perished in Nazi concentration camps from 1940 to 1945. You step down into a series of granite chambers with narrow, iron-barred windows, horribly reminiscent of the actual killing pens. And just as bare. Hewn into the stone walls are the nightmarish names of the camps, each one like the tolling of a funeral bell: Auschwitz—Bergen-Belsen—Dachau—Buchenwald—Mathausen—Treblinka. . . .

Back on ground level, you'll see an iron bridge leading over to the Île St-Louis. This smaller and even quieter of the river islands has remained almost exactly as it was in the 17th century, after it had been divided up into private building lots. Sober patrician houses stand along the four quays, and the fever-beat of the city seems a hundred miles away.

PLACE VENDÔME: This is *the* textbook example of classical French architecture, a pure gem set in the fashionable heart of the Right Bank. The pillared palaces encircling the square include the Ritz Hotel as well as the Ministry of Justice. The center is crowned by a 144-foot-high column, erected to commemorate Napoleon's greatest victory—Austerlitz. The actual column is stone, but the enclosing spiral band of bronze was cast from the 1200 cannon (a fantastic number) captured by the emperor at the battle. The statue on top of the pillar is, of course, Napoleon, restored there after being pulled down twice: once by Royalist reactionaries, the second time by Communard revolutionaries . . . an odd combination.

A WALKING TOUR OF LE MARAIS: Very few cities on earth boast an entire district that can be labeled a sight. Paris has several. The one visited on this walking tour is the vaguely defined maze of streets north of the **Place de la Bastille** known as Le Marais, or the marshland.

During the 17th century, this was a region of aristocratic mansions, which lost their elegance when the fashionable set moved elsewhere. The houses lost status, but they remain standing. Although Le Marais is still considered unfashionable by today's standards, many artists and crafts people are moving in, and the government is restoring some of the mansions.

You can take the Métro to the Place de la Bastille to begin your tour. The actual Bastille, of course, is gone now (currently a hub of traffic). However, as you know, the mob attack on this fortress on July 14, 1789, touched off the French Revolution. To commemorate the storming, Bastille Day on July 14 is a major French holiday. Once the prison contained eight towers, housing such illustrious tenants as "The Man in the Iron Mask" and the Marquis de Sade.

If you don't mind risking your life, you can cross the square to look at the **Colonne de Juillet,** which, surprisingly, honors the victims of the July Revolution of 1830 that marked the supremacy of Louis-Philippe. The winged god of Liberty crowns the column.

From the Place de la Bastille, head up the rue Saint-Antoine, cutting right on the rue des Tournelles, with its statue honoring Beaumarchais *(The Barber of Seville).* Take a left again onto the Pas-de-la-Mule, "the footsteps of the mule," which will carry you to. . .

Place des Vosges

An enchanted island rather than a city square, this silent, serenely lovely oasis is the oldest square in Paris and—for our money—the most entrancing.

Laid out in 1605 by order of King Henry IV, it was once called the "Palais Royale" and was the scene of innumerable cavaliers' duels. The Revolutionary government changed its name but—luckily—left its structure intact. In the middle is a tiny park, and on three sides an encircling arcaded walk, supported by arches and paved with ancient, worn flagstones.

That's all, but the total effect is so harmonious, so delicately balanced between mellow stone and green trees, that it works like a soothing balm on the nerves. Spend half an hour there and you're ready to face the traffic again.

At No. 6 on the square is the. . .

Maison de Victor Hugo

The house in which Victor Hugo lived and worked from 1832 to 1848 has been turned into a miniature museum. You probably know Hugo as a literary great, but here you'll also see his drawings, carvings, paintings, and pieces of furniture he made. The windows of his study overlook the square, and it's easy to see where he drew his inspiration. The museum is open daily, except Monday, Tuesday, and legal holidays, from 10 a.m. to 5:40 p.m. It charges 7F ($1.25) admission; free on Sunday. For information, telephone 272-16-65.

Continuing the Walk

After your visit, you can pick up the trail again by taking the rue des Francs-Bourgeois, which will lead you to the **Hôtel Carnavalet,** on the same street. This Renaissance palace—entrance on 23 rue de Sévigné, named after the madame of letter-writing fame—is now owned by the City of Paris, which has turned it into the **Musée Carnavalet,** described in the following chapter under "Historical Museums."

Following a stopover here, looking at relics of the French Revolution, you can continue up the same street to the **Palais Soubise,** housing the **National Archives** of France, also described in the following chapter under "Historical Museums." The palace, at 60 rue des Francs-Bourgeois, was named for the Princess Soubise, mistress of Louis XIV.

After such a prestigious stopover, you can double back a block to the rue Vieille-du-Temple and the **Hôtel de Rohan,** at no. 87. The mansion was once occupied by the fourth Cardinal de Rohan, involved in the diamond necklace scandal implicating Marie Antoinette. The interior is open to the public only for guided tours on Monday, Wednesday, Thursday, and Friday at 3 p.m. In the courtyard (open Monday to Saturday from 9 a.m. to 6 p.m.), you can see a stunning bas-relief depicting a nude Apollo and four horses against a background exploding with sunbursts.

On the same street, at 47 rue Vieille-du-Temple, stands the **Hôtel des Ambassadeurs de Hollande,** where Beaumarchais founded the Rodriguez Hortalez Company financed by the French and Spanish governments to help the American settlers fight the English government, and where he wrote his immortal play, *The Marriage of Figaro.* Again, you have to be content with a look from the outside.

From this street, turn down the **rue des Rosiers** (the street of rose bushes), the main street of the old Jewish quarter of Paris, still filled with kosher delicatessen stores and Hebrew inscriptions.

At the end of this street, you'll be on the rue Mahler. Take a sharp right onto the rue Rivoli, then branch off to the left onto the rue St-Antoine.

The **Hôtel de Sully,** 62 rue St-Antoine, was begun in 1625. The duc de Sully, Henry IV's minister of finance, acquired it in 1634. He planned to live there with his young bride, who turned out to prefer a more virile lover (Sully was 74 years old). It's very difficult to get inside without special passes unless you're there for the Festival du Marais.

The rue St-Antoine leads into the rue François-Miron, where at no. 68 stands the 17th-century **Hôtel de Beauvais,** which was built by Louis XIV as an abode for a lady named Catherine Bellier, allegedly his first-ever mistress. Mozart lived there in 1763, by the way.

Leaving the hotel, continue down the street, turning left onto the rue de Jouy, which leads to the rue du Figuier and the **Hôtel de Sens** at no. 1. Construction began in 1470 on the mansion for the archbishop of Sens, and it is—other than the Cluny—the only domestic architecture that remains from 15th-century Paris. It was once inhabited by the notorious Queen Margot, wife of Henri IV, who had an interest in young lovers. Today, it houses the **Forney Library.** You can walk inside the gate during the day—about all you'll have energy to do at the end of this.

THE ST. GERMAIN DES PRES AREA

QUARTIER LATIN: Now we cross over the Seine to the Left Bank. The Latin Quarter lies in the Fifth Arrondissement and consists of the streets winding around the Paris University, of which the **Sorbonne** is only a part.

We have already been to several restaurants here, and we'll come back again to drop in on some of the nightspots that make this area hum after dark. Right now, we'll just stroll.

The logical starting point is the **Place Saint-Michel,** right on the river, decorated by an impressive fountain. This was the scene of some of the most savage fighting during the uprising of the French Resistance in August 1944. Here—as in many, many other spots—you'll see the moving little name tablets, marking the place where a Resistance fighter fell: *"Ici est Tombé . . . le 19 Août 1944. Pour la Libération de Paris."*

Running straight south is the main thoroughfare of the quarter, the wide, pulsating **Boulevard St-Michel** (called Boul' Mich' by the locals). But we'll turn left and dive into the warren of dogleg alleys adjoining the river—**rue de la Huchette, rue de la Harpe, rue St-Séverin.** Thronged with students, tingling with the spice smells of Arabian, African, and Vietnamese cooking, narrow, twisting, and noisy, the alleys resemble an Oriental bazaar more than a European city. This impression is aided by the incredibly garish posters advertising horror movies, belly dancers, and sticky Algerian sweets, the crush of humanity, the honking of cars bullying a path through the swarming crowds.

We emerge at the **Church of St-Séverin** and are back in Paris again. Dating from the 13th century, this flamboyant Gothic edifice acts like a sanctuary of serenity at the edge of an antheap.

Head down the **rue St-Jacques** and Paris reasserts herself completely. The next crossing is the **Boulevard St-Germain,** lined with sophisticated cafés and some of the most avant-garde fashion shops in town.

MONTMARTRE: This name has spread chaos and confusion in many an unwary tourist's agenda. So just to make things clear—there are three of them.

The first is the **Boulevard Montmartre,** a busy commercial street nowhere near the mountain. The second is the tawdry, expensive, would-be-naughty, and utterly phoney amusement belt along the **Boulevard de Clichy,** culminating at **Place Pigalle** (the "Pig Alley" of World War II GIs). The third—the Montmartre we're talking about—lies on top, and on the slopes of the actual **Mont.**

The best way to get there is to take the Métro to **Anvers,** then walk to the nearby rue de Steinkerque, and ride the curious little funicular to the top. Operated between 6 a.m. and 11 p.m., the funicular charges 3F (54¢).

Montmartre used to be the artists' village, glorified by masters such as Utrillo, painted, sketched, sculpted, and photographed by ten thousand lesser lights. The tourists, building speculators, and nightclub entrepreneurs came and most of the artists went. But a few still linger. And so does some of the village charm that once drew them. Just enough to give you a few delightful hours, and leave you nostalgic for a past you wish you'd known.

The center point, the **Place du Tertre,** looks like an almost-real village square, particularly when the local band is blowing and puffing oompah music. All around the square run terrace restaurants with dance floors and colored lights. And gleaming through the trees is the Basilica of **Sacré-Coeur.** Built in an oddly Oriental neo-Byzantine style, the church, which is a center of perpetual prayer, is visited not only by pilgrims from many places but by tourists as well. From the white dome and also from the steps, you get an unsurpassed view of Paris as it lies spread out beneath the "mountain of martyrs" (that is to say, "Montmartre"). The crypt and its dome are open from 9 a.m. to 5:30 p.m. year round.

Behind the church and clinging to the hillside below are steep and crooked little streets that seem—almost—to have survived the relentless march of progress. The **rue des Saules** still has Montmartre's last vineyard, plus a wonderful cabaret which we'll visit later. And the **rue Lepic** still looks—almost—the way Renoir and the melancholy Van Gogh and the dwarfish genius Toulouse-Lautrec saw it. Which—almost—makes up for the blitz of portraitists and souvenir stores and postcard vendors up on top.

PÈRE-LACHAISE CEMETERY: This graveyard, the largest in Paris, contains more illustrious dead than any other place on earth. Métro stop: Père-Lachaise.

A map available at the main entrance will help you find the tombs, and they read like a roll call of international renown. There are Napoleon's marshals Ney and Masséna, and the British admiral Sir Sidney Smith who, by holding the fortress of Acre, made the Corsican taste his first defeat.

There are the poets, playwrights, and novelists Beaumarchais, Balzac, Oscar Wilde, Colette, La Fontaine, Molière, Apollinaire, and Daudet, the composers Chopin and Rossini, the painter Corot, the singer Edith Piaf, and a legion more.

But the most sombre note in Père-Lachaise is a piece of wall called *Mur des Fédérés*. It was among the graves of this cemetery that the last-ditch fighters of the Paris Commune—the world's first anarchist republic—made their final desperate stand against the troops of the regular French government in May 1871. They were overwhelmed, stood up against this wall, and shot in batches. All died except a handful who had hidden in vaults and lived for years in the cemetery like wild animals, venturing into Paris at night to forage for food. Now, turning from general vistas we take in particular sights.

The Major Sights

EIFFEL TOWER: Strangely enough, this symbol of Paris wasn't meant to be a permanent structure at all. Erected specifically for the Universal Exhibition of 1889, it was destined to be pulled down a few years later. But by then, wireless telegraphy had appeared on the scene and the 985-foot tower—the tallest on earth—presented a handy signaling station. Radio confirmed its role. During the German advance on Paris in 1914, the powerful beam from the top effectively jammed the enemy's field radios.

You could write a page with nothing but figures about the tower. The plans for it covered 6000 square yards of paper, it weighs 7000 tons, contains 2½ million rivets. Its base extends more than . . . etc.

But enough of that. Just stand underneath the tower and look straight up. It's like a rocket of steel lacework shooting into the sky. If nothing else, it is a fantastic engineering achievement.

Gustave Eiffel, "the universal engineer," who had previously constructed hundreds of bridges and even the inner structure of the Statue of Liberty, had the overall responsibility for the project of building the tower. Architects and aesthetes hated it. ("That damned lamp post ruins the skyline.") The Parisians loved it. Almost overnight it became a part of local legendry. A dozen poems were written about it and at least as many ghastly pieces of music, including an "Eiffel Tower Waltz." By 1910, its permanence had been confirmed—the "lamp post" was there to stay.

The first and second levels are open from 10 a.m. to 11 p.m. The third level is open from 10 a.m. to 6 p.m. An elevator costs 8F ($1.43) to the first level, 18F ($3.21) to the second level, and 26F ($4.64) to the third level.

Even for Paris, the tower is unusually well equipped with restaurants. Two dining rooms, one deluxe, a snackbar, and a drinking bar at various levels await your decision. On the ground level, the 1891 lift machinery is open to visitors in the western pillar for a fee of 5F (89¢). On the first level, a ciné museum showing films on the tower is open, charging 10F ($1.79). Eiffel's office has been newly recreated on the fourth level, with wax figures of the engineer receiving Thomas Edison.

But it's the view most people go up for and this extends for 42 miles, theoretically. In practice, weather conditions tend to limit it. Nevertheless, it's fabulous, and the best time for visibility is about an hour before sunset. Métro: Trocadéro, École Militaire, or Bir-Hakeim.

NOTRE-DAME: The Cathedral of Paris and one of civilization's greatest edifices, this is more than a building—it's like a book written in stone and wood and glass. It can be read line by line, the Virgin's Portal alone telling four different picture stories. The doors of Notre-Dame did, in fact, take the place of religious textbooks during the ages when few of the faithful were literate.

The cathedral replaced two Romanesque churches (Ste. Mary and St. Stephen), which stood on the spot until 1160. Then Bishop Maurice de Sully, following the example of Suger, the abbot of St. Denis, undertook the new structure, and building continued for more than 150 years. The final result was a piece of Gothic perfection, not merely in overall design but in every detail. The rose window above the main portal, for instance, forms a halo 31 feet in diameter around the head of the statue of the Virgin.

More than any other building, Notre-Dame is the history of a nation. Here, the boy-monarch Henry VI of England was crowned king of France in 1430, during the Hundred Years War when—but for Joan of Arc—France would have become an English dominion.

Here, Napoleon took the crown out of the hands of Pope Pius VII, and crowned himself and Josephine emperor and empress.

Here, General de Gaulle knelt before the altar on August 26, 1944, to give thanks for the liberation of Paris—imperturbably praying while sniper bullets screeched around the choir galleries.

Because of the beauty of its ornaments and of its symbolic meaning of redemption of all evil, Notre-Dame is a joyous church. However, those devils and gargoyles grinning from its ledges add a genuinely macabre touch. You can almost see Victor Hugo's hunchback peering from behind them.

There are many cathedrals larger than Notre-Dame, but the interior has a transcending loftiness that makes it seem immense.

The flat-topped twin towers flanking the entrance rise to 225 feet. You can climb the 387 steps, leading to a magnificent view, every day except Tuesday from 10:30 a.m. to 4:15 p.m. You can visit the tower for 8F ($1.43). Incidentally, on national holidays and feast days, you can hear the brass thunder of the "Bourdon," the 16-ton bell that hangs in the South Tower. Requiring a 5F (89¢) entrance fee, the Treasury (Trésor) is open from 10:30 a.m. to 4 p.m. daily, except Sunday. The cathedral is generally open from 8 a.m. to 7 p.m. However, it is advised to refrain from visiting during Sunday mass from 10 a.m. to 11:30 a.m. For information, telephone 354-00-04. The complete address is 6 Place du Parvis Notre-Dame (4e), but it's such a landmark no one needs a street number to find it. Métro: Cité.

ARC DE TRIOMPHE: This is the third of the trio of great Paris symbols, the largest triumphal arch in the world, and the centerpiece of the entire Right Bank. It stands as the focus of 12 radiating avenues on the Place Charles de Gaulle, formerly the Place de l'Étoile, giving it an unequalled position and making it pretty difficult to reach for the uninitiated. The best—in fact, the only—way to get there through the traffic is to use the underground passage leading from the Champs-Élysées.

The arch was begun on Napoleon's orders in 1806 to commemorate the victories of his Grande Armée. But it was not completed until 1836, when the Grande Armée had long been shattered. Ever since then, the arch has born witness to France's defeats as well as her triumphs.

Twice—in 1871 and 1940—German troops tramped through it in their moments of victory. And twice—in 1919 and 1945—Allied armies staged victory parades through those buttresses.

The arch is 162 feet high and 147 feet wide—a stone fanfare of military glory . . . and its price. It's ornamented with martial scenes and engraved with the names of the 128 victories of Napoleon and the 600 generals who participated in them.

But underneath burns the Flame of Remembrance that marks the tomb of France's Unknown Soldier. The effect at night is magical—if only that light weren't burning for millions of young men who lost their lives in war.

A stairway and an elevator take you to the top of the arch, which houses a small museum, admission 7F ($1.25). It is open daily except Tuesday from 10 a.m. to 5 p.m. Métro: Étoile (Charles de Gaulle).

HÔTEL DES INVALIDES: This is not a "hotel," rather a palace and a church combined, which today houses a great museum, dozens of military administration offices, and the tomb of Napoleon.

The monumental ensemble was originally built by Louis XIV as a stately home for invalid soldiers (hence the name). There are still a few living there, but most of the enormous space is taken up by the **Musée de l'Armée** (see our next chapter), various army bureaus, and the crypt beneath the dome in the rear that makes it one of Paris's greatest showpieces.

It's a shrine, and, like most shrines, impersonal. No trace of the man here—everything is in symbols. Napoleon rests in a sarcophagus of red granite on a pedestal of green granite. Surrounding the tomb are 12 figures of victories and six stands of captured enemy flags. The pavement of the crypt consists of a mosaic of laurel leaves.

It took 19 years for the British to release the body of their most illustrious prisoner, who had originally been buried near his house of banishment. Finally, on December 15, 1840, Napoleon's second funeral took place in Paris. The golden hearse was taken through crowds of mourners who had braved a snowstorm to pay their last respects to the nation's hero.

The same golden dome also covers the tombs of Napoleon's brothers, Joseph and Jerome, his son (who was never crowned), and Marshal Foch, who led the Allied armies to victory in 1918. Métro: Invalides.

THE CONCIERGERIE: The most sinister building in France squats on the north bank of the Île de la Cité (near the Pont au Change) and forms part of the huge Palais de Justice. Its name is derived from the title *concierge* (constable), once borne by a high official of the Royal Court. But its reputation stems from the Revolution.

Even on warm days, a chill wind seems to blow around its two bleak towers, and the gray, massive walls feel eternally dank. Here, as nowhere else in Paris, you can see the tall, square shadow of the guillotine.

For, after the fall of the Bastille, this became the country's chief prison. And when the Reign of Terror got under way, the Conciergerie turned into a kind of stopover depot en route to the "National Razor."

You forget everything else as you enter those courtyards and passages. There are the splendid remnants of a medieval royal palace in there, complete with refectory and giant kitchen. But the only features that imprint themselves on the mind are the rows of cells and the doghouse hovel in which prisoners—shorn and bound—sat waiting for the dung cart that was to carry them to the blade.

There were hundreds and hundreds of them, and their names reflect the inexorable process by which the Revolution devoured its own children.

First came the "aristos"—led by Marie Antoinette, the duc d'Orléans, brother of the king, and the notorious Madame du Barry. Then came the moderate liberals known as "Girondins." Then followed the radicals with their leader Danton. At their heels were the ultra-radicals along with their chief, the frozen-faced Robespierre. Finally, as the wheel turned full circle, it was the turn of the relentless public prosecutor Fouquier-Tinville, together with the judges and jury of the Revolutionary Court.

They all had their brief stay in those cells, followed by the even briefer ride to the guillotine. Among the few who stayed there, but lived to write about it, was America's Thomas Paine, who remembered chatting in English with Danton.

It is open daily from 10 a.m. to 4:25 p.m. Guided tours are given every 30 minutes. Admission is 8F ($1.43); on Sunday, 4F (71¢). Métro: Cité.

Within the same building complex, but spiritually a thousand miles away, is . . .

La Sainte Chapelle

One of the oldest, most beautiful, and oddest churches in the world, La Sainte Chapelle was built in 1246 for the express purpose of housing the relics of the Crucifixion, which had been sent, at tremendous expense, from Constantinople. But the relics were later transferred to Notre-Dame, leaving La Saint Chapelle as an empty showcase, although a magnificent one.

Actually, it consists of two separate churches, one humble, the other superb. The lower chapel was for the servants, the upper for the gentry—and one glance will tell you the difference.

The gentry, in fact, were the royal household, and you can still see the small grated window from which Louis XI could participate in the service without being noticed.

The outstanding feature of the chapel is the 15 great stained-glass windows, flooding the interior with colored light—deep blue, ruby red, and dark green—and depicting more than a thousand scenes from the Bible.

The church is open daily except Tuesday from 10 a.m. till noon, then from 1:30 to 5 p.m. The price of admission is 4F (71¢).

PANTHÉON: This strangely splendid cross between a Roman temple and a Gothic church has at some time been both and is now neither. But it towers impressively on the Left Bank as one of the city's most illustrious landmarks.

Originally the site of a Roman temple which grew into a medieval abbey, it was constructed as the Church of Ste-Geneviève in the 18th century, finishing up with a capitol-like dome, as well as noble Roman pillars.

Then the Revolutionary government decided to convert it into a purely patriotic shrine for the nation's greats. Under Napoleon it again became a church. Since 1885, however, it has reverted to being a nonreligious temple—a worthy receptacle for those the nation wished to honor.

The interior is stark and bare, with an austere grandeur all its own. It houses the tombs of Rousseau and Voltaire, of Victor Hugo and Émile Zola, of Louis Braille, who enabled the blind to read, and of the African Felix Eboué, who rallied his Equatorial colony to the colors of de Gaulle at a time when no other French administrator dared to do so.

It is open daily except Tuesday from 10 a.m. to 4:30 p.m. Admission is 8F ($1.43), reduced to 4F (71¢) on Sunday. Métro: Saint-Michel.

LA MADELEINE: Much more than somber Notre-Dame, this is the patron church of Paris, reflecting the mood, character, and charm of the city. Standing at the most fashionable focal point, between the Opéra and Place de la Concorde, it could pass as a handsome palace just as well.

Begun as an 18th-century church, the Madeleine was—at some stage or other—earmarked as a Napoleonic "Temple of Glory," a library, stock exchange, theater, municipal building, courthouse, and the Bank of France. Only in 1842 was it finally completed as a house of worship.

Yet despite these dubious beginnings, it became an outstandingly beautiful edifice—superlative when the west doors are open and the light is streaming in. The interior is roofed by three domes, lined with 52 Corinthian pillars, and decorated with rich, lively religious scenes.

Once a month there is a concert, sometimes an exceptional one. Metro: Madeleine.

CITÉ UNIVERSITAIRE: This is the only one of our sights which is still in the building stage. But then it has been since 1925, and will probably continue so for another half century. For the city's great, international students' campus isn't really meant ever to be completed. Its purpose is to keep on growing and expanding as long as the space lasts and the students keep coming.

Sprawling just south of Montsouris Park on the Left Bank,

this city of colleges, pavilions, and hostels resembles a nonbickering U.N. or a scholastic World's Fair. Only two-thirds of the students living there are French. The rest come from 83 different countries and are housed in buildings suggesting their national origins.

The community center—something like City Hall—is the huge Maison Internationale, built from the funds contributed by John D. Rockefeller, Jr. It has a theater, swimming pool, meeting hall, and club rooms.

All around this center lie the students' buildings, some of them architectural gems. Both the Swiss and the Brazilian pavilions were designed by Le Corbusier. There are also a British college, a Japanese hostel, a Moroccan college, a Norwegian house, and the elegantly French Institut Agronomique. Métro: Cité Universitaire.

THE SEWERS OF PARIS: Some say Baron Haussmann will be remembered mainly for the vast, complicated network of Paris sewers he erected. The *égouts* of the city are constructed around a quartet of principal tunnels, one of them 18 feet wide and 15 feet high. It's like an underground city, with the street names clearly labeled. Further, each branch pipe bears the number of the building to which it is connected (guides are fond of pointing out Maxim's). These underground passages are truly mammoth, containing pipes bringing in drinking water as well as telephone and telegraph lines.

That these sewers have remained such a popular attraction is something of a curiosity in itself. They were made famous by Victor Hugo's *Les Misérables.* "All dripping with slime, his soul filled with a strange light," Jean Valjean in his desperate flight through the sewers of Paris is considered one of the heroes of narrative drama.

Tours begin at Pont de l'Alma on the Left Bank (Métro: Alma-Marceau). A stairway there leads into the bowels of the city. However, you often have to wait in line as much as 2½ hours. Visits are possible on Monday and Wednesday and on the last Saturday of each month, except for holidays. Hours are 2 to 5 p.m. A one-hour visit costs 7F ($1.25). *Warning:* Visiting hours are likely to change from those stated, and times and days of opening should be verified with the tourist office before you go there. Telephone 705-10-29 for more information.

A Garland of Gardens

After seeing this town, you'll be astonished to hear that Paris boasts far less parkland than, for instance, New York or London. You don't notice this, because the rows of trees along every boulevard create the illusion of vast green spaces. The impression is conscientiously fostered by the municipality, which replaces each tree the moment it dies (unlike certain other city governments, whose main ambition seems to be to hack down and concrete over as many trees as possible).

Although there are not many actual parks, those that exist are lovingly and meticulously maintained. Near the heart of the city lies the . . .

JARDIN DES TUILERIES: Stretching along the right bank of the Seine, from the Place de la Concorde to the court of the Louvre, this exquisitely formal garden was laid out as a royal pleasure park in 1564, but thrown open to the public by the French Revolution. Filled with statues and fountains and mathematically trimmed hedges, it's just a bit too artificial for comfort. The nicest features are the round ponds on which pleasantly disorderly kids sail armadas of model boats.

JARDIN DU LUXEMBOURG: This is the Left Bank equivalent of the above, bordering the Boulevard St-Michel. A masterpiece of Renaissance landscaping with a jewel of a central pond, it faces the Palais de Luxembourg, the Senate building of the French Republic. More intriguing than the senators, however, are the throngs of university students who come here to do their outdoor cramming and, incidentally, to enlarge their acquaintance with the opposite sex.

PARC MONCEAU: The most fashionable park in Paris lies in the plush district northeast of the Arc de Triomphe. It has a colonnade of artificial Roman ruins, a Chinese bridge, a tiny river, and a great many upper-class toddlers guarded by attractive nurses and amiable dogs.

BUTTES-CHAUMONT: Napoleon III transformed an abandoned quarry into an artificial lake with an island in the middle, raised a mountain, and erected a suspension bridge. The park is rather like a stage setting, but a delightful one, and more of a fun place than the formalized landscaping of the Tuileries.

BOIS DE VINCENNES: Stuck on the southeastern fringe of the city (Métro: Picpus), this is a big, popular patch of woodland with fine trees, two boating lakes, and a racecourse. Its zoo you'll find described in our children's chapter. A favorite spot for family outings, it adjoins the 14th-century Castle of Vincennes, which is open to visitors.

JARDIN DES PLANTES: The botanical garden of Paris is set in a rather drab area near the Gare d'Austerlitz on the Left Bank. It contains a not-too-difficult maze and more than 11,000 different plants. Also, it offers the Museum of Natural History and a dreary little zoo. A large, open, and vastly more interesting menagerie is in the . . .

BOIS DE BOULOGNE: Covering 2500 acres, this area of woods, lakes, playgrounds, and sportsfields is Paris's favorite outdoor amusement zone. Bordering on the northwestern edge of the city (Métro: Pte. Maillot), the Bois is no longer quite the promenade of top-class elegance it was in the "Gay Nineties." But on race days at Longchamp, you can still admire the best-dressed women of the capital displaying their finest dresses. Otherwise it's relaxed and bourgeois, with family groups and lovers enjoying the lakes and waterfalls and discreetly hidden glens. Read about the compact Jardin d'Acclimation in our children's chapter.

Paris Tours

Paris is paradise for freelance wanderers. But the process takes both time and energy in large quantities, and even if you have both, chances are you'll miss out on some indispensable sights ("What—you *didn't* see the whatyoucallit?").

Therefore, here is a choice selection of conducted tours and trips, designed to combine the maximum of scenery with the minimum of strain. The ideal thing is to use them in combination with your own explorations, but in any case they'll show you the essentials and a few extras.

For a look at a different side of the city, the tour of **Modern Paris** passes by the Place de la Concorde and the Place Vendôme, leaving daily at 2:30 p.m. in the summer (2 p.m. in winter). You see the Invalides, where Napoleon is buried, the Arc de Triomphe, the artists' quarter of Montmartre, Sacré-Coeur, and the Opéra. More recent sites include the UNESCO Building, as well as the inevitable Eiffel Tower. A complete visit to the western and northern parts of the city costs only 80F ($14.28)—(readers of this book receive a 10% discount).

When the sun goes down, you can book a **Tour of Paris by Night ("Lido"),** spending a spectacular evening at three different cabarets in three different districts. You go first to the Bastille to see the famed "Apaches" dances, then on to Montmartre for a "Pigalle" show. You end up—where else?—at the Lido. Shows, dancing, music, champagne, transportation, and guide service are included in the 400F ($71.40) price (readers of this book will receive a 5% discount). Departure is at 9 p.m. every night of the year. You return at 2:30 a.m. Another evening tour is the **Illuminations Tour,** taking you past Paris's brightly lit monuments (Notre-Dame). Music and commentary are provided along the way. Departure is at 9 p.m. every night in summer, only on weekends in winter. The cost is 80F ($14.28)—(readers of this book will receive a 10% discount).

Before leaving Paris, you should explore some of the rich sights in the environs, the Île de France. The most popular trip is the **Tour of Versailles,** a morning or afternoon excursion to that symbol of ultimate French glory. You can visit the magnificent palace of the kings, see the lavishly decorated apartments and the chapel. In the celebrated **Hall of Mirrors,** the 1919 peace treaty was signed. Finally, you can explore the gardens where Marie Antoinette romped with her perfumed lambs. The 3½-hour tour leaves four times daily: 10 and 11 a.m., and 1:15 and 2 p.m. in summer. In winter, the departures are limited to two times a day: 10 a.m. and 2 p.m. The price is 100F ($17.85)—(readers of this book receive a 10% discount).

A **Tour of Chartres** goes via Versailles and Saint-Cyr through the rich farming country of the Beauce, for a visit to the magnificent cathedral. You will marvel at the architecture, the sculpture, and especially the stained-glass windows dating from the 12th and 13th centuries. The return trip is via Maintenon, site of a château, and Rambouillet, summer residence of the French president. The six-hour tour runs on Tuesday, Thursday, and Saturday all year round, costs 140F ($24.99), and departs at 1:15 p.m. (readers will receive a 10% discount on the price).

Another trip to the environs is a **Tour of Fontainebleau and Barbizon,** a five-hour jaunt leaving every day except Tuesday at

2 p.m. In winter, tours are conducted on Wednesday, Friday, and Sunday only. The cost: 125F ($22.31), (readers receive a 10% discount). You drive through farmland to Barbizon, the village that became world famous as a 19th-century art center, sheltering the studios of Millet and Rousseau, among others. Then you're taken through the forest of Fontainebleau to the great palace where you will see the collections of furnishings and artworks representing 700 years of French history.

Below you will find information on the river cruises of Paris. Readers of this book will receive a 10% discount off the price of the Bateaux-Mouches.

By Invitation Only

The presidential palace, the **Palais de l'Élysée,** occupies an entire block along the chic Faubourg St-Honoré. But you have to have a personal invitation from the president to visit.

The palace was built in 1718 for the count d'Evreux and knew many owners before becoming the residence for the presidents of the Republic in 1873. Madame Pompadour purchased it and in time bequeathed it to the king when she had "the supreme delicacy to die discreetly at the age of 43." Voltaire presented the world première of his play, *The Chinese Orphan,* there. After her divorce, Josephine spent a brief time there. Napoleon III lived here as president from 1848 until he went to the Tuileries as emperor in 1852. Distinguished English visitors have also been lodged here, everybody from Wellington to Queen Victoria to Queen Elizabeth II.

The palace contains many works of art, including 18th-century Beauvais tapestries, paintings by Leonardo da Vinci and Raphael, Louis XVI furnishings, plus a grand dining hall built for Napoleon III, a lavish ballroom, a portrait gallery, and the former orangerie of duchesse du Berry which has been converted into a winter garden.

Bateaux Parisiens Tour Eiffel, Port de la Bourdonnais, 7e (tel. 551-33-08). This is one of the companies running boat rides on the Seine. The streamlined, glass-encased luxury cruisers with English-speaking commentators depart daily every 15 minutes, from 9:30 a.m. to noon, and from 1:30 p.m. to 6:30 p.m. Tours leave from Pont d'Iéna, the bridge directly in front of the Eiffel Tower.

This is a truly memorable river trip, giving you a view of Paris you'll never get from dry land—some of the world's most beautiful bridges, the quays, Notre-Dame, and the dreamy Île St-Louis, the whole panorama of the city that grew from the river.

On Saturday and Sunday evenings, the company also runs a special **"Illuminations Cruise,"** showing you the floodlit city at night. Departure, also from Pont d'Iéna, is at 9 p.m. The cost of day and evening tours is the same: 20F ($3.57). Children under 10 years pay half fare.

Bateaux-Mouches (tel. 225-96-10). More luxury cruises on the river are offered. The launches vary—some boast a delightful open sundeck; others, well-stocked bars and restaurants. All provide commentaries in five languages, including English.

Departures are from the Pont de l'Alma, at the Place de l'Alma, on the Right Bank. Boats leave every 30 minutes from 10 a.m. to noon, from 2 to 7 p.m., and from 9 to 11 p.m., for rides lasting one hour and 15 minutes. The cost is 12F ($2.14) during the day, rising to 18F ($3.21) at night. Luncheon cruises leave at 1 p.m., offering a tourist menu for 150F ($26.78). Dinner cruises leave at 8:30 p.m. with a gourmet meal for 300F ($53.55).

Meet the French

No, this isn't a conversation club, but one of the most personal and stimulating tourist services available anywhere. Its purpose is to offer you Paris-as-you-like-it, with the assistance of one of its friendly but professional driver-guides with whom you view, explore, shop, eat, tour, and generally enjoy yourself. He or she will be fluent in your language, an expert driver, and as knowledgeable about the city as only a native can be.

Your guide suggests activities, but *you* choose them. They may be sightseeing drives, or shopping sprees, or cultural jaunts embracing theater, opera, and concerts, or a round of cafés and nightspots. Whatever your choice, your guide will pick you up at your hotel and deliver you there afterward.

Rates come on a sliding scale, but all of them include unlimited mileage in Paris, plus all car expenses. They do not include your meals and entrance fees.

Readers who want to know the best of French life may also book one of the three-day, deluxe châteaux vacations in the Loire Valley, including not only visits to the châteaux, but nights spent in the deluxe châteaux hotels, as well as two gourmet meals a day.

Meet the French, at 3 rue Vignon (tel. 742-66-02), offers its tours in several languages including English, and its guides, ranging from college students to middle-aged women, are qualified to expound and discuss French history, art, music, gastronomy, and all things Parisian.

Place des Pyramides Jeanne d'Arc

Chapter VII

MUSEUMS AND EXHIBITIONS

THERE ARE PEOPLE—and you well might agree with them—who find visiting museums in Paris redundant. Why sacrifice the sunshine to pursue art and culture through dim museum corridors when every Seine-side stroll brings you vistas the masters have painted and every city square is a model of architectural excellence?

If that's your view, stick with it. Of the almost 100 highly worthy Paris museums, only one is required matter for the world-traveler: the Louvre. All the rest can be guiltlessly left to people with serious and specific interests, or saved up for that proverbial (and inevitable) rainy day or for your next trip here.

Paris museums fit into three categories: city museums *(C)*, national museums *(N)*, and those run by private organizations. The municipal and national museums have fairly standard hours. They are closed on Tuesday and national holidays. Fees vary, but average a generous 8F ($1.43) per person. Half-price tickets are usually provided to students, children age 3 to 7, and extra-large families or groups. If you want to museum-hop in earnest, pick a Sunday, when the majority of the museums let you in for half price.

Whatever time of the year you come, Paris seems to be deeply involved with one or another outstanding exhibition—touted madly from the lamp posts by huge and colorful posters. The largest and most comprehensive are showcased at the **Grand Palais,** between the Seine and the Champs-Élysées on Avenue Winston Churchill, built for this purpose for the 1900 Exposition. More modest collections are set out across the street in the **Petit Palais.** In the halls and museum rooms across the city, there are at least 15 special shows on any given week—a Chagall retrospective, Giacometti sculptures, Art of the Workers' Movement, the public life of Napoleon. Fees charged depend on the exhibit. To find out what's showing while you're in town, stop into the **Welcome Office,** 127 Avenue Champs-Élysées, and pick up a free copy of the English-language booklet, "Paris Weekly Information," published by the National Tourist Office.

Fine Arts Museums

Paris is well stocked with artworks, from Tang Dynasty crockery to crushed-automobile sculpture. But of all its museums, none has quite the fantastic scope of the Louvre.

THE LOUVRE: The largest palace in the world, housing a collection of up to 208,500 works of art, the **Musée du Louvre** (N; tel. 260-39-26) is both impressive and exhausting. There's so much to see, so many endless nightmare hallways to get lost in, that—regardless of how much you may enjoy exploring a museum on your own—here we'd suggest you start with the guided tour. At least do so until you get the lay of the land. Then you can always go back and see what you missed. Or sit down in one favorite room and spend the day.

Tours in English are given daily except Sunday and Tuesday at 10:30 a.m. and 3 p.m. They leave from a desk staffed by multilingual hostesses inside the large entrance hall. The tours last for one hour and 15 minutes and cost 9F ($1.61) per person, over and above the 9F museum admission fee. And they're well worth the cash outlay.

First, your guide will tell you something about the museum buildings, which are immensely interesting in themselves. French kings have lived on this site by the Seine since the 13th century, but much of the present grand residence was built by Napoleon I and his nephew, Napoleon III. The palace was converted to a museum after the Revolution; the royal art collections provided the first exhibits. The palace rooms don't function perfectly as skillfully-lit museum rooms (for which the Louvre apologizes), but they provide a sumptuous setting, especially for the statuary, that at times even competes with the displays. The splendid **Galerie d'Apollon,** where the royal jewels are on show, is lavishly reminiscent of the Hall of Mirrors at Versailles. The central panel of the ceiling was painted by Delacroix.

Next, the guide will tour you through the major rooms of the Louvre, stopping to discuss works of interest and making sure you see at least the highlights of the collection. Of these, there are three that top everybody's request list. To the left of the main entrance, at the crest of a graceful flight of stairs, stands *The Winged Victory,* cloak rippling in a wind that blew two centuries before the birth of Christ. In the Department of Greek Antiquities, on the ground floor, stands the supple statue of *Venus de Milo,* the warm marble subtly tinted by sunlight. Upstairs, in the Salle Denon, covered with bulletproof glass and surrounded by art students, photographers, and awe-struck tourists, hangs the gently chiding portrait of the *Mona Lisa.*

Altogether, there are six museum departments: Egyptian Antiquities, Oriental Antiquities (the world's most complete collection), Greek and Roman Antiquities, Objets d'Art and Furniture, Paintings, and Sculpture.

If you have time, don't let the Louvre go with just the guided tour. There are so many other things to see: six more da Vincis (nearby the *Mona Lisa*), voluptuous Titians, Franz Hals's *The Gypsy,* the enormously lifelike Egyptian *Seated Scribe.* But one can't even start to list the items in this museum. Nor could you see them all if you took three days and brought your lunch. The only blessing is that there is a cut-off point—the collection doesn't go beyond the 19th century.

The Louvre is open daily except Tuesday from 9:45 a.m. to 6:30 p.m. As mentioned, admission is 9F ($1.61), free on Sunday. Some of the less important rooms are closed daily between 11:45 a.m. and 2 p.m. Métro: Louvre, Palais-Royal.

The Impressionists—Galerie du Jeu de Paume

If the Louvre is impressive, it can also be pompously staid and overbearing, with its rows and rows of dark, sober portraits giving rise to the thought that here is where all good paintings go when they die. The rebels—those men who couldn't even get a rusty picture-hook in the Louvre during their lifetime and suffered to the point of starvation through that rejection—are displayed at the other end of the Tuileries Gardens in the Louvre's **Galerie du Jeu de Paume (N;** tel. 260-12-07), on the corner of the rue de Rivoli and the Place de la Concorde. See this museum after the Louvre because only then will the enormity of this group's breakthrough strike you.

Back in the Paris of the 1870s, when the young painters Manet, Renoir, Monet, Degas, Sisley, Pissarro, and Cézanne gathered at the Café Guerbois on the Boulevard Clichy to discuss ideas and buttress each other's morale, they were the outcasts of the tight Paris art community, the avant-garde who promulgated such "way-out" ideas as the use of bright colors, open-air painting, subjects taken from daily life, and the ever-present study of light. Contemporary artists leapt from this springboard into unexplored orbits, and today the wild men of yesteryear are comfortably tabulated and awarded their slot in art history. There's a scholarly aspect to the Jeu de Paume that almost overwhelms the released life of the paintings. But not quite. You can still hear a faint, beard-muffled cry of "Look! There are other ways to see things!"

The two-story museum is easy to visit, compact, and studded with famed paintings of the period. In the first room is Fantin-Latour's portrait of his friends, *The Studio at Batignolles*. On the first floor you'll find Manet's once-scandalous *The Picnic*, with its two fully-clothed men and plump nude by a stream. There are more of Manet's full-blooded nudes, as well as his portrait of Zola. Look for Renoir's delicately tinted *Moulin de la Galette* —the garden and windmill still exist on the slopes of Montmartre. Go upstairs for Van Gogh and Gauguin. Van Gogh's *Room at Arles* and *The Church of Anvers* hang in the room at the top of the stairs. Flanking one door are two identical glass cases, one enclosing the palette of Van Gogh, the other safeguarding Gauguin's palette and water jug—mementoes so humble they catch at your heart. There's an excellent selection of horse-racing pictures by Degas, as well as his dancing girls and *The Laundresses*. Rousseau is represented by two fever-dream canvases, *War* and *Portrait of a Woman*. Take a look at Monet's five paintings of the Rouen cathedral in changing lights. They're magnificent.

The museum is open daily except Tuesday from 9:45 a.m. to 5:15 p.m. Admission fee is 7F ($1.25), half price on Sunday. Métro: Concorde.

Musée de l'Orangerie

When you leave the Jeu de Paume, turn left and walk to the river edge of the Place, where you'll find the **Musée de l'Orangerie (N)**. Usually set aside for special exhibits (which are announced outside the Jeu de Paume), this museum has one permanent display: Claude Monet's exquisite *Nymphéas*, executed between 1890 and 1921, a light-filtered tangle of lily pads and water, paneling the two oval, ground-floor rooms. The museum, as of this writing, is still under renovation but may have reopened by the time of your visit.

On into the 20th Century

CENTRE GEORGES POMPIDOU: It was Georges Pompidou's dream to create a large cultural center in Paris that would include every form of 20th-century art. As president of France (in 1969), he launched the project for a "temple devoted to art" on the Plateau Beaubourg, east of the Boulevard de Sébastopol (4e). That center was finally inaugurated in 1977 by yet another French president, Valéry Giscard d'Estaing.

The building housing the center has been called "the most avant-garde building in the world" because of its radical exoskeletal design, but Parisians are more likely to refer to it as "the refinery." The colorfully painted pipes and ducts which crisscross the transparent facade do indeed create a toy factory-like impression, but the pipes are actually the practical housings for the intricate electrical, heating, and telephone systems which service the center. Even the escalators are housed in worm-like tubes on the outside of the building. Thus, the vast interior has no need for walls, and a grand feeling of open space is created. When walls are needed for exhibits, moving partitions are rolled into place.

All this uniqueness has made the Pompidou Center Paris's favorite sightseeing attraction, surpassing even the Eiffel Tower in the number of tourists who visit.

The **Musée National d'Art Moderne (N)** has been moved to the new center and now forms its most important part. Minor Cubists are represented alongside such giants as Braque and Picasso (many of his harlequins). The museum has beefed up its permanent collection considerably with many recent acquisitions, including its first Mondrian. A large part of the collection is devoted to American artists.

The permanent old collection includes works ranging from the Fauves to Icelandic Conceptual art. Among the sculpture, which leans heavily on the use of 20th-century metals, is a walkthrough Calder and his ironic wire portrayal of the late Josephine Baker. Other sculpture includes works by Henry Moore and Jacob Epstein.

Seasonally, special exhibitions are organized, including retrospective showings of the works of individual artists, periods, and movements.

In addition to the modern art museum, the center contains the first public library in Paris, with more than a million volumes and documents. Its Center for Industrial Design contains exhibits and research facilities in the field of architecture, space planning, publishing, and visual communications. A cinémathèque offers visitors a historical tour of filmmaking. The top-floor restaurant and cafeteria offer a panoramic view of Paris.

The Centre Georges Pompidou is open daily, except Tuesday, from noon to 10 p.m., and from 10 a.m. to 10 p.m. on weekends. Admission is 16F ($2.86) for an all-day pass which permits you access to any part of the center. Admission to the museum of modern art only costs 8F ($1.43), with free admission on Sunday. Persons under 18 and more than 65 years of age enter free at all times. Métro: Rambuteau.

MUSÉE D'ART MODERN DE LA VILLE DE PARIS: Just across the marble plaza at 11 Avenue du Président Wilson, this museum houses the City of Paris collections of 20th-century art and also organizes temporary exhibitions. Other sections of the museum are: **ARC,** which shows work of young artists and new trends in contemporary art, and the **Musée des Enfants,** with exhibitions and animations for children. The museum is open daily, except Monday, from 10 a.m. to 5:30 p.m., charging 9F ($1.61) for admission (free on Sunday), half price for children and students. On Wednesday it remains open until 8:30 p.m. Métro: Iéna or Alma.

UNESCO BUILDING: If your interest in contemporary art is not yet sated, visit the **UNESCO Building,** 7 Place de Fontenoy, not far from the Eiffel Tower on Avenue de Suffren (Métro: Ségur). International in theme and decor, it has murals by Picasso, a mobile by Calder, a statue called *Silhouette at Rest* by England's Henry Moore, even a stylized Japanese garden. There is no charge for admission, and you can visit from 9 a.m. to 6 p.m. by announcing yourself at the reception desk.

Other Museums of Interest

NATIONAL MUSEUM OF FRENCH MONUMENTS: Up the hill from the modern art museum, in the complex of the Palais de Chaillot on the Trocadéro, is the unusual and strangely atmospheric **Musée des Monuments Français (N).** There are no original works of art in this museum. The sculptures are full-scale plaster casts which enable you to study at eye-level such exalted creatures as the sword-brandishing angel on the Arc de Triomphe. But most fascinating are the meticulously reproduced (even the colors are aged) murals from the most ancient abbeys and churches in France—all in reconstructed settings. Within the awesome museum with its echoing crypts, you can view the great works now in the cathedrals of Chartres, Reims, and Amiens, without ever losing sight of the Eiffel Tower outside the museum-room windows. The museum is open daily except Tuesday from 9:45 a.m. to 12:30 p.m. and from 2 to 5:15 p.m. Admission is 7F ($1.25), 5.50F (98¢) on Sunday. Métro: Trocadéro.

THE MUSEUM OF CLUNY: An enchantress of a museum, with some of the most beautiful medieval art extant, the **Musée de Cluny (N),** 6 Place Paul-Painlevé (tel. 325-62-00), stands back from the intersection of Boulevards St-Michel and St-Germain in a walled courtyard—one of the two Gothic private residences of the 15th century left in Paris.

Dark, rough-walled, and evocative, the Cluny is devoted to the church art and castle crafts of the Middle Ages, but mainly to tapestries—among them the world-famed series of the *Lady and the Unicorn* gracefully displayed in a circular room on the second floor. The painstakingly depicted *Life of St. Stephen* hangs in the shadowy chapel, while a third series is concerned with the colorful life at court.

In recent times, it was discovered that in 200 B.C. a Roman bathhouse stood on this site. Already uncovered is the well-preserved "Frigidarium."

The Cluny is open daily except Tuesday from 9:45 a.m. to 12:30 p.m. and from 2 to 5:15 p.m. Admission is 7F ($1.25), 3.50F (63¢) on Sunday. Métro: St-Michel or Odéon.

LES GOBELINS: If you enjoyed seeing the tapestries, you might also enjoy watching how they are made. Tapestry work is still being done at **Les Gobelins,** 42 Avenue des Gobelins (tel. 570-12-60), in the same way and on looms like those used at the founding of the factory in 1662. You will be toured through the workshops where weavers sit behind huge screens of thread, patiently thrusting stitch after stitch into work that may take up to three years to complete. The tours are given only on Wednesday, Thursday, and Friday between 2 and 3:45 p.m. And they are given in French. But to the person truly interested in the craft, all that needs to be known can be seen. Métro: Gobelins.

THE RODIN MUSEUM: Auguste Rodin, the man credited with freeing French sculpture of classicism, once lived and had his studio in the charming 18th-century mansion **Hôtel Biron,** 77 rue de Varenne (tel. 705-01-34), across the boulevard from Napoleon's Tomb in the Hôtel des Invalides. Today the house and garden are filled with his works, a soul-satisfying feast for the Rodin enthusiast. In the cobbled Court of Honor, within the walls as you enter, you'll see *The Thinker* crouched on his pedestal to the right of you; *The Burghers of Calais* grouped off to the left of you; and to the far left, the writhing *Gates of Hell,* atop which *The Thinker* once more meditates. There's a third *Thinker* inside the museum before a second-floor window. In the almost too-packed rooms, men and angels emerge from blocks of marble, hands twisted in supplication, and the nude torso of Balzac rises up from a tree. Wander back from the house through the long wooded garden where more sculptures await you under the trees. The **Musée Rodin** is open daily except Tuesday from 10 a.m. to 6 p.m. (till 5 p.m. off-season). Admission is 8F ($1.43), reduced to 4F (71¢) on Sunday. Métro: Varennes.

MUSÉE GUIMET: Becoming increasingly popular what with the upsurge of interest in Eastern mysticism is the excellent **Musée Guimet** (N) on the Place de la Ville de Paris, diagonally across from the modern art museums and down the boulevard from the Trocadéro. The Guimet and its annex at 19 Avenue d'Iéna feature a splendid selection of artworks from India, Indochina, Afghanistan, Tibet, China, and Japan. Included are the entire Far East collection of the Louvre, bronzes dating back to 1300 B.C., plump and placid Buddhas, and ancient Indian figurines of religious import set off nicely on simple wooden pedestals. Many of the monuments are displayed with maps of the area where they were unearthed, plus photographs of the excavation. The jewels of the collection are on the first floor, the Rousset collection and the Michel Calmann room on the top floor (take the elevator), which contains some exceptionally lovely porcelain pieces, pottery statues, plates and vases, dating from the earliest Chinese Dynasties, including many from the T'ang Dynasty. The museum is open daily except Tuesday from 9:45 a.m. to noon and 1:30 to 5:15 p.m. Admission also includes the annex and is 7F ($1.25), half price on Sunday. Métro: Iéna.

DELACROIX MUSEUM: From 1857 through 1863, the great Romantic painter Delacroix had his final studio at 6 Place de Fürstenberg, one of the most bewitching small squares in all Paris. The artist's apartment and rear garden "atelier" have been transformed into the **Musée Eugène Delacroix (N),** and hung with sketches, lithographs, watercolors, and oils. This is no poor artist's shabby studio, but the very tasteful creation of a solidly established man. A few personal mementoes are about, including a lovely mahogany paint box.

The museum is open daily except Tuesday and holidays from 9:45 a.m. to 5:15 p.m. Admission is 7F ($1.25). Métro: St-Germain-des-Prés.

To see the work that earned Delacroix his sure niche in art history, go to the Louvre for such passionate paintings as his *Liberty Leading the People on the Barricades,* or to the **Church of St. Sulpice** (Métro: Mabillon) for the famed fresco, *Jacob Wrestling with the Angel,* among others.

MARMOTTAN MUSEUM: Time was, when nobody but a stray art scholar ever visited the **Musée Marmottan,** 2 rue Louis-Boilly, on the edge of the Bois de Boulogne. Nowadays, it is one of the most popular museums in Paris. The rescue from obscurity actually occurred on February 5, 1966, when the museum fell heir to more than 130 paintings, watercolors, pastels, and drawings of Claude Monet, the painter considered the father of Impressionism. A gift of Monet's son, Michel, an octogenarian safari-lover who died in a car crash, the bequest is valued at $10 million. Of the surprise acquisition, one critic wrote, "Had an old widow in Brooklyn suddenly inherited the fortune of J. P. Morgan, the event would not have been more startling."

The owner of the museum, the Académie des Beaux-Arts, was immediately embarrassed with a lack of space. The Marmottan was just a small town house, adorned with First Empire furniture and objets d'art (although it did own Monet's *Impression,* which named the movement). The house had once been owned by a dilettante, Paul Marmottan, who had donated it, along with his treasures, to the academy. The solution was to go underground.

Now you can trace the evolution of Monet's art, especially his eternal obsession with water lilies. Presented are about 30-odd pictures of his house at Giverny that inspired him so much. Exceptional paintings include his celebrated 1918 *The Willow,* his 1905 *Houses of Parliament*, his undated *African Lilies*, as well as paintings by Monet's masters, Boudin and Delacroix, and by his fellow impressionists (see especially a portrait of the 32-year-old Monet by Renoir). The donation has been accurately hailed as "one of the great art treasures of the world."

The museum is open daily, except Monday, from 10 a.m. to 6 p.m., and charges 10F ($1.79) for admission. Métro: La Muette.

Historical Museums

Once you've become acquainted with the Paris of today, it can be of tremendous interest to go back and putter around among the souvenirs of its past. The **Musée Carnavalet (C)**, in the Marais district at 23 rue de Sévigné, covers the history of the city to the present time. There are rooms filled with models of the old quarters of Paris—detailed down to the lace on the cap of the baker's girl. You can see the Bastille, of which there is now not a trace. One room is crammed with signposts of the 17th and 18th centuries, designed to let the unlettered know that here at the sign of the tree worked a carpenter, and here where a pig was portrayed you could buy your cold-cuts. The striking collection of memorabilia from the French Revolution includes the chessmen with which Louis XVI passed time while imprisoned in the Temple, as well as the boyish diary of the dauphin and some effects of Marie Antoinette.

There is more, such as antique furniture of various periods—in all a total of 22,000 exhibits. Not the least of the exhibits is the mansion that houses them, built in 1545 and considered a prime example of Renaissance architecture. The museum is open daily except Monday from 10 a.m. to 5:30 p.m. Admission: 9F ($1.61); free on Sunday. For more information, telephone 272-21-13. Métro: Saint-Paul.

When you leave the museum, take a few moments to walk up the rue des Francs-Bourgeois two blocks to the aged arcades of the **Place des Vosges** (described in the previous chapter), where you may sit and rest a while within the fenced park or visit the home of Victor Hugo. Alternatively, turn right down the rue des Francs-Bourgeois and walk three long blocks to no. 60, where an elegant 18th-century apartment in the majestic Palais Soubise contains the **Musée de l'Histoire de France** (tel. 277-11-30), installed by Napoleon in 1808. The rooms are open from 2 to 5 p.m. daily except Tuesday. Admission is 4F (71¢), half price on

Sunday. What you see are mainly documents—some so gloriously inscribed they become works of art—chronicling the history of France from its origins. Once again, the building vies in interest with the displays within.

ARMY MUSEUM: The Musée de l'Armée in the Hôtel des Invalides is the finest military museum in the world—outdistancing even Britain's Imperial War Museum in amassed martial relics. Its collection of arms dates back so far it seems to include the first rock thrown by Neolithic man. With the prideful bluster of a victory parade, the museum sets out the war paraphernalia of every age—bronze spearheads and medieval crossbows, intricately engraved armor and doughboy drabs—leading up with a flourish and the recorded strains of "Tipperary" to the bugle that sounded the cease-fire on November 11, 1918. The shrine-like aura is distressing. The detail is fascinating.

The museum occupies a building created by Louis XIV as a home for disabled soldiers. You aren't left guessing about the subject under study. Cannon lurk among the classic colonnades surrounding the vast, cobbled court. The west wing, on your right as you enter the courtyard, houses exhibits from World War I and II. The east wing, on your left, predates 1914 and is the more interesting. Off the entrance hall in the hushed Salle Turenne (a plaque at the door cues you to proper respect), fly the battleflags of France, including those of Bonaparte's regiments and some shredded remnants of standards from 1940. Opposite, in the Salle Vauban, 18 mounted figures illustrate the showy uniforms of the French Cavalry. Go upstairs to view the bed in which Napoleon died, as well as the personal effects from his island exile.

The Salle Orientale in the west wing shows arms from the Far East and from Muslim countries of the Mideast, from the 16th to the 19th centuries. Turkish armor and weapons, as well as Chinese and Japanese armor and swords, are on exhibit.

The gloss of the show tends to veil the truth that war is a matter of death and heartbreak. But occasionally it comes through, simply and effectively, as in the display of a silvery cuirass, pierced by a jagged wound the size and shape of a softball—the breastplate of a Carabinier downed by a cannon at Waterloo.

Admission is 12F ($2.14), with no Sunday discount. The ticket covers admission to the Army Museum, Napoleon's Tomb (see

"Daytime" chapter), and the **Musée des Plans-Reliefs,** under the fourth-floor dormers, a unique collection in scale model of French villages, towns, and monuments. It's in French but compiled of old international newsreels. The Army Museum is open daily except January 1, May 1, November 1, and December 25, from 10 a.m. to 5 p.m., from October 1 through March 31; 10 a.m. to 6 p.m., April 1 through September 30. In July and August, the Royal Dome (Napoleon's Tomb) is open till 7 p.m. Métro: Invalides, Latour-Maubourg, Varenne, Saint-François-Xavier.

A Bouquet of Esoterica

Those with more time to spend in Paris may want to seek out one of the following museums. Each is decidedly off the beaten path.

MUSÉE JACQUEMART-ANDRÉ: This 19th-century town house at 158 Boulevard Haussmann, 8e, with its gilt salons and elegant winding staircase, contains one of the best small collections of 18th-century decorative art in Paris. The building and its contents were a bequest to the Institut de France by the late Mme. Nélie Jacquemart-André, herself an artist of some note. She and her husband, Edouard André, formed a fine collection of rare French decorative art, adding to it a rich collection of painting and sculpture from the Dutch and Flemish Schools, as well as paintings and objets d'art from the Italian Renaissance and the 18th-century French School.

The museum, open every day except Monday and Tuesday from 1:30 to 5:30 p.m. (closed in August), is entered through an arcade which opens onto an inner courtyard. Through the main entrance, flanked by two stone lions, is a world of paintings, antiques, Gobelin tapestries, Savonnerie carpets, Slodtz busts, Della Robbia terracottas, and Donatello torchères. Many of the greatest painters of the Northern Schools and the Italian Renaissance are represented: Rembrandt (*The Pilgrim of Emmaüs*), Van Dyck, Rubens, Tiepolo, and Carpaccio. The art of 18th-century France is well represented by the works of Watteau and Boucher. Admission to the museum is 8F ($1.43). Métro: St-Philippe-du-Roule.

MAISON DE BALZAC: This unpretentious house on the slope of a hill in Passy, a residential district of Paris, was the home—or more accurately, the hideaway—of the great French novelist, Honoré de Balzac, from 1840 to 1847. At 47 rue Raynouard (tel. 224-56-38), the Balzac museum is almost completely unfurnished, but it does contain mementoes, documents, manuscripts, and other items associated with the writer. Throughout the house are scattered caricature drawings of Balzac, whose amusing appearance and eccentric dress lent itself to ridicule. Among the other better known mementoes is the famed Limoges coffeepot that Balzac's "screeching owl" kept hot during the long nights while he wrote *La Comédie Humaine.*

The house also contains a small courtyard and garden. While the main entrance is on the rue Raynouard, the back door leads to the rue Berton—a fortunate situation for Balzac who often had to make hasty retreats from his many creditors. The museum is open daily except Tuesday from 10 a.m. to 5:45 p.m. Admission is 7F ($1.25). Métro: Passy or La Muette.

NISSIM DE CAMONDO MUSEUM: At 63 rue de Monceau, near the Musée Cernuschi, this museum is a jewel box of elegance and refinement, evoking the days of Louis XVI and Marie Antoinette. The pre–World War I town house was donated to the Museum of Decorative Arts by Comte Moïse de Camondo (1860-1935) in memory of his son, Nissim, a French aviator killed in combat in World War I.

Entered through a courtyard, the museum is like the private home of an aristocrat two centuries ago—richly furnished with needlepoint chairs, tapestries (many from Beauvais or Aubusson), antiques, paintings (the inevitable Guardi scenes of Venice), bas-reliefs, silver, Chinese vases, crystal chandeliers, Sèvres porcelain, and Savonnerie carpets. And, of course, a Houdon bust (in an upstairs bedroom). The Blue Salon, overlooking Parc Monceau, is impressive. You wander without a guide through the gilt and oyster-gray salons.

Open all year, the museum can be visited from 2 to 5 p.m. daily except Monday and Tuesday for an admission of 8F ($1.43). Métro: Villiers.

Chapter VIII

PARIS FOOTLIGHTS

WITH FIVE NATIONAL THEATERS, including its own opera house, and 55 theaters of lesser renown, Paris is both the hub of French culture and host to all the best on the international circuit. Whatever the season, the choice is fantastic: top pop stars, French classics, chamber concerts, lavish music-hall spectaculars. In one cavernous hall, an American singer might be belting out a standard to a packed crowd of Parisians. While in a shabby Left Bank lane, a young playwright anxiously watches his first work performed on the same small stage that launched Ionesco or Beckett.

The only limitation to your enjoyment of French theater is, as always, language. Those of you with modest French can still delight in a lively, sparkling Molière at the Comédie Française. But those with no French at all might prefer an evening that is longer on melody and shorter on speech.

Announcements of shows, concerts, even the opera programs are plastered all around town on kiosks. A less hit-and-miss method of finding out what's playing is to consult the English-language *Paris Weekly Information,* available at newsstands or free from the Welcome Offices. Ardent music aficionados can track down every projected drumbeat and piano chord through *Le Guide du Concert et du Disque,* a weekly.

Ticket agents are dotted all over Paris and clustered thickest near the Right Bank hotels. Avoid them if possible. You'll get the least expensive tickets at the theater box offices. Remember to tip the usher who shows you to your seat a minimum of 1F (18¢) for one or two persons, 50 centimes per person over that. This holds true in movie houses as well as theaters. Performances start later in Paris than in London or New York—anywhere from 8 to 9:30 p.m.—and Parisians tend to dine after the theater. You don't have to follow suit, as many of the modest, less expensive restaurants shut up shop as early as 9 p.m.

OPERA, LIGHT AND GRAND: The most glorious thing about "l'Opera" (tel. 266-50-22) in Paris is the building itself. What a fitting set for the overstatement of grand opera—sweeping stair-cases and a Chagall ceiling. Go for the glamor of it and the spectacle of the staging. Tickets cost from 80F ($14.28) to 200F ($35.70). Métro: Opéra. The Opéra closes from the end of July to mid-September.

Less expensive and more consistently excellent are the light-opera productions of the **Opéra-Comique,** 5 rue Favart, 2e (tel. 296-12-20), where seats range from 60F ($10.71) to 110F ($19.64). The box office is open from 11 a.m. to 6:30 p.m. one week ahead of a scheduled performance. On Sunday, hours are from 10 a.m. to 1 p.m. Métro: Richelieu-Drouot.

CONCERTS: The concert-going public is kept busy year round in Paris, with daily offerings taking up full newspaper columns. Organ recitals are featured in the churches (the largest organ is in St. Sulpice); jazz shatters the peace of the city's modern art museum. The best orchestra in France belongs to Radio France, and top-flight concerts with guest conductors are presented in the **Radio France Auditorium,** 116 Avenue Président-Kennedy (Métro: Passy). The price of seats depends on who is performing.

Concerts, ballet, and opera are performed at the **Théâtre des Champs-Élysées,** 17 Avenue Montaigne, 8e (tel. 723-36-86). National and international orchestras appear here. The box office is open daily except Sunday from 11 a.m. to 5:30 p.m. Tickets cost from 20F ($3.57) to 200F ($35.70). Métro: Alma-Marceau.

One of the largest concert halls, with an organ second in grandeur only to the one in St. Sulpice, is in the **Palais de Chaillot** (Métro: Trocadéro), with programs announced on big showboards out front.

MUSIC HALLS: That old music-hall format of sing a little, dance a little, juggle a few balls, and sprinkle generously with jokes, is very much alive and doing well in Paris today. And the combina-tion, slickly carried off, adds up to a top value in entertainment for the visitor. The two first-rank city music halls offering packed programs of professional talent and international stars are the **Olympia,** 28 Boulevard des Capucines (tel. 742-25-49; Métro: Opéra), and the **Bobino,** 20 rue de la Gaieté (tel. 326-68-70; Métro: Gaieté). The Olympia is that "cavernous hall" referred to at the beginning of the chapter, where the likes of Charles

Aznavour make frequent appearances. On one occasion Yves Montand appeared, but you had to reserve a seat four months in advance. A typical line-up would include an English rock duo singing its latest record hit, a showy group of Italian acrobats, a well-known French crooner, a talented dance troupe, a triple-jointed American juggler/comedy team (doing much of their work in English), plus the featured Big Name, all laced together neatly by a witty emcee and backed by an on-stage band. Tickets dip as low as 50F ($8.93) and climb up to about 130F ($23.21). We rushed in late one night and got seats so high we were leaning against the rear walls, and still we could see and hear well. The Bobino, which has a reputation for being the place where all great French stars make their debut, gives a similar show at prices a little cheaper: 40F ($7.14) to 120F ($21.42).

THEATER: If you've a taste for fine theater, don't let the language barrier scare you off—spend at least one night of your Paris stay at the **Comédie-Française,** Place du Théâtre-Français (tel. 296-10-20). Nowhere else will you see the French classics—Molière, Racine—so beautifully staged in their own language. As a national theater established for the purpose of keeping the classics in the cultural mainstream, the Comédie-Française usually prices its tickets at a low 14F ($2.50) and up to 70F ($12.50). Métro: Palais-Royal.

MOVIES: We don't know what you're doing going to the movies when there's all Paris out there to walk through at night. But if that's your wish (and you know it's a hard habit to break, even on a trip), you'll find English-language films listed in *Paris Weekly Information* and in the papers, where the letters "V.O." stand for "Version Originale" and mean that the soundtrack is in the original language and the film is subtitled, not dubbed, in French. Movies run from 2 p.m. to midnight daily, not always continuously, and you often have to line up before a theater even during midweek.

Chapter IX

THE BRIGHT LIGHTS
OF PARIS

THE MOST REMARKABLE THING about the famed nightlife of Paris is its unremarkable normalcy. It's simply part of the city routine continued after dark.

There's none of the vacuum period you find in American towns between the time offices close and theaters start. Paris keeps humming on much the same beat until around one or two in the morning, when it finally curls up for a brief slumber. The main boulevards remain thronged, noisy, and traffic-clogged at all hours without a noticeable break.

The chief cause of this cycle is the younger set's habit of not going home after work and meeting in cafés instead. But quite apart from this, Parisians tend to work later, date later, eat later, and get to bed later than Anglo-Americans. One reason for this is undoubtedly their long midday break.

Paris today is still a nirvana for night-owls, even though some of her once-unique attractions have become gluts on the market. For the fame of Parisian nights was established in those distant days of innocence when Anglo-Americans still gasped at the sight of a bare bosom in a chorus line, and free love was something you only whispered about in polite transatlantic circles.

The fact is that contemporary Paris has less nudity than London, less vice than Hamburg, and less drunkenness than San Francisco.

Nevertheless, both the quantity and the variety of her nocturnal pleasures still beat those of any metropolis on earth. Nowhere else will you find such a huge and mixed array of clubs, bars, discos, cabarets, jazz dives, music halls, and honky-tonks, ranging—in the subtlest of gradations—from the corniest tourist traps to the most sophisticated connoisseurs' fare.

Some of the best and most genuinely Parisian attractions are, unfortunately, outside the scope of this book. They are the so-called *boîtes* in which chansonniers sing ballads and ditties intended only for local consumption. A few performers, like Edith Piaf and Juliette Greco, graduated to international fame from these places. But the lyrics that delight the patrons there are so slangy, so topically witty, so heavily laced with verbal innuendoes and double-entendres that they're incomprehensible to foreigners. Your French wouldn't just have to be good, but Pigalle-perfect. In which case you aren't likely to be reading this guidebook.

Luckily, there are hundreds of other establishments where lingual ignorance is of no consequence. Sometimes it can even be an advantage, because the verses perpetrated by, say, a French rock group are every ounce as inane as their Stateside brethren's.

The bright lights of Paris come in highly concentrated clusters, each one big enough to fill the requirements of a large American city. So let's proceed with a geographical survey of what to expect, where, and for how much. Although the borders are by no means airtight, these districts generally cater to distinct taste and pocketbook brackets, which it's handy to know about in advance.

Many of the Right Bank—but few of the Left Bank—hosteries are lavishly sprinkled with unattached belles whose job it is to push your tab up to astronomical heights. They're incomparably more skillful at it than American hookers, and once you've allowed one of those smiling sharks to keep you company, you're in for a staggering bill including champagne, cigarettes, candy, teddy bears, and what-have-you. Under their gentle touch, an evening that might have cost you the equivalent of five bucks can rapidly mount up to $100 and more—much more. Don't be afraid to respond with a firmly polite "No" to an unsolicited approach. The girl's only reaction is usually a regretful Gallic shrug, and she'll rarely try again. And you'll retain control of your night's expenditure.

The other general rule to remember is that the Right Bank, by and large, is plusher, slicker, and more expensive than the Left, which contains more of the avant-garde entertainment, the younger clientele, and a minimum of professional "lady companions."

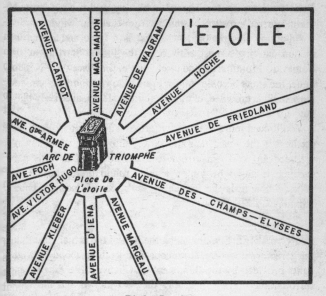

Right Bank

L'ÉTOILE DISTRICT: The region around the Arc de Triomphe and along the Champs-Elysées is the most glamorous—and expensive—of the city's night haunts, home of the Lido and the world's greatest strip spot, the "Crazy Horse Saloon."

Most of the action is found in the side streets off the Elysées, such as the Avenue George-V, the rue de Marignan, and the rue du Colisée, plus half a dozen others. Clubs here are as svelte as mink coats and almost as expensive . . . Paris at her most seductive.

L'OPÉRA DISTRICT: The heart of the tourist center is almost as sparkling as the above. It extends from the Boulevard des Italiens in the northeast to the posh part of the rue de Rivoli in the southwest. It contains Harry's Bar (with shades of Hemingway) as well as Le Slow Club in the rue de Rivoli, an authentic haven for jazz aficionados.

Around here, the entertainment spots are rather more widely spaced than elsewhere, not cheek-by-jowl as in Montmartre.

Neon signs are discreet instead of blazing, and you get fewer of the motorized prostitutes smiling from their car windows.

Adjoining this region to the east is a huge and intriguing section catering almost entirely to the locals. Starting at the Boulevard Montmartre and stretching to the Place de la République, the spots become solidly French, lower middle class, and parochial—a crowded, cluttered, slightly sleazy, and lively playland for underpaid Parisians.

You'll need more than a smattering of French to follow proceedings in the music halls and variety shows here, so we haven't included any of them in our listing. But if you have a spare evening, it might be fun to amble around there and see for yourself how little the French person's idea of "popular entertainment" differs from ours.

MONTMARTRE: Snaking along the foot of the actual mountain, the garish, rainbow-hued, raucous, and jostling ribbon of bright lights provided by the Boulevard de Clichy, Place Pigalle, and surrounding alleys is probably the best known and most frequently cursed of the tourist regions. Some of its attractions—a few of which we'll drop in on—offer fair value for your money. A great many more are simply sucker traps, lavish in promise, lilliputian in delivery, using the stalest of conmanship to milk you of more than you intended to spend.

Take the trick habitually sprung by some of the wayside strip cabarets. The notice outside says admission is 5F (89¢) to 10F ($1.79). But once inside, you discover that there's also a one-drink minimum amounting from 40F ($7.14) to 50F ($8.93). This surprise sting is also displayed (the law is pretty strict hereabouts), but in such a darkened corner that only a bat could read it.

The sloping side streets boast bars strung together like fake pearls on a necklace. Most of them carry English or German labels, and all of them are equipped with an ample quota of sociable lasses ready to quadruple your bill, some of them looking as if they'd acquired the knack during World War II.

However, there are a few raisins in the Montmartre pie. We'll help you pick them out when we get down to particulars later.

Left Bank

ST-GERMAIN-DES-PRÉS: Centering around the church of that name, this is undoubtedly the most stimulating entertainment district in Paris. Although touristy and chi-chi in patches, it has somehow managed to retain enough genuine local color to avoid becoming a cardboard backdrop. Some of the bars and cafés are at least as amusing as the actual nightclubs—thanks to the cosmopolitan population of students, artists, writers, sculptors, and professional expatriates.

The best spots are mostly away from the main boulevards St-Germain and St-Michel, and crowd the ramshackle back streets like the rue de l'Abbaye, rue de Seine, and rue Monsieur-le-Prince. The weekend crush is murder, particularly in the discos, but on Wednesday and Thursday nights you have room to breathe as well as look around.

QUARTIER LATIN: This is the eastern neighbor of the above, the dividing line running—very roughly—along the Boulevard St-Michel. The Latin Quarter, revolving around the Sorbonne, is similar to St-Germain, but more so—the streets older and grayer, the crowds more academic, the atmosphere less smartly sophisticated and more evocative. Prices—perhaps—are a fraction lower.

The Quarter houses a pseudo-medieval cabaret installed in a medieval dungeon. It also boasts a couple of the best jazz dives in town, for contrast. And more bars, bistros, and boîtes are found here than we could count.

MONTPARNASSE: Southwest of the above sections, this curiously contradictory area has as its centerpiece the futuristic Gare Montparnasse, France's most modern railroad terminal. The district looks drab and ordinary, lacking both the elegance of the Right Bank and the charm of the Left. Yet for a quarter century it was *the* literary and artistic portion of Paris, stamping ground for a fabulous constellation of celebrities that included Picasso, James Joyce, Augustus John, Chagall, Ernest Hemingway, Mary McCarthy, and F. Scott Fitzgerald.

Currently Montparnasse appears to be regaining some of its old magnetism, which may account for its checkered complexion. It harbors both the rue de la Gaieté, a white-collar amusement strip, and the rue Vavin, specializing in resolutely "naughty" tourist shows. At the same time, it houses the last remnants of the Existentialists and more active painters' studios than any other quartier.

The **Maine-Montparnasse Tower,** 33 Avenue du Maine, overshadows the Left Bank quarter of Montparnasse where Gertrude Stein once reigned at her Saturday evening gatherings. The tower, completed in 1973, covers an entire block and houses some 80 shops, including Galeries Lafayette. Its 56 floors are serviced by ultra-rapid elevators which speed visitors from the lobby to the top floor in less than 40 seconds. Sightseers go to the observation deck on the 56th floor, where a panoramic view of Paris opens from every side. On a clear day, you can see as far as Orly Airport, 25 miles away. Maps, telescopes, and spoken commentaries in six languages help you to recognize the sights below.

The 56th floor also houses the Belvedere, a light snackbar and café, and **La Ciel de Paris,** the highest restaurant in Paris, open daily from 11 a.m. to 2 a.m. The observation deck is open daily from 9:30 a.m. to 11:30 p.m. from April 1 to September 30, and from 10 a.m. to 10 p.m. during the winter months. Admission is 17F ($3.04) for adults and 8.50F ($1.52) for children under 10. For bookings telephone 538-52-35. Access to the 58th floor is an extra 3.50F (62¢) per person.

Before starting our round of establishments, let us repeat that this is a town for genuine night-owls, meaning that few spots get swinging before 11 p.m. and acquire their full heads of steam around midnight—or later. Since the Métro stops running at 1 a.m., be prepared to use taxis, and sleep in the next morning.

Spectacles

Leading off is a quartet without which no Paris roll-call would be complete. While decidedly expensive, they give you your money's worth by providing some of the most lavishly spectacular floorshows to be seen anywhere. So, for a real night's splash, try the—

New Lido Cabaret Normandie, 116 bis Avenue des Champs-Élysées, 8e (tel. 563-11-61), is housed in a panoramic room with 1200 seats, having excellent visibility. This palatial nitery puts on an avalanche of glamor and talent, combined with enough showmanship to make the late Mr. Barnum look like an amateur. The permanent attraction is the Bluebell Girls, a fabulous precision ensemble of long-legged international beauties. The rest of the program changes, but the bill we last saw included an artful juggler, a couple on ice skates, the best antipodists in the world, and a real waterfall. And that's *one* show!

The dinner-dance at 8:30 nightly costs 335F ($59.80), including half a bottle of champagne. However, you can go solely for "La Revue" at either 10:30 p.m. or 12:30 a.m., and pay a minimum of 230F ($41.06), which also includes the half-bottle of champagne, taxes, and service. And if you perch at the bar, you get two glasses for 160F ($28.56). Métro: George-V.

According to legend, the first G.I. to reach Paris at the Liberation in 1944 asked for directions to the **Folies Bergère,** 32 rue Richer, 9e (tel. 246-77-11). His son does the same today. Even the old man comes back for a second look. Although the Folies has been closed for several months as of this writing, it should have reopened by the time of your visit, and predictions are that it will feature more nudity than ever—if such a thing is possible.

A roving-eyed Frenchman would have to be in his second century to remember when the Folies began. Apparently, it's here to stay, like Sacré-Coeur and the Eiffel Tower. The affection of Parisians for it has long turned into indifference (but try to get a seat on a July night). Some, however, recall it with sentimentality. Take, for example, the night the "toast of Paris," Josephine Baker, descended the celebrated staircase, tossing bananas into the audience.

Ever since 1914 the Folies Bergère has stood as the symbol of unadorned female anatomy. Fresh off the boat, Edwardians—starved for a glimpse of even an ankle—flocked to the Folies to get a look at much more. Yet the Folies also dresses its girls (at least 1600 costumes at the last revue we saw) in those fabulous showgirl outfits you associate with Hollywood musicals of the 1930s.

The big musical revue begins nightly, except Monday, at 8:45 p.m. You can go to the box office anytime between 11 a.m. and 6:30 p.m. for tickets. Prices at press time have to be estimated, but the orchestra or balcony loge seats are likely to run about 225F ($40.16), with the *galerie* going for 120F ($21.42). For the first and second balcony tiers, you will likely pay from 150F ($26.78). A scale model at the box office shows locations. Métro: rue Montmartre or Cadet.

The **Moulin-Rouge,** Place Blanche, Montmartre, 18e (tel. 606-00-19). Toulouse-Lautrec, who put this establishment on the map about a century ago, probably wouldn't recognize it today. The windmill is still there and so is the cancan. But the rest has become a super-slick, gimmick-loaded variety show with the accent heavy on the undraped female form. You'll see underwater ballets in an immense glass tank, a magnificent cascade, young women in swings and on trick stairs, all interspersed with animal acts, comic jugglers, and song trios. These are just a smattering of the acts usually found on the daily bill of fare. This technicolored candy-floss stuff is expertly staged, but any connection with the old Moulin-Rouge is purely coincidental.

If you go around 8:30 p.m. for dinner, you can stay and see the revue at 10:30 p.m. at a cost of 295F ($52.66). Attending the revue only costs 200F ($35.70), including the obligatory champagne. There's no minimum if you sit at the bar, where the average drink costs 100F ($17.85). Of course, the view is nothing like what you get at the tables. Métro: Place Blanche.

The Milliardaire, 68 rue Pierre-Charron (off Champs-Élysées), 8e (tel. 225-25-17). Smaller and less spectacular, but more stylishly elegant, this velvety night-nest is reached through a backyard that contrasts intriguingly with the plush interior. Despite the tag, the program doesn't dwell exclusively on dishabille, but includes comics, jugglers, and first-rate dance interludes. Two drinks at your table are 180F ($32.13). At the bar, each libation costs 80F ($14.28). Two different spectacles are staged nightly—the first at 10:30 p.m., the second at 12:30 a.m. Métro: Champs-Élysées–Clemenceau.

Son et Lumière: "Shades of Glory," the great Sound and Light spectacle at the Hôtel des Invalides, allows you to participate dramatically in some of the great moments in French history, through the eras of Louis XIV and Napoleon. Sponsored by the French government, the shows are performed at 9:30 p.m. and again at 11:15 p.m. in English and at 10:30 p.m. in French (except from May 15 to August 9 when there is only a 10:30 p.m. performance in French and an 11:15 p.m. spectacle in English). The show runs from mid-April to mid-October. The cost is 22F ($3.93) for adults, 16F ($2.86) for children. Reservations aren't necessary. Just take the Métro to Invalides, Latour-Maubourg, or Varennes.

Songs and Sentiment

We had to find a special lable for the next group because the spots wouldn't fit under any other. A cross between our familiar American folk cellars and modified French *boîtes,* they have an appeal depending entirely on your digging their brand of tunes. Chances are you will—mightily.

The He and She Mystery

Madame Arthur, 75 bis rue des Martyrs, 18e (tel. 264-48-27). This one is risqué with a vengeance, so be careful who you take here. It's a rendezvous for transvestites, many female, some belonging to the staff, others to the clientele. Lots of aloof, serenely pretty dolls with pageboy cuts can be seen dancing earnestly together. The floor-show is tailored to their taste.

One of the leading female impersonator cabarets of Europe, this Place Pigalle showplace is directed by Madame Arthur, who is no lady. At the bar, your first drink costs 50F ($8.93), increasing to 80F ($14.28) at a table. The cabaret is open until 3 a.m. Métro: Pigalle.

Au Caveau de la Bolée, 25 rue de Hirondelle, 6e (tel. 633-33-64 before 7 p.m.; afterward, tel. 354-62-20). You descend into the catacombs of the early 14th-century Abbey of Saint-André, once a famous literary café, drawing such personages as Verlaine and Oscar Wilde, who downed (or drowned in) glass after glass of absinthe here.

The elegant and beautiful Renée Devainegie shows you to a seat for an evening of listening to what she calls wittytellers and fancy fellows. The French songs are good and bawdy and just what the young students, who form a large part of the audience, like. Occasionally, the audience sings along.

Performances begin at 9:15 and 10:30 p.m. on Wednesday, Thursday, and Friday nights, but at 10 p.m. and again at 12:45 a.m. on Saturday. Soft drinks or "baby whiskey" range in price from 25F ($4.46) to 40F ($7.14), tax and service included. Dinner, served from 9 p.m., costs from 140F ($24.99). The place is closed Sunday through Tuesday, and in August. Metro: St-Michel.

Au Lapin Agile is perched near the top of Montmartre, at 22 rue des Saules, 18e (tel. 606-85-87). This tiny rustic cottage was once a celebrated haunt of writers, impressionist painters, and their models. Some of their spell still lingers. You sit at carved-up wooden tables in a low, dimly lit room, the walls covered with Bohemian memorabilia, and listen to your hosts sing, play, and recite.

They sing—singly or in groups—old French folk tunes, love ballads, army songs, sea chanties, and music-hall ditties. They sing so simply, so naturally, with so much esprit and talent, that you desperately want to join in, even if you can't speak a word of French. And before you know it you're belting out the "oui, oui, oui—non, non, non" refrains of "Les Chevaliers de la Table Ronde," and humming along with "Larilette" and "Madelon." And while these merry and sad and incredibly catchy songs last, you feel as one with the nation that produced them.

It's at its best out of the tourist season and on a weeknight. The admission and the price of one drink ranges from 45F ($8.03) for regular customers. A second drink goes for 20F ($3.57). Closed Monday. Métro: Lamarck.

Caveau des Oubliettes. It's hard to say which is more interesting in this place—the program or the environment. At 1 rue St-Julien-le-Pauvre, 5e (tel. 354-94-97) in the Latin Quarter, just across the river from Notre-Dame, this nightspot is housed in a genuine 12th-century prison—complete with dungeons, spine-crawling passages, and scattered skulls. Oubliettes, by the way, were the portholes through which prisoners used to be pushed into the Seine to drown.

Performers in medieval costumes sing French folk songs and tavern choruses—sentimental, comic, and bawdy—to exclusively tourist audiences. It's rather artificial and stagey, but with charm. There's nothing artificial, however, about the adjoining museum, which displays a working guillotine, chastity belts, and instruments of torture. Drinks begin at 65F ($11.60), including service. Métro: St-Michel.

Nude Dancing

Crazy Horse Saloon, 12 Avenue George-V, 8e (tel. 723-32-32). Texans in ten-gallon hats are fond of "Le Crazy," which is considered by many to be the leading nude dancing joint in the world. Alain Bernardin parodies the American West in the decor, but only purists claim that Cheyenne was never like this.

Two dozen performers do their acts entirely nude. Sandwiched between the more sultry scenes are three international variety acts. The first show goes on at 9 p.m., the second one at 11:20 p.m. At a table, the charge is 270F ($48.20) for two drinks, 180F ($32.13) for two drinks at the bar. On Friday and Saturday, three shows are presented—one at 8:20 p.m., another at 10:30 p.m., and a final at 12:45 p.m.

Supper Clubs

As widely varying as Ms. Deneuve is from Ms. Bardot, the following are still uniquely Parisian.

Villa d'Este, 4 rue Arsène-Houssaye, 8e (tel. 359-78-44). When Amalia Rodrigues, Portugal's leading fadista and an international star, is in Paris, she's likely to appear at this supper club. Its owners book top talent from both Europe and America. A short stroll from the Champs-Élysées, the Villa d'Este has been around for a long time, and the quality of its offerings remains high. If you go for dinner, expect to pay at least 140F ($24.99), plus 20% for service. The tab goes up to 180F ($32.13) on weekends. Closed in July and August.

Offbeat: For Friends of Rabelais

Au Mouton de Panurge, 17 rue de Choiseul, 2e (tel. 742-78-49), is the "official" association of the friends of Rabelais, out to preserve those lusty medieval days. Just like the master French author, the restaurant likes to poke fun at sacred objects. It's very French, and out-of-towners find it "naughty"—at least for one visit—although Parisians seem bored with it. If it's your thing, you might enjoy a dinner here immensely—that is, if you're amused by such items as a phallic-shaped "loaf of love" or escargots (snails) served in miniature chamber pots.

You can spend an evening here, ordering an à la carte dinner that will cost you from 160F ($28.56) to 210F ($37.49), depending on your wine selection. A set menu goes for 110F ($19.64). Go between 8 and 9 p.m. You never know what you'll encounter: perhaps an old woolly sheep going from table to table with the waiters in medieval garb hawking roses from a basket on its back. A "drinking trough" is on the ground floor, the "mangers" on the second.

Dance Halls and Discos

Although Paris is supposedly the cradle city of discothèques, the labeling process has become so indiscriminate that nobody seems to know what, precisely, constitutes one. Originally the discos were small, intimate dives where patrons danced to records—hence the term. Now, however, the tag is applied to anything from playground-size ballrooms with full orchestras to tiny bars with taped tunes—where they don't let you dance at all.

We, therefore, have had to make up our own definition for this bracket, since "discothèque" has lost whatever classification value it might have had. The samples below are a few of the hundreds of spots where people go chiefly to dance—as distinct from others where the main attraction is the music.

Le Palace, 8 rue du Faubourg Montmartre (tel. 246-02-56), is the leading disco of Europe. Right in the heart of the Boulevards, it was once a theater, and many of the old trappings still remain. The main hallway is decorated in light brown with large mirrors, and the former foyer on the left (as you enter) is a bar, drawing fashionable Parisians who often finish the evening here after a première at a Right Bank theater.

From the bar you can climb to the balcony which is now filled with tables and chairs. Or from the main entrance you can join the disco dancing in the hall, the scene reflected in a wide mirror at the end. There you'll find another bar, this one with bartenders dressed as "punk angels" in psychedelic orange coveralls.

The music is quite loud but of good quality, and you will likely be dancing to everybody from Diana Ross to Paul McCartney, from Grace Jones to Pink Floyd. Colored light rays flash around you, and an illuminated mobile rises and falls. A curtain rises, revealing erotic but humorous posters, along with pictures of the great Hollywood film stars. Most of the crowd is young, but all ages patronize the place. The entrance fee, including your first drink, is 80F ($14.28) on weekdays, rising to 100F ($17.85) on weekends. After that, your next drink is 30F ($5.36). The disco temple is closed on Monday and Tuesday.

Le Chat Qui Pêche ("The Fishing Cat"), 4 rue de la Huchette, 5e (tel. 326-23-06), is still on most everybody's list as one of the best known citadels of jazz on the Left Bank. After an overhaul, it has found new life as a restaurant/bar/disco/caveau. Set meals are offered nightly, ranging in price from 35F ($6.25) to 60F ($10.71). The chef specializes in couscous, the typical dish of North Africa. If you're going just for dancing to records, you'll find whiskeys beginning at 35F ($6.25) during the week, 40F ($7.14) on weekends.

Riverside Club, 7 rue Grégoire-de-Tours, 6e (tel. 354-46-33), attracts an international crowd of young people to its precincts where they dance to recorded music. Meeting fellow companions is fairly easy. It opens nightly at 10. From Sunday to Thursday, the entrance fee is 32F ($5.71), but this goes up to 40F ($7.14) on Friday and Saturday nights.

Wonder Club, 38 rue du Dragon, 6e (tel. 548-90-32), is part of the same Left Bank grind, with the musical accent on pop and jazz. Its regular admission ranges from 35F ($6.25) to 40F ($7.14). The cover charge includes not only your admission, but your first drink as well. On weekends, matinees begin at 3 p.m. and usually last until 7 p.m. The cost then is only 20F ($3.57).

This entire region opposite and around the church of St-Germain-des-Prés is so honeycombed with dance dives of one sort or another, and they are so ephemeral (some have the life spans of sickly butterflies), that it's almost impossible to keep track of their coming and closing. What's hopping at the time of writing might be a hardware store by the time you get there. But chances are there'll be two new joints in the same block.

La Coupole, 102 Boulevard Montparnasse, 14e (tel. 320-14-21). One of the big Montparnasse cafés is a former Bohemian stronghold turned staid. This is also reflected in the large basement ballroom where dancing goes on till 2 a.m., but very formally, in a kind of late-night tea-dance atmosphere. It's ideal for couples who want to dance to an excellent orchestra. The minimum charge is 40F ($7.14), which is the price of your first drink. Métro: Vavin.

Mainly Music

At a few spots, you sit and listen, despite the fact that some of them title themselves "discothèques."

L'Escale, 15 rue Monsieur-le-Prince, 6e, is one of the true charmers of St-Germain-des-Prés. It's not exactly cheap, but worth every cent in terms of atmosphere and artistry. The bar is semidark and very intimate. The Mexican mural on the wall is almost invisible in the dim light. Musicians play Latin American songs, not the diluted stuff you usually hear, but the really melancholy and wild gaucho airs, with the particular smouldering fire that is their special idiom. The first drink, which you can nurse as long as you like, costs 50F ($8.93). The club also has a "cave" where you can dance to a Cuban combo. Métro: Odéon.

Jazz and Rock

You can probably listen and dance to more jazz in Paris than in any U.S. city, with the possible exception of San Francisco. The great jazz revival that swept America 20 or so years ago is still going full swing in Paris, with Dixieland or Chicago rhythm being pounded out in dozens of jazz cellars, mostly called "caveaux."

This is one city where you don't have to worry about being a self-conscious dancer. The locals, even young people, are not particularly good. The best dancers on any floor are usually American. And although Parisians take to rock with enthusiasm, their skill does not match their zest.

The majority of the jazz/rock establishments are crowded into the Left Bank near the Seine between the rue Bonaparte and the rue St-Jacques, which makes things easy for syncopation-seekers. Herewith are a few sample spots out of perhaps a dozen similar ones. Our first is on the **rue de la Huchette,** a narrow, semi-Oriental thoroughfare leading from the Place St-Michel.

Club Saint-Germain, 13 rue Saint-Benoît, 6e (tel. 222-51-09), stands right in the heart of St-Germain-des-Prés, evoking memories of the glory that was existentialism. A long time ago Jean-Paul Sartre and Simone de Beauvoir could be seen here, watching their friend, Juliette Greco. Nowadays, sophisticated Parisians go here to hear some of the best jazz on the Left Bank. The film *Paris Blues* was shot here. If you pass admission by ringing a bell and being stared at through a peephole you'll be admitted to the club. You have a choice of going downstairs to the jazz cellar where drinks are stiff—60F ($10.71) for your first one and 30F ($5.36) thereafter. However, there is no admission charge, and the entertainment is usually expensive talent. Or you can go upstairs to **Le Bilboquet** (tel. 584-81-84), the restaurant, where the Gallic vocalist, Robert Martin, has been singing for more than 17 years. There drinks are cheaper—a beer costing 28F ($5) to 40F ($7.14), depending on the time of your arrival. In addition, you must pay a 12% service charge.

Caveau de la Huchette, 5 rue de la Huchette, 5e (tel. 326-65-05), is a celebrated jazz cave, drawing a young crowd, mostly students, who listen and dance rapturously to the hot stuff poured out by well-known jazz combos. This is a cellar hideaway, reached by a winding staircase. In prejazz days, it was frequented by Robespierre and Marat. The fun starts at 9:30 p.m. and lasts until 2 a.m., except on weekends when the action may stretch out till 3. The basic entrance ticket is 35F ($6.25) for men, although students and women pay only 25F ($4.46). With that ticket, a beer costs 7F ($1.25).

Les Trois Mailletz, 56 rue Galande, 5e (tel. 354-00-79), is a haven for real aficionados of all nationalities, one of the few places in the district where students don't predominate. Jazz celebrities such as Memphis Slim or Bill Coleman are often imported from America. They perform for experts—would-be or genuine. The first drink costs 50F ($8.93), and there is no entrance fee. It opens at 10 p.m. and closes on Sunday and Monday. Métro: Maubert-Mutualité.

A quick sweep over the rest of the jazz field would include the **Slow Club**, 130 rue de Rivoli, 1er (tel. 233-84-30), a stylish and smart stronghold of New Orleans fare featuring the well-known French jazz band of Claude Luter, who played for 10 years with the late Sidney Bechet. The regular entrance price is 45F ($8.03). Drinks begin at 7F ($1.25). It's open every night except Sunday and Monday, from 9:30 p.m. till 2 a.m.

The **Caméléon**, 57 rue St-André-des-Arts, 6e (tel. 326-64-40), in a Left Bank "caveau," is yet another disco-jazz citadel. On the street floor is a bar, but in the downstairs dive a top-notch band plays for "cave dancing." The Caméléon is popular with young people who pay a regular entrance fee, including the first drink, of from 40F ($7.14), going up to 50F ($8.93) on weekends. An additional whiskey costs from 35F ($6.25) and up. Métro: Odéon.

Le Patio, Hotel Méridien, 81 Boulevard Gouvion Saint-Cyr, 17e (tel. 758-12-30), isn't just for patrons of France's largest hotel, situated at Porte Maillot. Anybody can drop in, going directly to the hotel's central courtyard, where they can hear some of the best jazz bands in the French capital from 10 p.m. to 2 a.m. The setting is of palms and fountains, an impressive backdrop for musicians (some of those who appear here have worked for the Count Basie band). A piano player—naturally, a smooth one—takes over during intermissions. You're not charged an admission fee and there's no minimum, but you will pay around 45F ($8.03) for the average alcoholic beverage.

Péniches, Quai Conti

Chapter X

CAFÉS AND BARS

TO LEAVE OUT CAFÉS from any description of Paris would be like writing about London without mentioning a pub. Worse—because the role of the café in Parisian life is incomparably greater than those played by either drugstores, coffeeshops, or saloons in urban America.

Contrary to general belief, the coffeehouse is not a French invention. It began in 17th-century Vienna and flourished in London long before taking root in France. But when the Parisians adopted it, they infused it with such Gallic flair and local flavor that it became an accepted symbol of their inimitable brand of joie de vivre.

It's almost impossible to venture a guess at the number of cafés in Paris. A single block in the central arrondissements may house three or four. They thin out a little in the farther suburbs, but still remain far more numerous than, for instance, hamburger stands in the U.S. And somehow each gets its quota of customers.

And it's nearly as difficult to define their precise function. They aren't restaurants, although the larger ones may serve complete and excellent meals. They aren't bars, although they offer an infinite variety of alcoholic potions. And they aren't coffeeshops in the Anglo-American meaning, because they'll serve you a bottle of champagne just as readily as an iced chocolate.

Parisians use them as combination club-tavern-snackbar, almost as extensions of their living rooms. They are spots where you can read your newspaper or meet a friend, do your homework or write your memoirs, nibble at a hard-boiled egg or drink yourself into oblivion. At cafés you meet your dates to go on to a show or to stay and talk. Above all, cafés are for sitting and people-watching.

Perhaps their single common denominator is the way they let

THE CAFÉS AND BARS OF PARIS

you sit. Regardless of whether you have one small coffee or the most expensive cognac in the house—nobody badgers, pressures, or hurries you. If you wish to sit there until the place closes, *eh bien,* that's your affair. For the café is one of the few truly democratic institutions—a solitary soda buys you the same view and sedentary pleasure as an oyster dinner.

A French philosopher once called them "the greatest man-made contribution to happiness ever conceived," and after sampling a few in Paris you may incline to agree with him.

All cafés sport an outdoor portion. Some, merely a few tables on the pavement; others, immense terraces, glassed in and heated in winter. Both categories, however, fulfill the same purpose: they offer a vantage point from which to view the passing parade.

Café-sitting is a pleasure rather like gum-chewing or cross-word puzzle solving: you either fail to see any fun in it or you become an addict. For the latter category, here are a few of the items you can imbibe while, well . . . sitting.

Coffee, of course, is the chief potion. It comes black in a small cup, unless you specifically order it "au lait." Tea (*thé*, pronounced tay) is also fairly popular, but not on the same level of quality.

The famous apéritifs, French versions of the predinner cocktail, are the aniseed-flavored, mild-tasting Pernod, Ricard, and Pastis, all mixed with ice and water. Also there are St. Raphael and Byrrh, tasting rather like port wine, and the slightly less sweet Dubonnet.

If you prefer beer, we'd advise you to pay a bit more for the imported German, Dutch, or Danish brands, incomparably better than the local brew. If you insist on the French variety, at least order it *à pression* (draft), which is superior. A great local favorite as an apéritif is the Italian Campari, drunk with soda and ice, very bitter and refreshing. Try it at least once.

In the teetotal bracket, you get a vast variety of fruit drinks, as well as Coca-Cola and the specifically French syrups, like Grenadine. They're about on the same level as the stuff you get at home. But French drinking chocolate—either hot or iced—is absolutely superb and on a par with the finest Dutch brands. It's made from ground chocolate, not a chemical compound.

Finally, there's water (but you'll have to order it with something). The Parisians tend to avoid it, but it's every drop as drinkable as the U.S. version. Considering our pollution problem, maybe more so.

Cafés keep delightfully flexible hours, depending on the season, the traffic, and the part of town they're in. Nearly all of them stay open till one in the morning, some till two, a few all night.

Now just a few words on café etiquette. You don't pay when getting your order, but only when you intend to leave. Payment indicates that you've had all you want. Unless your check is "Service compris," you tip about 15%.

You'll hear the locals call the garçon, but as a foreigner it would be more polite to use "Monsieur." *All* waitresses, on the other hand, are addressed as "Mademoiselle," regardless of age and marital status.

In the smaller establishments, you may have to share your table. In that case, even if you haven't exchanged one word with them, you bid your table companions good-bye with a perfunctory "Messieurs et Dames," on leaving.

And now, a small—a microscopic—selection of Paris cafés, including some, but nowhere near all, of the famous ones. We could, in fact, fill an entire chapter of this book with nothing but café descriptions and still leave a couple of thousand unmentioned.

Some Famous Cafés

Café de la Paix, Place de l'Opéra, 9e (tel. 260-33-50). This hub of the tourist world virtually commands the Place de l'Opéra, and the legend goes that if you sit there long enough, you'll see someone you know passing by. Huge, grandiose, and frighteningly fashionable, it harbors not only Parisians, but, at some time or the other, every visiting American, a tradition that dates from the end of World War I. Once Émile Zola and Oscar Wilde sat on the terrace; later, Hemingway and F. Scott Fitzgerald frequented it. You pay 22F ($3.93) to 28F ($5) for a whiskey, 10.50F ($1.88) for a Coca-Cola, and 7.50F ($1.34) for a café espresso. Add 15% for service. It's open from 10 a.m. until 1:30 a.m. Métro: Opéra.

The two following cafés are next to each other and so alike in fame and clientele that we'll treat them as twins. They are the **Deux Magots** and the **Flore,** at respectively 170 and 172 Boulevard St-Germain, 6e, right in the legendary St-Germain-des-Prés. Both made history as the haunt and hatching place of the Existentialists and have hosted nearly all of the French intellectuals who shaped the world's philosophical innovations during the postwar years.

Sartre, Camus, and Ms. de Beauvoir have vanished from the

scene, as have Brigitte Bardot and Juliette Greco. But their shadows still linger. The crowd is still on the highbrow side, richly sprinkled with devastating damsels and the more sophisticated Anglo-American visitors. Both get fearfully packed in the evenings, and the best time to enjoy their charms is around 10 in the morning.

Neither is what you'll call economical. Expect to pay 5.60F ($1) for coffee, 7F ($1.25) for domestic beer. Métro: St-Germain-des-Prés. The Flore closes in July, the Deux Magots in August.

Across the street is the world-famous **Brasserie Lipp**, 151 Boulevard St-Germain, 6e (tel. 548-53-91). On the day of Paris's liberation in 1944, owner Roger Cazes spotted Hemingway, the first man to drop in for a drink. But famous men—then and now—customarily drop into the Lipp for its sauerkraut, beer, wine, and conversation. Food is secondary, of course, yet quite good, providing you can get a seat (an hour and a half waiting time is customary on many occasions if you're not a "friend of the management"). The specialty is sauerkraut garni at 55F ($9.82). Each day the Lipp features about four plats du jour, ranging in price from 55F ($9.82) to 70F ($12.50). You can perch on a banquette, enjoying your face reflected—along with that of, say, Françoise Sagan—in the "hall of mirrors." The Lipp was opened in 1870–1871, following the Franco-Prussian war, when its founder, Monsieur Lippman, fled German-occupied territory for Paris. It's been a Parisian tradition ever since. Even if you don't drop in for a drink, you can sit at a sidewalk café table, enjoying a cognac at 28F ($5) and people-watching. It's closed on Monday and in July.

Le Dôme, 108 Boulevard du Montparnasse, 14e (tel. 354-53-61). After an unsuccessful attempt as a drugstore, Le Dôme, the most famous of the Montparnasse cafés, is back in business as usual. Totally changed and completely redecorated in the belle époque style, it, nevertheless, contains photographs on the walls, revealing the café in its heyday. The memories of Hemingway linger long here—some of the most celebrated names in the world of art sat on the terrace in the years between 1920 and 1925. A regular beer goes for 7F ($1.25) to 12F ($2.14), an espresso for 5F (89¢). You can also order food such as a potage du jour at 9F ($1.61), or sauerkraut garni, 32F ($5.71). A sorbet rounds the meal off at 20F ($3.57). Métro: Vavin.

La Coupole, 102 Boulevard du Montparnasse, 143 (tel. 320-14-20), was once a leading center of Parisian artist life. This big and attractive café has, however, grown more fashionable with the years, attracting fewer locals, and nary a struggling artist. But some of the city's most interesting foreigners show up. Reputations are long to fade. The sweeping outdoor terrace is among the finest to be found in Paris. An espresso goes for 5F (89¢), a cognac VSOP for 19F ($3.39). You can also order food inside: the fried sole is 58F ($10.35). Most main dishes cost from 50F ($8.93) to 60F ($10.71). Métro: Vavin.

La Rotonde en Montparnasse, 105 Boulevard du Montparnasse, 6e (tel. 326-48-26), stands at the intersection of the Boulevards Montparnasse and Raspail. Another of the large, lush Montparnasse cafés, it was mentioned in Hemingway's *The Sun Also Rises.* In its heyday, it attracted what one biographer called the "Bronco Bills of Montparnasse"; now it's merely a shade of its former self. It charges 5F (89¢) for coffee on the terrace, and from 8F ($1.43) for a bottle of beer. Métro: Vavin.

Le Sélect, 99 Boulevard du Montparnasse, 6e (tel. 222-65-27), may be down the social ladder from the other glittering cafés of Montparnasse, but we find it the liveliest and friendliest. It opened in 1923, and really hasn't changed all that much. At one time it was the favorite hangout of Jean Cocteau. A beer costs 7F ($1.25); coffee, 5F (89¢).

Wild Boar Pâté at the Pont-Neuf

Le Henri IV, 13 Place du Pont-Neuf, 1er (tel. 354-27-90), is quite different from our other recommendations. This one is called both a *taverne* and *bistro à vin.* The location couldn't be more magnificent—in a 17th-century building at the Pont-Neuf, on the Île de la Cité. The patron, Monsieur Cointepas, does his own bottling, or at least some of it. His prize wines are listed on a blackboard menu. A glass of his special beaujolais goes for 4F (71¢); a glass of his Chinon, 4F also. You can even snack here. Sandwiches cost 9F ($1.61) to 15F ($2.68). A special farmer's lunch is offered for 35F ($6.25). Try to arrive for an apéritif at sunset. Closed Saturday, Sunday, and in August. Métro: Pont-Neuf.

WHERE THE PARISIANS GO: La Tartine, 24 rue de Rivoli, 4e, was beloved by Tito, Trotsky, and Lenin. A formidable trio like that hardly prepares you for the warm welcome you receive here. The special wines offered include a Pouilly-Fumé, Beaujolais, les Bordeaux Saint Emilion et Pomerol, Sancerre, and a Châteauneuf-du-Pape, at costs that range from 4.50F (80¢) to 8F ($1.43) per glass. Insert mirrors, brass decorative details, and frosted globe chandeliers form the decor. The atmosphere is most unpretentious.

Ma Bourgogne, 19 Place des Vosges, 4e (tel. 278-44-64), is a fine café with a good selection of wines. But the real reason to go here is to sit and contemplate this dreamy square, following in the footsteps of Victor Hugo. Under the arcades you can enjoy an espresso at 4.50F (80¢), or for 9F ($1.61) you can have a large glass of Châteauneuf-du-Pape. There are rattan sidewalk tables for summer sitting and a cozy enclosure if you're there for a winter visit.

Bar des B.O.F., 7 rue des Innocents, 1er (tel. 236-75-54), overlooks an attractive square at Les Halles with gardens and a beautiful old fountain from the 17th century. Wine here is loved with a passion. The owner, Jean Cetton, always posts signs when the new beaujolais arrives. He always bottles the wine himself. His well-selected wines begin at 6F ($1.07) a glass, ranging upward to 10F ($1.79) a glass. The bar is open daily from 11 a.m. to midnight except on Sunday and Monday.

AT STRATEGIC POINTS: Café de Cluny, 20 Boulevard St-Michel or 102 Boulevard St-Germain, 5e (tel. 326-68-24), is placed strategically at the intersection of these two famous avenues, overlooking the hub of the Left Bank and the Museum de Cluny. One of the main meeting places for visitors and locals alike, this large, bustling oasis attracts a striking proportion of pretty girls, mostly, alas, waiting for their boyfriends. Local beer goes for 8F ($1.43), a glass of beaujolais for 6.50F ($1.16), or bordeaux for 7F ($1.25). Métro: St-Michel.

Le Mandarin, 148 bis Boulevard St-Germain, 6e, is an elegantly decorated corner café thronged with young people of the Left Bank or else visitors soaking up the atmosphere of St-Germain-des-Prés. At the brass bar you can order fine wines, certainly a coffee. But the café also serves good food—omelets at 14F ($2.50), sandwiches which begin at 8F ($1.43), and a raw steak filet with french fries at 40F ($7.14). Métro: Odéon or Mabillon.

And Now the Bars

These are Anglo-American imports to France and—with few notable exceptions—strike an alien chord. They're about equally divided between those trying to imitate Stateside cocktail bars and those pretending to be British pubs. Some go to amazing lengths in the process.

Most bars serve American cocktails, although they don't always taste the way you remember them. On the other hand, most of them are considerably more comfortable than either their American or British prototypes. They have neither the Stygian darkness of the U.S. models nor the built-in drafts of the English. And the quality of the snacks they provide is infinitely superior.

Bar-hopping has become the "in" thing with Paris's smart set, as distinct from café-sitting, which is practiced by the entire populace. Bar prices, therefore, are generally a fraction higher, a biggish fraction if the place boasts a well-known bartender.

THE MOST FAMOUS: Harry's New York Bar, at 5 rue Daunou, 5e (tel. 261-71-14) ("Sank roo doe Noo," as the ads tell you to instruct your cab driver), is the most famous bar in Europe—quite possibly in the world. It's sacred to Hemingway disciples as the spot where Ernest did most of his Parisian imbibing. To others it's hallowed as the site where White Lady and Sidecar cocktails were invented in, respectively, 1919 and 1931. Also, it is the birthplace of the Bloody Mary and French '75, as well as headquarters of the International Bar Flies (I.B.F.).

Opened on Thanksgiving Day in 1911, Harry's closes one day each year, December 25, otherwise it stays open from 10:30 a.m. till . . . till . . . well, till. The upstairs bar is excessively hearty and masculine, but it gets smoother down below under the influence of an excellent pianist. The bar is always crammed with Anglo-Americans and their Gallic admirers. A dry martini costs 24F ($4.28) and whiskeys generally range in price from 26F ($4.64) to 32F ($5.71).

TO BE CHIC: Rosebud, 11 bis rue Delambre, 14e (tel. 326-95-28), has taken on a new meaning. Originally, it was based on Orson Welles's greatest film, *Citizen Kane*. Nowadays, it refers to Otto Preminger's unsuccessful movie which marked the screen debut of John Lindsay. The screenplay was based on a novel published in French by Paul Connecarrère and Joan Hemingway (granddaughter of Ernest). Rosebud is just around the corner from the famous cafés of Montparnasse. It has often attracted such devotees as the late Jean-Paul Sartre, Simone de Beauvoir, Eugene Ionesco, and Marguerite Duras. Drop in at night for a beer at

14F ($2.50), or perhaps something to eat, maybe steak tartare at 25F ($4.46) or chili con carne at 25F also.

The Cobra Under a Tiger's Leer

La Factorerie, 5 Boulevard Malesherbes, 8e (tel. 265-96-86). In a city where the trend setters sometimes seem bored with their sophistication, only a "jungle" like this would do. Where else in Europe can you sip a drink called "The Cobra" while a roving tiger leers over your shoulder? Fortunately, the latter is behind thick glass that the management claims is "foolproof."

The food is nominal in price, but everybody here looks too thin to eat mere food anyway. Most of the exotic concoctions from the bar cost 22F ($3.93) with alcohol, 19F ($3.39) without. Underneath is one of the most curious boutiques in Paris, and outside your window you can gaze upon Paris's Parthenon, the Madeleine. Métro: Madeleine.

A TOUCH OF BRITAIN: Sir Winston Churchill. At 5 rue de Presbourg (tel. 500-75-35), a fashionable Right Bank street in the 16th Arrondissement, this is the most authentic-appearing pub in Paris. It uses English advertising posters and serves Watney's ale and imported British tea brands—along with roast beef and Yorkshire pudding, so help us. All the elements of an Edwardian decor are here, too—cut-glass mirrors, plush banquettes, highly polished dark wood. You can order your Red Barrel—that is, Watney's Keg on draft—at 16F ($2.86) for a half pint. Complete meals are served with a special tourist menu costing 48F ($8.57). A real English breakfast is served here for 45F ($8.03). Métro: Place Charles-de-Gaulle (Étoile).

Pub Saint-Germain-des-Prés, 17 rue de l'Ancienne-Comédie, 6e (tel. 329-38-70), is the only one in the country to offer 15 draft beers and 250 international beers. Leather niches render drinking discreet. The decor consists of gilded mirrors on the walls, hanging gas lamps, and a stuffed parrot in a gilded cage. Also, leather-cushioned handrails are provided for some mysterious purpose—guidance perhaps? You'll need it. There are seven different rooms and 500 seats, which makes the pub the largest in France. The atmosphere is quiet, relaxed, and rather posh, and it's open day and night. Genuine Whitbread beer is sold, and Pimm's No. 1 is featured. You can also order snacks or complete meals here. Drinks start at 7.20F ($1.29), menus at 52F ($9.28). Métro: Odéon.

A Drink with Your Renault

If you like to combine your hamburgers with shopping for a Renault, you'll be at the right place if you drop in at **Pub Renault**, 53 Avenue Champs-Élysées, 8e. At first you'll think you've come to an automobile showroom . . . and you have. But proceed to the rear, where a bar of "horseless carriages" is waiting. Here you can either order set meals ranging in price from 40F ($7.14) to 50F ($8.93), or just have a drink.

LOCAL COLOR ON THE LEFT BANK: Le Village, at 7 rue Gozlin, 6e (tel. 326-80-19), just off St-Germain-des-Prés, caters mainly to upper-bracket Frenchmen and women. Don't expect Anglo trappings, despite the label. The decor is kept in soothing deep browns, and even the art exhibition and travel posters on the walls are unobtrusive. The atmosphere is quiet and amiable, service impeccably polite, in keeping with the pleasant clientele. A scotch goes for 20F ($3.57), a Carlsberg for 14F ($2.50). In the back, a complete set meal is offered for 40F ($7.14). On the à la carte you can enjoy such specialties as escargots (one dozen), followed by a cassoulet Landais or perhaps a platter of sauerkraut with all the trimmings. If you order what we have suggested, expect to spend around 85F ($15.17) to 100F ($17.85). Métro: St-Germain-des-Prés.

Tea and Tarts

If you're not a heavy drinker, but prefer mouth-watering, creamy, and most fattening pastries as well as a pot of nicely brewed tea, then patronize the following:

Boulangerie, 73 Avenue Franklin D. Roosevelt, 8e. Croissants, sandwiches, brioches, chocolates, confectionery items—this place has them all. It is, perhaps, one of the best known of the "grandes pâtisseries" of Paris. Its tarts, averaging around 10F ($1.79), are among the best in town. The pastry chef also specializes in macaroons with almonds (d'Italie). Sandwiches begin at 5F (89¢).

Drugstores

Le Drug Store, 149 Boulevard St-Germain-des-Prés, 6e, is an upbeat, totally Parisian version of that old corner drugstore and

A Left Bank Students' Hangout

Le Bar. That's the actual name of this small and intimate hangout at 10 rue de l'Odéon, 6e, right off the Place de l'Odéon on the Left Bank. This place is permanently thronged with swarms of noisy, friendly, amorous, and argumentative university students and is an ideal spot to make contact with them—if that's what you desire. Plastered with posters, both antique and pop, it reverberates to the strains of an overworked jukebox. Lots of friendly girls, singly and in pairs, are around; not hunting, but open to agreeable approaches. Drinks range in price from 10F ($1.79). Métro: Odéon.

soda fountain back home . . . but vive la différence! Unlike its American cousin, this establishment is sophisticated, stylish, and super-slick. It still sells shampoo and toothpaste, and has an ice-cream soda fountain, but that's only the beginning. Behind the rather staid facade is a carnival of activity with lots of little boutiques selling everything from baby powder to costume jewelry. The decor is centered around a series of bronze molds of the lips of Moreau, Dietrich, Monroe, Bardot, Greco, and Sagan. At the soda fountain, you can order a banana split or a Coca-Cola float, but champagne and caviar are also available. There's also a cocktail lounge, a coffeehouse, and a snackbar. Set meals are offered from noon to 2:30 p.m. and from 7 to 9 p.m., priced from 40F ($7.14), including drink and service. A club sandwich costs 20F ($3.57); a hamburger, 13F ($2.32). Desserts are served under a blanket of whipped cream.

You'll find several other Les Drug Stores, all quite similar to the one at St-Germain, throughout Paris: at 53 Avenue Champs-Élysées (Métro: Franklin D. Roosevelt); and 1 Avenue Matignon (Métro: Franklin D. Roosevelt), just off the Champs-Élysées. All are open daily till 2 a.m., even on Sunday.

Chapter XI

PARIS FOR CHILDREN

PARIS IS A GROWNUP TOWN, dedicated to adult pleasures. And we don't know an adult who won't say *"Vive!"* to that. The French spend little sentiment on their homegrown small fry. Children are expected to earn their future privileges by studying Latin quietly for long hours and being unfailingly polite to their superiors in age and wisdom. Family outings almost invariably include a four-course dinner at some special restaurant, relished as thoroughly by *la petite fille* of seven as by her mama and papa.

So there are fewer special spots for children in Paris than there are, say, in Amsterdam or Copenhagen. But there are some. And others that will charm both sides of the generation gap equally. When you're weary of dragging the kids on your rounds, forcibly inculcating culture, try refreshing the family spirit with a few of these:

Museums

The only problem for parents in Paris museums is that all the exhibits are identified in French and unless you managed to struggle past that silly aunt's plume in high school or are an expert on the subject under study, you aren't going to distinguish yourself with explanations.

Some exhibits are self-explanatory or of interest in themselves. If your kids have sea water in their veins, take them to the **Musée de la Marine** in the Palais de Chaillot (Métro: Trocadéro), which features a kaleidoscopic collection of models, maps, figureheads, and whole craft, tracing the development of shipping from Columbus's *Santa Maria*. The most magnificent item on show is the actual "Boat of the Emperor," a gilt-crowned, oar-driven longboat built in 1811 for Napoleon's trip to Anvers. The museum is open daily except Tuesday from 10 a.m. to 6 p.m.; admission is 8F ($1.43). For information, telephone 555-31-70.

The building also contains the **Musée de l'Homme** (tel. 505-

70-60), with an admission fee of 10F ($1.79), same hours. This has a large and important collection of artifacts illustrating the way different peoples live the world around. There is plenty of scope here for a little instructive lecturing. In the rooms dealing with anthropology and paleontology, you can point out characteristics all human races share and view such fascinating fossils as the skeleton of the Menton man. One wing deals exclusively with prehistoric Africa. Less needful of elucidation is the rich collection of costumes, weapons, tools, jewelry, and household goods from every corner of civilization—Eskimo sleds, African totems, a sinuous gold-spangled matador's suit contrasting with the heavy garb of the Slovak peasant.

A guaranteed child-pleaser (and you can use the kids as an excuse to go yourself) is Paris's wax museum, the **Musée Grevin,** at 10 Boulevard Montmartre (Métro: Montmartre). Unlike some wax museums which take themselves too seriously, this one has some delightful camp touches, such as its "Hall of Mirrors" of Versailles-like splendor where the mirrors irreverently distort rather than reflect. The museum is open daily from noon to 7 p.m., and on holidays from noon to 8 p.m. Admission is 20F ($3.57) for adults, 14F ($2.50) for children up to 14.

The charge includes two short shows. One, called *Le Cabinet Fantastique,* features a rather good magician who—after the usual birds fly out of bandanas—burns a 100-franc note collected from a person in the audience and, with many Gallic grimaces of sorrow at its loss, manages to make it reappear in an un-cracked walnut. The other show is exaggerated in the extreme. You are herded into a circular, mirror-walled room, called *Le Palais des Mirages,* which vaguely resembles the temple of Brahma the museum claims it to be. And then darkness descends and lights start to flicker, reflecting down the endless mirror corridors while sitar music echoes through the chamber. Suddenly the scene shifts and you are in an enchanted forest, with glowing stars and butterflies jerking fitfully above your head and a thunderstorm howling around you. And finally, with a whirling crescendo of light and sound, you are deposited within a "Fête à l'Alhambra," with barely clothed wax native women on pedestals around you. And all the time the German tourist beside you is murmuring, "Wunderbar! Wunderbar!"—while the kids (up to a certain blasé age) are truly transported.

The wax figures aren't of Tussaud standard, but they're worthy enough, and some of the settings are impressive. The pride of the museum is *Une Soirée à la Malmaison,* which features 48 famed French figures as they might have looked attending a party at Josephine's house. Bonaparte and his beautiful lady are, of course, the focal point. A quieter scene depicts Napoleon on his deathbed. Twenty-five scenes deal with the history of France from Charlemagne to Napoleon III. Joan of Arc calmly leaves the prison for the marketplace. Louis XIV throws a do at Versailles. The Revolution is represented by such sights as the murder of Marat. But there is no chamber of horrors to frighten the littler ones into nightmares. The tableaux are not identified with placards, but with numbers, and you are pretty well forced to purchase a program to tell the people apart. English-speaking guides are on hand to aid you.

Grevin Museum has opened a subsidiary, **Serelor,** at Forum des Halles, the new heart of Paris (Métro: Les Halles). This is a sound-and-light show devoted to La Belle Époque, the period between 1885 and 1900. The show is open from 11 a.m. to 10 p.m. weekdays; from 1 to 8 p.m. Sunday and holidays. Entrance fee is 22F ($3.93) between 1 and 6 p.m.; 18F ($3.21) from 11 a.m. to 1 p.m. and after 6 p.m. Children up to 14 are admitted for 16F ($2.86).

Among the other museums frequented by the children of Paris is the **Musée National d'Histoire Naturelle,** 57 rue Cuvier, in the Jardin des Plantes (Métro: Jussieu or Austerlitz). Its history dates back to 1635, when it was founded as a scientific research center by Guy de la Brosse, physician to Louis XIII, but that period is a fleeting moment compared to the eons of history covered inside the huge museum complex. In the Galleries of Paleontology, Anatomy, Mineralogy, and Botany, your little genius can trace the history and evolution of life on earth, wondering at the massive skeletons of dinosaurs and mastodons, and staring fascinated at the two-headed animal embryos floating forlornly in their pickling jars. These galleries are open daily except Tuesday from 1:30 p.m. to 5 p.m., Sunday from 10:30 a.m. to 5 p.m. Admission is 8F ($1.43) for adults, half price for children.

Within the museum grounds are tropical hot houses containing thousands of species of unusual plant life. These are open from 9 a.m. to 5:30 p.m. daily except Tuesday. You'll pay 6F ($1.07) for admission to the menagerie hot houses and vivarium, where you can view small animal life, including plenty of reptiles, in glass cases designed to recreate their natural habitats.

Science fanatics would delight in the **Palais de la Découverte** in the Grand Palais on Avenue Franklin Roosevelt (Métro:

FDR)—if they knew French. This is a full fun-house of things to do—displays to light up, machines to test your muscular reactions, live experiments to watch. White-coated technicians give more than 50 lectures a day using a large number of experiments in physics, chemistry, and biology. You can also visit and listen in on astronomy, space, geology, science, history, and other lectures. You can find special temporary exhibitions, and there is a planetarium. But, as we've said, all is in French. If your little science nut is fanatical enough, take him or her anyway. He or she can explain the exhibits to *you*. Admission is 14F ($2.50) if you include the planetarium show. The museum is open daily except Monday from 10 a.m. to 6 p.m. Planetarium shows are held at 11 a.m., and 2, 3, and 4 p.m. on weekdays, with an additional show at 5:45 p.m. on Sunday.

Parks and Zoos

The definitive children's park in Paris is the **Jardin d'Acclimation,** a 25-acre zoo-cum-amusement park on the northern edge of the Bois de Boulogne (Métro: Pte-Maillot). This is the kind of place that satisfies tykes and adults alike—but would be regarded in horror by anyone in his or her teens. The visit starts with a ride from Porte Maillot to the Jardin entrance, through a stretch of wooded park, on a jaunty, green-and-yellow narrow-gauge train. A one-way fare costs 4F (71¢), plus an additional 4F for the entrance fee. Inside the gate, there is an easy-to-follow layout map. The park is circularly shaped and if you follow the road in either direction it will take you all the way around and bring you back to the train at the end. En route you will discover a house of funny mirrors, an archery range, miniature golf, zoo animals, an American-style bowling alley, a puppet theater (only on Thursday, Saturday, Sunday, and holidays), playground, hurdle-racing course, and a whole conglomerate of junior-scale rides, shooting galleries, and waffle stalls. You can trot the kids off on a pony or join them in a boat on a mill-stirred lagoon. On most afternoons at 3, 4, and 5, you can attend the dolphins' spectacle. The cost is 8F ($1.43) for adults, but only 6F ($1.07) for children. Fun to watch (and a superb idea for American cities to copy), is "La Prévention Routière," a miniature roadway operated by the Paris police. The youngsters drive through it in small cars equipped to start and stop and are required by two genuine Parisian gendarmes to obey all street sign and light changes. The Jardin is open daily from 9 a.m. to 6:30 p.m. (on Sunday till 7:30 p.m.).

There is a modest, rather motheaten zoo in the Jardin des Plantes, near the natural history museum. But without a doubt, the best zoo this city has to offer is in the **Bois de Vincennes**—on the outskirts, but quickly reached by subway (Métro: Pte-Dorée). Open daily from 9 a.m. to 5:30 p.m. (on Sunday to 7 p.m.), it charges an admission fee of 15F ($2.68); children between 4 and 10, 10F ($1.79). This ultramodern zoo displays its animals in settings as close as possible to their natural habitats. Here you never get that hunched-up feeling about the shoulders from empathizing with a leopard in a cage too small to stalk. The lion has an entire veldt to himself, and you can view each other comfortably across a deep protective moat. On a cement mountain reminiscent of Disneyland's Matterhorn, lovely Barbary sheep leap from ledge to ledge or pose gracefully for hours watching the penguins in their pools at the mountain's foot. Also at the foot, burrowed cave-like into the mountain, is a restaurant extending out into a stone-paved café. The animals seem happy here and are consequently playful. Keep well back from the bear pools or your drip-dries may be dripping wet.

While visiting the **Marine Museum** (mentioned earlier) in the Palais de Chaillot, you can always take a cool break by walking down into the gardens where there is a small **aquarium.** Built on the style of the Vincennes zoo structures, it resembles a rough-walled rock underground cave. The exhibits aren't exceptional; they represent the river fishes of France. We've looked in vain for "truite aux amandes." The aquarium is open daily from 10 a.m. to 6 p.m. charging an entrance fee of 3F (54¢).

The large inner-city parks all have playgrounds with tiny merry-go-rounds and gondola-style swings. If you're staying on the Right Bank, take the children for a stroll through the **Tuileries Gardens,** where there are donkey rides, ice-cream stands, and a marionette show. At the circular pond, you can rent a toy sailboat with a prod from two enterprising young sprouts. On the Left Bank, equivalent delights exist in the **Luxembourg Gardens.** If you take in the gardens of the **Champ de Mars,** you can combine a donkey ride for the children with a visit to the nearby Eiffel Tower for the entire family.

Puppet Shows

Whether or not you take in a puppet show while visiting the above-mentioned parks is a matter of knowing your own children. Because, once again, all the words are in French. But they're a great Paris tradition and worth seeing, almost for the people-to-people joy of sharing a French child's typical experience. The shows are given in the Tuileries Gardens at 3 p.m. and 3:30 p.m. on Wednesday, Saturday, and Sunday, all summer long. At the Luxembourg Gardens, you'll see puppet productions of sinister plots set in Gothic castles and Oriental palaces. Prices vary depending on the extravagance of the production, ranging from 6F ($1.07) to 15F ($2.68). Some young critics think the best puppet shows are held in the Champ de Mars. Performance times in both the Luxembourg Gardens and the Champ de Mars vary with the day of the week and the production being staged. But all are colorfully and enthusiastically produced—and received. You may have to whisper the story line to your monolingual offspring as you go along, but when Red Riding Hood pummels the Wolf over the head with an umbrella, they'll be contorted in glee like the rest of the half-pint audience. That's international kid-talk.

An Afternoon on Montmartre

On Sunday afternoons whole French families crowd up to the top of the Butte Montmartre—to join in the fiesta atmosphere. Start by taking the Métro to Anvers and walking to the **Funiculaire de Montmartre.** You'll run the gamut of several balloon-sellers before you get there. The funiculaire is a small, silvery cable car that slides you gently up the steep, grassy hillside to the Sacré-Coeur on the hillcrest for the price of 3F (54¢) round trip. Once up top, follow the crowds to the **Place du Tertre,** where a Sergeant Pepper–style band will usually be blasting off-key and where you can have the kids' pictures sketched by local artists. Funny how even the shyest child will preen when a crowd is watching.

Signs lead from the Place to the **Musée de Cire de la Butte Montmartre,** 11 rue Poulbot, 18e (tel. 606-78-92), a wax museum illustrating the history of Montmartre. All the neighborhood characters—Toulouse-Lautrec, Renoir, Liszt, Chopin—make their somewhat stiff appearance in settings of their time. A recent addition is the tableaux, Le Bateau Lavoir, the meeting place of painters since 1830. Admission is 12F ($2.14) for adults,

8F ($1.43) for children under 16. There are guided tours in English if the demand is large enough. It is open daily from 10 a.m. to noon and from 2 to 6 p.m. in summer; 2 to 6 p.m. from November 1 to Easter. Before returning to the cable car, take in the views of Paris from the various vantage points, and have an ice cream in an outdoor café on the Place.

Montmartre, with the Basilica of Sacré-Coeur

Chapter XII

A PARIS SHOPPING SPREE

SHOULD YOU BUY anything in Paris? Are there any good buys? Is there any item purchased here that you can't duplicate better back home?

Good questions. It is quite true that shopping abroad can be fraught with pitfalls. For example, it's perfectly conceivable that you might buy something comparable for less in your own home city. But that leaves out a persuasive argument. Not everyone has access to the wide and multifarious offerings found in Paris. There are items unique to France, rarely and not easily found in America.

Not to be ignored is the joy of bringing "something back from Paris," a reminder of your stay. There can be no substitute for memories of strolling along one of the chic boulevards of Paris, browsing in the smart boutiques, and finally, purchasing a scarf or handbag.

Naturally, as everywhere, you'll have to be careful, even shrewd in your shopping. It's easy to buy something shoddy anywhere in the world. On the other hand, if you're careful and adventurous, you'll find many wonderful items in Paris.

Shopping Tips

THE GOOD BUYS: There are exceptions to the rule. Perfumes in Paris are almost always cheaper than in the States. And that means all the famed brands: Guerlain, Chanel, Schiaparelli, Jean Patou. Cosmetics bearing French names (Dior, Lancôme) also cost less. Gloves are a fine value.

TOURIST DISCOUNTS: And then you can take advantage of a special discount offered to foreigners, which simply means you are exempt from French purchase taxes. This entitles you to a 15% discount off list prices, although it does entail some red tape. First, if you're taking your purchases with you, ask if the store allows tourist discounts (most do). Then you must purchase a minimum of 400F ($71.40) total in each shop to be eligible. You pay the full price to the store, and it in turn will give you a receipt in triplicate—one green copy (for your personal records) and two pink ones for the French customs—and a stamped, self-addressed envelope. When you leave the country you hand the two pink receipts along with the envelope to the Customs official. He mails one back to the store and keeps the other to give the shop tax credit. Eventually, you will receive a check in the mail from the store for the discount due you. And don't worry about it—all good Paris shops follow through.

If you mail your purchases through a store, the discount will be immediately taken off your payment at the cashier's desk. Major department stores have hospitality desks on the street level to assist in handling tourist discounts, and to help you with any other shopping problems.

AIRPORT TAX-FREE BOUTIQUES: Further choice: Should you do your shopping within the city proper or wait until you fly out to make some of your purchases? In the tax-free shops at Orly and Charles de Gaulle Airports, you will get a minimum discount of 20% on *all* items and up to 50% off on such things as liquors, cigarettes, and watches. Among the stock on sale: crystal and cutlery, French bonbons, luggage, wines and whiskeys, pipes and lighters, filmy lingerie, silk scarves, all the name perfumes, knitwear, jewelry, cameras and equipment, French cheeses, and antiques. Remember that what you buy must travel with you, and you are allowed to bring into the States the retail value of $300 in overseas purchases without paying customs duty.

SHOPPING DAYS AND HOURS: Shops are open from around 9 a.m. to 7 p.m. Small shops take a two-hour lunch break. Most close on Sunday and Monday. The flea market and some other street markets are open Saturday, Sunday, and Monday. That intriguing sign on shop doors reading "Entrée Libre" means you may browse at will. "Soldes" means Sale. "Soldes Exceptionel" means they're pushing it a bit.

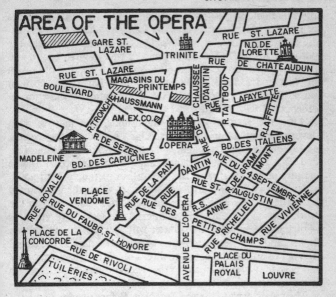

Shopping Guide

RIGHT BANK SHOPS: Start at the Havre-Caumartin Métro stop to begin your tour of two *Grands Magasins*. On the corner is **Au Printemps** (tel. 285-22-22), the city's largest department store. Actually, it consists of three stores and one supermarket connected by bridges on the second and third floors. Go to Brummel for clothing for men, both sports and dress. Printemps-Havre is mainly for books, furniture, and housewares, while Printemps Newstore sells clothes for young people and children (the ground floor is mainly for perfume, cosmetics, gifts, and Paris "handicrafts"). Interpreters stationed at the Welcome Room on the main floor will help you claim your discounts, guide you to departments, and aid you in making purchases. Extra services include a travel agency, advance booking for shows and theaters, a hairdresser, lockers, a rent-a-car service, babysitting arrangements, counters to repair watches or make keys in a hurry, a shoe repair, and even a self-service restaurant.

Another of the great department stores of Paris is the **Galeries Lafayette**, 30 Boulevard Haussmann (tel. 282-34-56). Inside most doorways is a Welcome Service telephone to direct you to the merchandise you're interested in. Of the three buildings comprising this department store, Lafayette offers the most exciting merchandise for visitors. On the ground floor are the perfumes for which Paris is famous, as well as gifts, books, and records. The third floor has an exceptional collection of dresses for women. Incidentally, the top of Galeries Lafayette is open on sunny days. We suggest you take the elevator up there for an exceptional view of Paris.

After the vastness of these emporiums, you may want to devote your attention to some specialty shops. Up the avenue, at 73 Boulevard Haussmann, is the century-old **Trousselier** (tel. 265-32-23). You'll think first it's simply a florist shop, with some artfully displayed sprays. But look again or touch—and you'll see that every flower is artificial, shaped in silk and hand-painted by crafts people, who pursue this famous French craft in the workshops in the rear. And what exquisite work! Everything is lifelike in the extreme. One cluster will bear a bud, a full-blown flower, and then one just past its prime and fading at the edges. The prices are worthy of the quality. This recently renewed store has been in the same family for three generations. Mlle. Trousselier is actually there to welcome you.

Then walk back to the **rue Tronchet.** Before turning down the street, stop in at the corner establishment, **Aux Tortues,** 55 Boulevard Haussmann (tel. 265-56-74), across from Au Printemps. Offbeat and charming, this is one of the most delightful specialty shops of Paris, offering items unique and unusual made in ivory and semiprecious stones. Look especially for the ivory miniatures. The prices aren't cheap, but then you wouldn't expect them to be.

Turning down the street, flanked by young boutiques, you'll arrive at the "youngest" shop of them all, the **Soldes Enfantines,** 17 rue Tronchet, 8e, specializing in clothing for children.

The rue Tronchet leads to the Place de la Madeleine, where stands the most popular sight in the city—not the church, but **Fauchon,** 8e (tel. 742-60-11), a vast shop crammed with gastronomical goodies. Never have we seen faces so rapt—not even before the *Mona Lisa*—as those of Parisians gazing at the Fauchon window display. Plump chickens coated in a glazing of sliced almonds, a thigh of lamb opening out like a cornucopia, filled with bright, fresh vegetables made to look like fruits. It's the French person's version of "The Garden of Eden." Incidentally, two decorators are employed to keep this window display filled with delectable items.

At Fauchon, there is both a main store and an annex across the street. English-speaking hostesses will assist you, if needed. In the fruit-and-vegetable department, you'll find such items as rare mushrooms and fraise des bois (wild strawberries). In another department you'll come across such items as escargots (snails), stuffed pig's feet, Hawaiian bread, more than a dozen types of pâté, foie gras de canard, small birds in gelatin, corked bottles containing oils for fondue, clay pots of herbs from the provinces, even dozens of varieties of mustard.

The annex features different types of pastry, candies, and a self-service stand-up bar. The candies, incidentally, are divine, including glazed tropical fruits, whiskey truffles, stuffed dates, and chocolate-dipped ginger. After seeing the self-service bar, you'll probably decide to stay for lunch. Go first to the display case, make your decision, then tell the cashier what you want. She'll give you a check for each item which you in turn surrender to the serving woman. You may order an omelet for 12F ($2.14), a shrimp salad for 19F ($3.39), or even a club sandwich, 17F ($3.04). A "coupe" of ice cream makes a soothing dessert at 12F ($2.14). It's closed Sunday, but open otherwise from 9:30 a.m. to 6:30 p.m.

Across the square is the **rue Royale,** the street of the legendary Maxim's. Along the rue Royale, you can turn right onto the **Faubourg Saint-Honoré,** that platinum strip of the city, where the presidential palace shares space with the haute couture houses of Lanvin and Courrèges.

Lanvin, 22 Faubourg Saint-Honoré, 8e (tel. 763-80-21), specializes in women's fashions and accessories. On the second floor, Lanvin's marvelous haute couture dresses are presented in the house's salon. On the first floor, chic and contemporary *prêt-à-porter* (ready-to-wear) day and evening dresses and ensembles are to be found together with beautiful Lanvin shawls.

Hermès, 24 Faubourg Saint-Honoré, is a legend, of course. The shop is especially noted for its scarves, made of silk squares that are printed with antique motifs. Three well-known Hermès fragrances, two for women and one for men, make excellent gift choices. The gloves sold here are without peer, especially those for men in reindeer hide, doeskin, or supple kid. The leather-goods store at Hermès is the best known in Europe. The crafts-people working on the premises turn out the Hermès handbag, an institution that needs no sales pitch on these pages.

Courrèges, 40 rue François 1er, 8e (tel. 720-70-44), is a bright, modern shop, with lots of high-quality knitwear, along with a well-chosen collection of items made, for the most part, of cotton, wool, and silk. It's a great place to drop in, especially if you're out walking your poodle. The workmanship in some of the boutique items is flawless.

Of course, there are others—so many others! You can visit **Christian Dior,** world famous for its custom-made haute couture, at 26–32 Avenue Montaigne, 8e (tel. 743-54-44), with a wide selection of both women's and men's ready-to-wear, sportswear, and accessories, including separate salons for shoes and leather goods, furs, children's and juniors' clothing, and a variety of gift items, costume jewelry, lighters, pens, among other offerings.

The spirit of **Chanel** lives on, and her shop at 31 rue Cambon, 1er (tel. 261-54-55), across from the Ritz, is more than ever in business with the introduction of new accessories and new cosmetic lines.

And **Pierre Cardin** boutiques are popping up in every hotel and on every street corner. You can't miss them.

Emilio Pucci, 4 rue de Castiglione, 1er (tel. 260-89-42), is the Parisian showcase for this talented and temperamental Italian designer. Across the street from the Inter-Continental Hotel, this boutique carries a full line of accessories for women, all created with special flair. Included in the array are scarves, handbags, hats, belts, shoes, even his own perfume. Of course, Pucci enjoys one of the most outstanding reputations in Europe for his blouses and slacks.

Gucci, 350 rue Saint-Honoré, 1er (tel. 295-83-27), is yet another showcase for a fabled Italian designer. Gucci, of course, is noted for his leather goods, including shoes and handbags. This boutique also has an excellent collection of scarves and two-piece ensembles. Its sweaters are especially outstanding. Another address is 27 rue du Faubourg Saint-Honoré, 8e (same telephone number).

If your tastes are not traditional, you may want to avoid all these deluxe citadels and seek out exotica supreme at **La Factorerie,** 5 Boulevard Malesherbes, 8e (tel. 265-96-86), reached by heading up the Boissy d'Anglas from the Faubourg Saint-Honoré. This is one of the most unusual and offbeat boutiques on the Right Bank, with a selection of items from Sumatra, the Philippines, Tibet, Ethiopia, and Singapore, to name only a few points of geography.

Here's a roundup of other Right Bank shopping establishments you might want to take a peek at:

For Stylish Hats

One of the most distinguished outlets for hats for both men and women in Paris is the chapeliers of **E. Motsch,** 42 Avenue George-V, 8e, right off the Champs-Élysées. In this sedate corner store, the staff offers almost every type of headgear, ranging from berets to Scottish tam-o-shanters. The section for women contains some of the most stylish, although conservatively sedate, hats in Paris.

For Books

W. H. Smith & Son, 248 rue de Rivoli, 1er (tel. 260-37-97), is the English bookshop in Paris. Books, magazines, and newspapers published in the English-speaking world are widely available. You can get *The Times* of London, of course. There's a fine selection of maps if you plan to do much touring. Across from the Tuileries Gardens, W. H. Smith also has a combined tearoom and restaurant.

For Unusual Engravings

Carnavalette, 2 rue des Francs-Bourgeois, 3e (tel. 272-81-82), off the Place des Vosges in the Marais sector, sells unusual one-of-a-kind engravings, plus complete old magazines, some dating from 1850. You can also obtain copies of *Frou-frou* and *Tutu* which sold for 20 centimes in 1903.

For Perfumes

Freddy of Paris, 10 rue Auber, 9e (tel. 742-63-41), near the American Express and the Opéra, offers moderate rates on all name-brand scents, top-fashion handbags, scarves, ties, French umbrellas, Limoges, crystalware, and costume jewelry. His shop is open daily except Sunday from 9 a.m. to 6 p.m.

For Antiques

Le Louvre des Antiquaires, Place Palais-Royal, 1er, is the largest antiques center in Europe, attracting collectors, browsers, and those interested in art nouveau and deco objects. For Americans, the art nouveau and deco objects are the best buys. However, they are taxable, regrettably, as only items which can be imported into the United States are duty free. The center stands across the street from the Louvre. Housing some 240 antique dealers, the showrooms are spread across 2½ acres of well-lit modern salons. The building, a former department store, was erected in 1852 according to Napoleon's plans for the rue de Rivoli. Arranged on three levels, the widely varied showrooms are a happy mélange, including everything from antiques to secondhand clothing items, from tapestries to books and stamps. Hours are Tuesday through Sunday from 11 a.m. to 7 p.m.

China and Crystal

Au Grand Siècle, 31 rue La Boetie, 8e, is an elegant shop presenting the final word on antiques and reproduction furniture, silver, and crystal, especially Lalique. A small place, it is nevertheless filled to the brim with every imaginable item, including a splendid collection of lamps and small gifts. No low-priced items are offered, but it is a memorable experience in exquisite taste. It is open Tuesday through Saturday from 9:30 a.m. to 6:30 p.m. On Monday, it is open from noon to 6:30 p.m.

Haute Coiffure

Jacques Dessange is a new star on the scene, offering unisex hair-styling in its several shops in Paris, including those at 37 Avenue F. D. Roosevelt, in the Montparnasse Tower, at 32 Avenue Mozart, and at 4 Avenue de la République. These luxurious salóns are a favorite with women around the world who demand the ultimate in style and service.

Gifts for Children

Au Nain Blue, 406 rue Saint-Honoré, 8e. Any child you love is expecting a present from Paris, and at the "Blue Dwarf" you'll be bedazzled by the choice. Nor can any adult withstand the temptation to browse through this paradise of playthings. It's a world of toy soldiers, stuffed animals, games, model airplanes, technical toys, model cars, even a "Flower Drum Kit." Puppets come in all shapes, sizes, and costumes.

Men's Wear

Olden, 189 rue Saint-Honoré, 8e, on the corner of the rue des Pyramides, offers the discriminating shopper the maximum choice in men's wear and accessories. The man who likes style will find high-fashion shirts, designer silk ties, sweaters, suits, sports jackets, sports shirts, belts, swimming suits, plus all manner of suede and leather.

Lenzo, 78 Avenue Champs-Élysées, 8e. In the Lido Arcade, this outstanding shop for men's apparel caters to a large number of international stage and screen personalities (ask to see the customer scrapbook). The decor—Florentine wood paneling, marble tables, crystal chandeliers—is reflective of the kind of taste you'll find here. Ties, shirts, sweaters, shoes, coats, and hats in the latest styles are offered. Lenzo also does custom tailoring.

Gifts

Eiffel Shopping, 9 Avenue de Suffren, 7e (tel. 566-55-30), offers you a free glass of cognac while you browse through the designer collection (Dior, St. Laurent, Lanvin, Cartier, Chanel, to name just a few) of handbags, ties, scarves, watches, sunglasses, jewelry, perfumes, Lalique crystal, and much more. This tax-free shopping center, only one block from the Eiffel Tower, offers top-quality merchandise at discount prices, and all the salespeople are bilingual. It is open daily from 9:15 a.m. to 8 p.m., and on Sunday from 11 a.m. to 8 p.m. A second shop is at the Paris Convention Center, Porte Maillot, Boulevard Gouvion St-Cyr, 17e (tel. 758-24-09), two floors above the Air Terminal, close to Concorde Lafayette and Meridien Hotels.

CUT-RATE SHOPPING: Paris no longer caters to just the well-heeled in its boutiques. Many formerly high-priced items are often on sale at tabs cut from 20% to 50% of their original price when displayed in a store along the Champs-Élysées. Several shops have opened which offer leftover merchandise from some of the better known fashion houses. Of course, the famous labels have been cut out, but it's still the same clothing.

Perhaps the best known of the cut-rate boutiques is **Le Mouton à Cinq Pattes,** 8 rue Saint-Placide, 6e (Métro: Saint-Placide, or Sèvres-Babylone), which is down in the Montparnasse area. Here you can find the creations of such well-known designers as Daniel Hechter and Sonia Rykiel, their clothing selling at a third of its original price. Two similar shops, **La Braderie** and **Credule,** are on the same street—so check them out, too.

Another shop that seems to have a "permanent sale" is **La Trouvailles,** 43 rue de la Convention, 15e (Métro: Javel). Here outfits sell at about one-fourth of their original price.

At last Paris has a hand-me-down shop, but the merchandise hardly qualifies for "Secondhand Rose." It's **Maxipuces,** 18 rue Cortambert, 16e (tel. 503-37-31; Métro: La Muette). Some of the wealthiest women in Paris, and some of the most chicly dressed, bring their high-fashion clothing to this shop. How does an Yves Saint-Laurent hand-stitched evening gown which originally sold for some 3800F ($678.30) strike you with a price tag of 1000F ($178.50)? Your friends back home may be dazzled when you appear at a party in such an original.

LEFT BANK SHOPS: Start your Left Bank shopping tour at the historic **Place de l'Odéon.** On a street branching off from here is **Lorenzi Frères,** 19 rue Racine, 6e (tel. 326-38-68), containing some of the most interesting sculpture reproductions, decorative accessories, and moulages (castings or moldings) d'art on the Left Bank. The house has been in business since 1871. You can also visit the studio of the talented craftsman-owner (in the rear, but wait for an invitation).

Right nearby is **Rigodon,** 13 rue Racine, 6e (tel. 329-98-66). This is a puppet-and-doll world for every child, even for those who are children only at heart. Hanging from its ceiling is one of the most varied and sophisticated collections of puppets in Paris. They come in all characters, sizes, and prices, and include everything from angels to witches on broomsticks to bat women with feather wings.

Rigodon also makes porcelain dolls. The painting on the faces and the costumes are unique for each model, be it a queen with all her power or the amazon of the hunt. There are marionettes (with strings) from French artisans as well as furry animals. The price of the dolls and marionettes begins at 200F ($35.70) and goes up to 3500F ($624.75).

Back at the Place de l'Odéon, you can strike out again—this time down the **rue de l'Odéon,** which contains the kind of items you might pick up at the Flea Market. Especially notable is a collection of jugs and pitchers, as well as turn-of-the-century bric-a-brac, even a sword collection. On the same street, at 22 rue de l'Odéon, stands **Seraphine,** which features framed embroideries and primitive artifacts.

At the end of the street, at the Car. de l'Odéon, you can turn onto the rue St-Sulpice, and there you'll find **Art Investigation,** 38 rue Saint-Sulpice, 6e. You enter the building through huge wooden doors leading into a courtyard. Proceed to the first floor, where a beautiful collection of woodcarvings, silkscreens, and lithographs is on display. Most of the work shown here is by contemporary international artists with the emphasis on graphics.

From here, you can walk to the **rue de Tournon,** 6e, one of the most interesting streets for shopping on the Left Bank. At 13 rue de Tournon is a fashion complex, featuring that *Vogue* look at **Tan Giudicelli** and stylish boutique items for both men and women at **Micmac St. Tropez.**

After walking back along the rue de Tournon for a while, you can cut onto the rue de Seine 6e, where art nouveau posters are sold cheek-by-jowl with genuine old masters. You pass along the **Buci street market,** where you can gather the makings of an unforgettable picnic under the shrill guidance of vendors.

The **Galerie Documents,** 53 rue de Seine, 6e (tel. 354-50-68), contains one of the most original poster collections in Paris. Many of them are inexpensive, although you could easily pay 1200F ($214.20) for an original. Your poster selection will be mailed back home in a tube.

Check the **Galerie Raymond Duncan,** 31 rue de Seine, 6e, a rather culty shrine to Isadora's brother, with an interesting exhibition of the looms he developed and the unique tapestry-like artwork he produced.

Farther along is **Robert Prouté,** 12 rue de Seine (tel. 326-93-22), which was founded in 1894 and has been offering ancient and modern prints ever since, at bargain prices.

Autographes, 14 rue de Seine, 6e, is a ten-foot-wide shop, with a bright-eyed collector of rare autographs, letters, and documents with famous connections. Often for very little money you'll pick up some celebrated signature to photograph (of course, you'll pay far more if that person happens to be, say, Anne d'Autriche). He's collected all the fun people, ranging from Henry Miller to Clemenceau, from Rodin to Somerset Maugham, from Marguerite de Navarre to Picasso.

If you want a photograph of any Paris scene, old or new, apply at **H. Roger Viollet,** 6 rue de Seine (at the foot of the street). Every inch of wall space is lined with green looseleaf notebooks containing archives of photographs, some seven million in all, from every country of the world. The shop has been stockpiling photos since 1880.

At the end of the rue de Seine, you can walk along the quays for galleries filled with graphics. On the river side of the street, open stalls dispense tourist prints, postcards, secondhand books, and funky antique postcards—but few real bargains or finds.

And **Le Monde En Marche,** 34 rue Dauphine, 6e (tel. 326-66-

53), has a large assortment of creative playthings for children at reasonable prices.

LES HALLES: Now that Les Halles is going through a rebirth, the produce market having moved elsewhere, a growing number of fashionable boutiques have taken over, opening on the side streets. The first of these avant-garde boutiques includes a random selection of the following:

Mauve, 3 rue des Prêcheurs, 1er, is the discovery of the year—that is, if you're seeking sophisticated, secondhand finery. Typical among its selection is a secondhand dress by Jean Patou or a wedding gown, circa 1880. Lanvin and Chanel are heavily represented, as is Mistinguett, the late French actress. And, of course, where can you find beaded Napoleon III hosiery on the spur of the moment? In addition, a large collection of delightful white nightdresses, sumptuously embroidered, is featured. They are from 50 to 150 years old. Other items include a good collection of famous-name reading lamps or decorator's vases (Daum, Gallée), as well as ancient boxes, flasks, and perfume bottles, for decorating homes.

Maurice Brocante, 4 rue des Prêcheurs, 1er, is two stores in one. One is a miniature flea market with soda siphons, decanters, coffee mills, flat irons, glass curtain rings, porcelain, clocks, jewelry, and art deco lighting fixtures.

Campagnie des Mers du Sud, 3 rue des Prêcheurs, 1er, is a miniature bazaar, with Moroccan caps, toys, a wicker basket of assorted spices, wall hangings, and vegetable colorings.

Sara Shelburne, 10 rue du Cygne, 1er (tel. 233-74-40), is what happens when a law student graduates but switches to couture instead. This is a ready-made boutique for women, with colorful dresses, separates, hostess gowns, hats from the 1920s, coats, sportswear, knits, and well-styled evening wear. An interesting detail: Sara designs and makes all her fabrics. She will make "on measure" for the same price as ready-to-wear. However, you must allow her two or three days. In addition, Sara Shelburne has opened a wedding dress department that attracts people from all over the world.

Antiquities, 18 rue de la Grande Truanderie, 1er (tel. 233-97-09), within full sight of the old market at Les Halles, and set back about 200 feet off rue Pierre-Lescot, displays a tiny but unusually imaginative collection of belle époque figurines, busts, and lamp statues. Although you may not be able to pack away one of the beaded chandeliers, there are a few of these now popular figurines which you might easily carry home with you. Most of the figures evoke an image of Isadora Duncan, with gowns that seemingly blow in gentle winds. Several heads are almost enclosed by large curling leaves.

THE MARKETS OF PARIS: The **Marché aux Puces (Flea Market)** is a landmark, adored and abused. Even if you don't purchase one item (an unlikely possibility), it's an experience to be savored. This is a complex of more than 2500 to 3000 open stalls and shops on the outer fringe of Paris, selling everything from antiques to junk, from new to secondhand clothing. Occupying a vast triangular area, it covers nearly four square miles and is almost impossible to cover entirely in just one visit.

The market is open only on Saturday, Sunday, and Monday. To reach it by Métro, take the train to Porte de Clignancourt. Bus 56 also goes to this point. When you emerge, walk to your left along Boulevard Ney. The first clues you are there will be the stalls of cheap clothing along that street. As you proceed, various streets will tempt you to walk down them. Some of these streets are narrow, lined with little shops that start pulling out their offerings around 9 a.m. and start bringing them in around 6 p.m. Monday is the traditional day for bargain seekers, as there is smaller attendance at the market and a greater desire on the part of the merchants to sell.

Naturally, you are supposed to bargain. Nobody pays the first price quoted to them. Many don't even pay the second or third price. Of course, a little basic French helps, too. The sound of an English-speaking voice is known to drive the price up right away. In addition to the permanent stalls, there are "drop-cloth" peddlers as well. They spread out their wares on canvas or sheets (as to be expected, they are viewed with scorn by the permanently installed vendors).

The big question everybody asks is "Do you get any real bargains at the Flea Market?" Or, conversely, "Will you get fleeced?" The questions are valid. Actually, it's all comparative. Obviously, the best buys have been skimmed by dealers (who often have a prearrangement to have items held for them). It's true, the same merchandise in the provinces of France will sell at less expensive tabs. But from the point of view of the visitor, who has only a few days to spend in Paris—and only half a day for shopping—the Flea Market is worth the experience.

Many of the items are a tremendous social comment on the discards of society. For example, "junk" discarded in garbage cans in the 1920s often commands high prices today. Incidentally, if goods are stolen in Paris or elsewhere, they often turn up at the Flea Market. We won't list the types of merchandise on sale, as it is ever changing.

The **Stamp Market** draws the avid collector. Nearly two dozen stalls are set up on a permanent basis under shady trees below Rond Point off the Champs-Élysées. The variety of stamps is almost unlimited—some common, some quite rare. The market is generally held on Thursday, Saturday, and Sunday. Take the Métro to Champs-Élysées.

The **Marché aux Fleurs** or Flower Market is the bouquet treat of Paris. Artists love to paint it; photographers love to click away. But, for the most part, travelers go there to refresh their souls, enjoying a feast of odor. The stalls are ablaze with color, each a showcase of flowers, usually from the French Riviera (those that escaped a fate of being hauled to the perfume factories of Grasse). The Flower Market is on the Île de la Cité in the Fourth Arrondissement, at the Place Louis-Lépine, along the Seine, in back of the Tribunal de Commerce. The market is open weekdays, but on Sunday the bird-sellers take over. Métro: Cité.

Even if you can't carry a bird back home with you, it's a delight to visit the **Bird Market** of Paris . . . and pretend. From the Louvre to the Hôtel de Ville, you can visit the long row of shops along the Seine. Both wild and tame birds are sold, including fantail pigeons, canaries, parrots, parakeets, and many rare birds. Some are displayed inside, but many can be seen hanging in cages along the sidewalk. Interspersed are shops selling greenery and houseplants, even pet fish and tortoises. On Sunday, birds are sold at the already-previewed Flower Market.

Village Suisse, 78 Avenue de Suffren, 7e, is a Left Bank complex of at least 100 antique shops and boutiques. The shops open onto sunny courtyards with fountains and sculptures. It's the hunting ground of interior decorators. Nothing sold here is shabby, broken down, or damaged (as is often the case in flea markets). Everything is super-restored, super-gleaming, and super-priced—ready to be flown home to your sitting room if you can afford it. Pewter, oil paintings, silver, copper, and furniture in seemingly all periods and styles are presented. The so-called Swiss Village is open Thursday through Monday from 10:30 a.m. to 12:30 p.m. and from 2 to 7 p.m. On the Métro, take the Place Balard line, getting off at the Champ de Mars station.

Walk along Avenue de la Motte-Picquet until you meet the Avenue de Suffren. The Swiss Village is near that corner.

Finally, **Cour aux Antiquaires,** 54 Faubourg Saint-Honoré, 8e (tel. 742-43-99), is an elegant Right Bank arcade of miniature shops and art boutiques, all opening onto a courtyard. Take the Métro to the Place de la Concorde. Nearly two dozen collectors are sheltered here, each operating independently.

Guisset-Bideau specializes in provincial furniture of the 18th century and faïences. **Chouky Bibas** offers unusual curios and pieces of furniture.

Gisèle Vaury has furniture of the 18th and 19th centuries, bibelots, and jewelry. At **Anne-Maris Vermeeren,** you'll find English 19th-century furniture, jewelry, faïences, and silverware.

A favorite is **Galerie Lear,** with its jade bottles, a cane collection, Wedgwood pieces, old flat silverwear, lithographs, original watercolors, and a changing exhibition of local artists.

Eileen Thierry has assembled a collection of Chinese ceramics, Japanese lacquers, bronzes, and other Oriental art. **Mmes. Vidal-Keller** specialize in porcelain, 19th-century jewels, and faïences. **Dominique Gouyon** features art nouveau and art deco; the **Galerie Arcadia** is the domain of Micheline Fodor who exhibits such 20th-century artists as Poliakoff, Delaunay, and Bryen; and, finally, **Marie-Alice Brazil** offers Staffordshire pottery and curios.

L'Étoile

Chapter XIII

ONE-DAY EXCURSIONS FROM PARIS

PARIS—THE CITY THAT GREW from an island—is herself the center of a curious landlocked island known as the Île de France.

Shaped roughly like a saucer, it lies encircled by a thin ribbon of rivers: the Epte, Aisne, Marne, and Yonne. Fringing these rivers are mighty forests with famous names—Rambouillet, St-Germain, Compiègne, and Fontainebleau.

These forests are said to be responsible for Paris's clear, gentle air, and the unusual lengths of her springs and falls. This may be a debatable point, but there's no argument that they provide the capital with a chain of super-excursion spots, all within easy reach.

The forests were once the possessions of kings and the ruling aristocracy, and they're still sprinkled with the magnificent châteaux or palaces of their former masters. Together with ancient hamlets, glorious cathedrals, and little country inns, they turn the Île de France into a tripper's paradise. And because of Paris's comparatively small size, it's almost at your doorstep.

The only difficult question is—where to go? What we're offering in this chapter is merely a handful of suggestions, a few out of hundreds of possibilities for one-day jaunts that will get you back to your hotel the same night. Let's start with the most illustrious of the lot:

Versailles

The town of Versailles, about 15 miles from Paris, is a stodgily formal place, but the palace is the sight of a lifetime.

The palace is unbelievably vast and as ornately artificial as a jewel box. The kings of France had built a whole glittering private world for themselves, as remote from the grime and noise and bustle of Paris as a gilded planet. Which helps to explain why there are no more kings of France. For viewing purposes, the palace is divided up into sections, one including the Hall of Mirrors (where the Treaty of Versailles was signed), the museum, and the Grand Apartments. The other contains the apartments of Madame de Pompadour, the queen's private suites, and the salons. Seeing all of it would take up an entire morning and leave you pretty exhausted. And perhaps you should skip some of the rooms to save energy for the park.

This is the ultimate of French landscaping perfection—every tree, shrub, flower, and hedge disciplined into a frozen ballet pattern and blended with soaring fountains, sparkling little lakes, grandiose steps, and hundreds of marble statues. More like a colossal stage setting than a park—even the view of the blue horizon seems embroidered on. It's a Garden of Eden for puppet people, a place where you expect the birds to sing coloratura soprano.

Between the hours of 9:45 a.m. and 5:30 p.m., the **Grand Apartments,** the **Royal Chapel,** and the **Hall of Mirrors** can be visited without a guide. The price of admission is 12F ($2.14), half that on Sunday. To see other parts of the château, you have to wait for certain opening times (there's a shortage of guards). For example, the **Opéra** is visited at 11:30 a.m., the **apartments of Mme. de Pompadour** at 2:45 p.m. For your same ticket, you'll be admitted to the **Museum of the History of France,** open daily from 2 to 5 p.m. Some of these sections may be temporarily closed, as the salons undergo restoration work.

Try to save time to visit the **Grand Trianon,** which is a good walk across the park. In pink-and-white marble, it was designed by Hardouin-Mansart for Louis XIV in 1687. The Trianon is furnished mostly with Empire pieces—certainly not the original. Charging 9F ($1.61) for admission, half price on Sunday, it is open daily except Monday, from 9:45 a.m. to 6 p.m. from April until the end of September (until 5 p.m. otherwise).

You can also visit the **Petit Trianon,** which was built by Gabriel in 1768. This was the favorite residence of Marie Antoinette, who could escape the rigors of court here. Once it was a retreat for Louis XV and his mistress, Mme. du Barry. It is open from 2 to 6 p.m. from April 1 until the end of September (otherwise, until 5 p.m.), charging 5F (89¢) for admission; half price on Sunday.

It's not necessary to book a guided tour to Versailles. You can take the Métro to the Pont de Sèvres exit. Get off there and catch a city-run bus, no. 171 (the stop is right near the point where you emerge from the underground). At a charge of 9F ($1.61), you'll be driven to Versailles in 15 minutes. If using tickets from your carnet pack, the charge drops to just 5F (89¢). The bus stops near the gates of the palace. Eurailpass holders or others can travel to Versailles by taking a commuter train which leaves about every 15 minutes. A one-way ticket goes for 4.50F (80¢). The station is connected to the Invalides Métro stop. Take the train to the Versailles–Rive Gauche station, turning right as you leave the station. At the first major street, go left and the palace will soon emerge. In all, it's about a five-minute walk.

WHERE TO DINE: For lunch, you can dine in regal style at the **Trianon Palace Hotel,** 1 Boulevard de la Reine (tel. 950-34-12). Set in a five-acre garden, the hotel became world famous in 1919 when it was the headquarters for the signers of the Treaty of Versailles, which included Woodrow Wilson. It still retains its old-world splendor, its dining room decorated with crystal chandeliers, fluted columns, and cane-backed Louis XVI–style chairs. You can order from an extensive menu that might begin with cold salmon with a green sauce, followed by coquilles St-Jacques Provençale (scallops in a garlic sauce), plus a selection of vegetables and salads, then a choice from the cheese board, and, finally, a rich-tasting dessert, such as meringue glacée Chantilly.

Two set menus are offered at 98F ($17.49) and 130F ($23.21), plus 15% for serivce. If you select the traditional dishes on the à la carte menu, expect to pay from 200F ($35.70) to 250F ($44.63) per person.

La Boule d'Or, 25 rue du Maréchal Foch (tel. 950-22-97), is the oldest auberge in Versailles, dating from 1696 and containing a rustic interior. At this "auberge of the grandfather clock," you can order a set menu at 110F ($19.64). A three-fork restaurant, you'll find the walls decorated with many fine paintings, including works by Mignard, Sorgue, Pesne, and Theniers. In addition to the already-cited set menu, you can also order many à la carte specialties as well from Franche Comté, that district between France and Switzerland. If you do so, expect to pay from 180F ($32.13) to 210F ($37.49) per person. La Boule d'Or is closed on Monday.

Finally, you'll enjoy one of your best bargains at an old-style establishment called **Le Dragon,** 30 bis rue des Réservoirs (tel. 950-70-02). Featuring such classic French dishes as snails Burgundy-style or frog legs à la Provençale, the chef is also proud of one of his set meals—just 38F ($6.78), although you pay extra for wine and service. For that low tariff, you'll be presented with an appetizer, a choice of a meat or fish course, topped by a dessert. A more plentiful menu is offered at 58F ($10.35). It is open every day except Tuesday.

Fontainebleau

Forty miles south of Paris on the main route to Lyon, a bit more than one hour by frequent train from the **Gare de Lyon,** is yet another royal palace. This one is surrounded by a superb forest of 50,000 acres, the hunting preserve of monarchs from François I to Napoleon.

Fontainebleau Palace is smaller and more intimate than Versailles and, for our money, more attractive. It's a product of the French 16th-century Renaissance, built before things were rococo. Napoleon later added most of the furnishings you'll see.

The surrounding forest is a magical retreat of ravines, wild gorges, Martian rock formations, and dark ponds. A beautiful area for hikes and picnics, it used to lure some of the greatest 19th-century painters—among them Millet and Rousseau—who turned the nearby village of **Barbizon** into an artists' colony.

The train station of Fontainebleau lies just outside the town in the suburb of Avon. A two-mile trip brings you to the château. You can take the town bus which makes a round trip every 10 or 15 minutes during weekdays, every 30 minutes on Sunday. The apartments at Fontainebleau are open daily except Tuesday, from 10 a.m. to 12:30 p.m. and from 2 to 6 p.m., April 1 to September 30; till 5 p.m., October 1 to March 31. Admission is 7F ($1.25), 3.50F (63¢) on Sunday.

WHERE TO DINE: Hôtel de l'Aigle Noir (Black Eagle Hotel), 27 Place Napoléon-Bonaparte (tel. 422-32-65), has been completely renovated, yet has retained its old charm. Opposite the château, the building was once the home of the cardinal of Retz. But it was converted into a hotel in 1720. All 26 of its bedrooms are with full baths and are individually heated. Each room is decorated in a period style with antique furniture. The tariffs for the doubles range from 370F ($66.01) to 445F ($79.43). In the redecorated dining room, you can order a set meal for 120F

($21.42). Specialties include terrine chaude d'écrevisses et son coulis, rognon de veau à la gousse d'echalotte, and gâteau Aigle Noir.

Napoléon, 9 rue Grande (tel. 422-20-39), is a classical formal hotel, across from the château. In the dining room you're faced with a choice of two set meals: 60F ($10.71) and 100F ($17.85), although you'll pay extra for wine, plus 15% for service.

A restaurant that functions as a restaurant and not a hotel is **Le Filet de Sole,** 5–7 rue du Coq-Gris (tel. 422-25-05). It features one of the most value-loaded set meals in Fontainebleau—90F ($16.06) including service, although your drink is extra. Behind a mock Norman facade, it offers pâtés, escargots, carré d'agneau, and crêpes suzette. Of course, the chef's specialty is filet de sole. A more elaborate menu costs 125F ($22.31). The restaurant is closed Tuesday for dinner, all day Wednesday, and during July.

Chantilly

This elegant little town 30 miles north of Paris boasts the finest racecourse as well as the most enchanting château in France. It's just an hour by train from the **Gare du Nord,** but take our tip and *don't* go during the racing season (first two weeks of June and September) unless you like getting stomped by turf fanatics.

The famed racing stables—almost as delightful as the palace—are decorated with carvings and sculptures that could grace any mansion. But the actual château, once the seat of the dukes of Condé, is a fairytale creation.

It lies about 1½ miles from the station, and you approach it through a shady forest glade. And suddenly it lies before you—dazzling white with blue roofs, reflected in the blue waters of the garden lakes, surrounded by lawns like green velvet. It's all turrets and towers and gables that seem to have been manufactured for a Hollywood epic. Inside are some of the country's greatest art treasures, including pictures by Holbein, Raphael, and Giotto.

The leading inn in town is **Hôtel d'Angleterre,** 9 Place Omer-Vallon (tel. 457-00-59). In the center of Chantilly, this is a pleasant inn, simply furnished, but not totally lacking in style. In fair weather you can enjoy a hearty meal in the small patio for only 70F ($12.50). Service and the cost of your wine are extra.

The best independently operated restaurant (outside of the inns or hotels) is **Tipperary,** 6 Avenue du Maréchal Joffre (tel. 457-00-48). Monsieur Oliveux will welcome you to his traditional establishment on the main floor of a town house. Café tables are placed outdoors, and in fair weather you can enjoy an apéritif here. The least expensive meal is about 75F ($13.39), including the cost of the house wine, although it's possible to order à la carte as well. Tipperary is closed Tuesday evenings in winter, Thursday, and in February.

Finally, your best bargain meal is at **Le Chantilly,** 9 Avenue du Général Leclerc (tel. 457-04-65). Also called "Chez Jean," this is a simple bistro outside town, about a mile from the center on N16. For only 50F ($8.93), you dine very well here. The food's not fancy, but it's well prepared—and the ingredients are of fine quality. On Sunday, the price of the set meal increases to 60F ($10.71). Closed Friday and in August.

Chartres

This medieval city 60 miles southwest of Paris houses one of the world's greatest Gothic cathedrals. Chartres is a one-hour ride by train from the **Gare Montparnasse.**

Even if you're tired of church architecture, Chartres is unforgettable. The cathedral was completed in 1220 and features all the painstaking artistry to which the craftsmen of the Middle Age devoted their lives. The Portail Royal, on the west side, is a piece of carving unmatched anywhere, while the vaulted interior is transformed into a stone fantasy by the light streaming in through the superlative stained-glass windows. The whole structure seems to change its form as the light varies during the day.

The city matches the cathedral—a huddle of gabled houses, some of them dating back seven or more centuries, sprinkled with equally ancient inns dishing up a memorable French provincial cuisine.

One such inn, and the finest of the lot, is **Henri IV,** 31 rue Soleil-d'Or (tel. 36-01-55). For years, that outstanding cuisinier, Monsieur Maurice Cazalis, has been welcoming gourmet-minded Parisians and foreigners who journey south to Chartres. Monsieur Cazalis, who is considered one of the master chefs of France, has been in the kitchen for more than half a century. He is definitely of the old school, deriding Cuisine Minceur. "Frenchmen may count calories at home," he says, "but when they eat out, they want to dine splendidly." The chef bought his restaurant after World War II. Many awards and citations have been presented to him. Specialties include duck with fruits, veal kidneys in his own special sauce, and a dessert named for his daughter, Brigitte, a resident of Boston, Massachusetts. On the second floor of a tiny town house, a few minutes' walk from Chartres cathedral, the restaurant has simple paneled walls and beams overhead, not enough decor, really, to distract from his *grande cuisine*. The cost-conscious will stick to the standard menu of 85F ($15.17), although a more elaborate repast is presented for 175F ($31.24). There is an à la carte menu as well. Incidentally, the restaurant has one of the best *carte des vins* in France. And don't just take our word for that. It's officially recognized as such. Closed Monday nights, Tuesday, and for part of February and July.

Another old-style inn is **Normand,** 24 Place des Epars (tel. 21-04-38). Even farther from the cathedral, but still within walking distance, this restaurant offers the personalized cuisine of Madame Normand. Plaster walls, timbers made of wood, lamps of wrought iron, even stained glass in the windows (none, however, that compete with those of the cathedral), form the backdrop for this cozy restaurant. Your best buy here is her 75F ($13.39) menu, although you can spend far more, of course. It's about 120F ($21.42) per person if you order à la carte. Closed Monday and holidays.

Rouen

The capital of Normandy lies beyond the Île de France, but so close that it makes our one-day excursion list. It's just 70 minutes by train from **St-Lazare station.**

Known as the "hundred-spired city," Rouen is a living museum of a town, showing every type of building erected in France, from fourth-century walls to 1970s office blocks. The modern impact is a result of the bomb damage suffered by Rouen during the Allied invasion of Normandy in 1944.

But standing intact is **Place du Vieux-Marché,** the gabled marketplace where Joan of Arc was burned at the stake on May 30, 1431. A mosaic marks the spot. An even more important site is **Rouen Cathedral,** whose spirit was captured in a series of paintings by Monet. It, too, was heavily bombed, but has been restored. The cathedral was originally consecrated in 1063, and it has seen many building crews over the centuries. It's distinguished by two soaring towers, one called the Tour de Beurre or Tower of Butter. The devout, willing to pay for the privilege of eating butter during Lent, financed its construction. It was built in the flamboyant Gothic style. Inside, the Chapelle de la Vierge is graced with the tombs of the cardinals d'Amboise in the Renaissance style. Also, Jean Goujon designed a tomb for Louis de Brézé, the husband of Diane de Poitiers. Richard the Lion-Hearted, incidentally, gave his "heart" to the people of Rouen as a token of affection.

Two other ecclesiastical monuments of interest include the **Church of Saint-Maclou,** in back of the cathedral. Built in the florid Gothic style, it contains handsome cloisters plus a step-gabled porch. This church is known for its panels of doors, dating from the 16th century. Rebuilt in 1432, Saint-Maclou was consecrated in 1521. The lantern tower, however, is from the 19th century. The other church is **St-Ouen,** reached by walking down the rue de la République to the Place du Général de Gaulle. Originally a seventh-century Benedictine abbey, it is now a Gothic church, one of the best known in France, with an octagonal lantern tower called "the ducal crown of Normandy." The stained glass inside is remarkable.

Two museums are important. One, the **Musée des Beaux-Arts,** Square Verdrel, is considered one of the finest provincial museums of art in the country. It includes works by Ingres, Delacroix, Veronese, Renoir, David, and especially a version of *Rouen Cathedral* by Monet. But even more fascinating to some is the unique **Le Secq des Tournelles,** a museum of wrought iron (entrance on rue Jacques-Villon). The museum is sheltered in the Church of St. Laurent, which dates from the 15th century. More than 12,000 pieces of wrought iron, including everything from Roman keys to sophisticated jewelry, are to be found here.

In food, Rouen is famous for its duck. The best place to sample it is at **La Couronne,** 31 Place du Vieux-Marché (tel. 71-40-90). This is the oldest restaurant in the city, dating from 1345. In fact, it claims to be the oldest auberge in all of France. On the square where Joan of Arc met her death, it is a half-timbered building. Dining is on several crooked floors. The dish everybody orders here is caneton (duckling) à la Rouennaise, 170F ($30.35) for two persons. The duck's neck is wrung so as not to lose any blood. It is then roasted, the breast slices flamed in Calvados. Then it is covered in a blood sauce. The drumsticks are grilled until crisp. Should this be too heavy for you, we'd recommend suprême de turbot hollandaise, 80F ($14.28), or filet de sole Normande, 80F also. The best dessert is profiteroles glacées at 25F ($4.46).

Dufour, 67 rue Saint-Nicolas (tel. 71-90-62), is also good. A 17th-century inn, it is a five-story corner building in the typical style of plaster and timbers. Under mellowed beams, you have your choice of several dining rooms. An excellent opening is stuffed mussels at 25F ($4.46). Turbot in béarnaise sauce is a fine dish at 90F ($16.06), although the chef's specialty is duck à la Roüennaise at 130F ($23.21) for two persons. Special attention is paid to desserts here. The restaurant is closed Sunday nights and Monday, and takes a vacation in August.

La Conciergerie

Chapter XIV

AFTER PARIS . . . WHERE?

THE QUESTION this chapter heading asks poses the knottiest problem of our entire book. The answer doesn't just entail an embarrassment of riches, but an inundation.

Covering 212,741 square miles, France is slightly smaller than Texas. But no other patch on the globe concentrates such a fabulous diversity of sights and scenery in so compact an area.

Within her borders, France houses each of the natural characteristics that make up Europe: the flat, fertile north, the rolling green hills of the central Loire country, the snow-capped Alpine ranges of the east, the starkly towering Pyrenees in the south, and the lushly semitropical Mediterranean coast of the southeast.

Name your taste and France has a spot for you. The château country around Orléans for castles and vineyards. Normandy and Brittany for rugged seashores and apple orchards. The Mont Blanc area for mountain-climbing and skiing. The Champagne for sun-warmed valleys and the greatest of all wines. Languedoc for Spanish flavor, olive groves, and Provençal cooking. The Riviera for golden sands, palm-fringed beaches, and bodies beautiful.

Because the country is—by American standards—not very large, all these contrasts beckon within easy traveling range. By train from Paris, it's just four hours to **Alsace,** five hours to the **Alps,** seven hours to the **Pyrenees,** and eight hours to the **Côte d'Azur.**

France's National Railroads (SNCF) actually *want* passengers and operate one of the finest services in the world. Most of the lines are electrified, the trains impeccably punctual, clean, and comfortable, the food excellent but expensive. They're also impressively fast to and from Paris, but more inclined to crawl on the transversal routes, i.e., those unconnected with the capital.

The French National Railroads is also the major promoter of

the remarkable **Eurailpass,** allowing you unlimited rail transportation in Western Europe, which can be purchased only in North America before you leave on your trip. Be sure to consult your travel agent about a Eurailpass if you plan to visit several European cities or countries.

There are some 44,000 miles of roadway at your disposal, most in good condition for fast, long-distance driving. But take our tip and don't stick to the Route Nationale network all the time. Nearly all the scenic splendors lie alongside the secondary roads, and what you'll lose in mileage you more than make up for in enjoyment.

But this still leaves us with the question—where to?

The answer depends entirely on your time, whim, and inclination. Here we'll give you merely a few sample tidbits, each from a contrasting area, to nudge your private decision computer.

The Château Country

About 120 miles southwest of Paris stretches the "green heart of France," the breathtakingly beautiful region of the Loire Valley. The towns of this area have magic names, but they also read like Joan of Arc's battle register—Orléans, Blois, Tours, Chinon. Every hilltop has a castle or palace, there are vineyards as far as your eye can see, the Loire winds like a silver ribbon, and the walled cities cluster around medieval churches.

Unless you're driving, we would advise you to take one of the organized tours of this region, since you couldn't see more than a fraction of its charms otherwise. **Cityrama** runs a two-day jaunt of the area, operated April through mid-November. The trip includes a visit to Chartres, Châteaudun, Tours, Langeais, Azay-le-Rideau, Vouvray, and a historical "Sound and Light" spectacle at Amboise. However, the best way to tour the Château Country is in your own rented car.

It is estimated that the average American spends only three nights in the Loire Valley. A week would be better. Even then, you will have only skimmed the surface. If you're severely hampered by lack of time, then try at least to see the following châteaux: Chenonceaux, Amboise, Azay-le-Rideau, Chambord, Chaumont, and Blois.

AMBOISE: The Loire town where the great Leonardo da Vinci died is dominated by its château, the first in the valley to show the influence of the Italian, not French, Renaissance. On a projecting rocky spur, the castle evokes the days of Charles VIII, the only child born to Louis XI. (He died at Amboise from a brain concussion after banging his head against a lintel as he was on his way to watch a fête planned for his amusement.)

The Cavalier king, François I, held court at Amboise, and invited Leonardo to come and take up residence. In 1560, the dreaded "Amboise Conspiracy" ruined all pleasant memories associated with the château. A plot by the Huguenots, protesting Catholic domination, was uncovered, and a series of mass hangings and savage decapitations followed. Reportedly, François II and his young queen (later Mary Queen of Scots) watched the executions with a certain wry amusement.

The Chapel of St. Hubert, erected on the ramparts in the 15th century, contains what are alleged to be the final remains of Leonardo (this claim is much disputed). The castle is open from 9 a.m. to noon and from 2 to 7 p.m. (till 5:30 p.m. in winter).

Before leaving Amboise, it's worthwhile to pay a visit to **Clos-Lucé,** a brick manor house of the 15th century, in which Leonardo died in 1519 after a residence of three years. Recently the room which was the scene of his death has been completely restored by the Ministry of Art. François I is said to have visited the artist through a subterranean tunnel connected with his own castle some distance away. The rooms are furnished with reproductions of the works of Da Vinci; downstairs are copies of some of his designs, including his plans for a parachute and an airplane. Amboise lies about 16 miles east of Tours, and is connected by a regular bus service.

CHENONCEAUX: The "dames of Chenonceaux" are forever linked in history with this Renaissance château. One of these ladies, Catherine Briçonnet, is largely responsible for its architecture. Another, Diane de Poitiers, the "older woman" mistress of Henri II, ruled the domain as early as 1547, and remained until she was evicted by Catherine di Medici, who became regent following the death of her errant husband. Louise de Lorraine, the widow of the effeminate king Henri III, lived at Chenonceaux and became known as "The White Queen" because of her devotion to the memory of her husband. The wife of the "farmer-general," Madame Dupin (the grandmother of George Sand) eventually acquired the château in the 18th century, and employed Rousseau as a tutor for her sons.

BLOIS: One of the most spectacular murders in French history took place here on a cold December morning, just two days before Christmas, in 1588. Fresh from the bed of his mistress, the duke of Guise was set upon by the hired assassins of the jealous Henri III. The king ordered that the Catholic leader's body be quartered and burned in one of the large fireplaces, still standing in the castle.

The "poet prince," Charles d'Orléans, is only one of the many residents who have occupied Blois. When he fathered the future Louis XII, the château began its new role as a royal residence, earning for itself the title "second capital of France." In time, François I adopted Blois as one of his many residences.

Marie di Medici was exiled to Blois by her unforgiving son Louis XIII, but she escaped by sliding down a rope and swimming across the moat. Blois was also the home of another exiled member of royalty, Gaston d'Orléans.

In the courtyard the span of centuries of French architecture can be dramatically witnessed; styles range from those of the 13th century to a wing built by François Mansart in the 1630s. Note especially the François I wing, with its celebrated spiral stairway.

CHAUMONT: Diane de Poitiers, mistress of Henri II, was banished here by Catherine di Medici after Henri died and she became regent of France. The legendary beauty—accused of working magic to keep Henri's affections from waning—didn't like Chaumont and didn't live there long. It's hard to understand her dislike.

In exile from Paris, Madame de Staël once lived here, hating "that man" (Napoleon). The château and its grounds were privately owned until they were acquired by the state in the years shortly before World War II. Inside, look for the stunning collection of medallions designed by the celebrated Nini of Italy (one is of Benjamin Franklin when he was a guest at Chaumont).

CHAMBORD: The largest château in the Loire Valley, Chambord represents the zenith of the French Renaissance. It was a favorite residence of the Cavalier king, François I. In time, it witnessed a parade of other bedfellows, ranging from Catherine di Medici to Henri III, to Gaston d'Orléans and his celebrated daughter, La Grande Mademoiselle, who used to gallop up and down the much-publicized spiral staircase. One night at Chambord, Molière's troupe of players performed *Monsieur de Pour-ceaugnac* for the Sun King, Louis XIV.

AZAY-LE-RIDEAU: A private residence of Renaissance France, Azay-le-Rideau is the favorite château of many. Its machicolated towers and moat, its white swans gliding by, and its parklike grounds, invite visitors to linger long. The château was built by Gilles Berthelot, the financial minister of François I. Subsequently, the Cavalier king—perhaps jealous—took over possession himself.

The interior is richly decorated, and contains an important banqueting hall with 17th-century Flemish tapestries. From the windows of the so-called Monarch's Chamber on the second floor, Balzac described the scenery in his *The Lily of the Valley.*

TOURS: Tours doesn't boast a château, but most Americans prefer it, nevertheless, as their center for exploring the eastern sector of the Loire Valley. It stands at the junction of the Cher and Loire Rivers, and was, in medieval days, the most famous pilgrimage center in all of Europe, attracting the faithful stopping off to honor St. Martin, the Apostle of Gaul. Visit at least the **Cathedral of St-Gatien,** with its flamboyant Gothic facade and 13th-century choir.

ANGERS: This former capital of Anjou, on the banks of the Maine River, has recovered from its extensive damage suffered in World War II. It makes a good center for exploring the château district in the west. The former home of the counts of Anjou, the **Castle of Angers** (tel. 87-43-47) is visited chiefly by those wishing to see the celebrated Apocalypse Tapestries, the most outstanding example of that art form to come down from the Middle Ages. The tapestries here were made by Nicolas Bataille in Paris between 1370 and 1380. The cost of entry is 8F ($1.43). Nearby stands the **Cathedral of St-Maurice,** dating from the 12th and 13th centuries, with stained-glass windows illustrating such scenes as the martyrdom of St. Vincent.

COUR-CHEVERNY: The 17th century lives on! Different from most of the châteaux of the Loire, Cour-Cheverny is still privately owned and inhabited by a descendant of its founding fathers, the marquis de Vibraye. Some of the most fashionable people of

Paris come to his estate for hunts. The château was constructed in a classic Louis XIII style, with two square pavilions. Interiors are richly furnished with antiques, tapestries, and a Jean Mosnier fireplace tracing the legend of Adonis.

LANGEAIS: One of the most impressive medieval fortresses remaining in the Loire, Langeais was built in the reign of Louis XI. Its greatest moment occurred on December 6, 1491, with the marriage of Anne of Brittany to Charles VIII. The event took place in the Wedding Chamber, which can be visited today on an organized tour.

VILLANDRY: This château melds the Middle Ages into the Renaissance. It is visited mainly for its gardens, which contain almost 11 miles of boxwood "sculpture"; the present gardens date from the 19th century, when they were restored by Dr. Carvallo, the founder of "La Demeure Historique." The different terraces are almost like a storybook, each illuminating a different theme.

Hours are from 8:30 a.m. to 8 p.m. without interruption. The garden is open all year long; the château, from March 30 to November 11.

VALENÇAY: Napoleon wanted Talleyrand to have a prestigious residence in which he could receive heads of state in a setting that would "reflect favorably upon the glory of France." Valençay was selected in 1803. Not all the guests were pleased with the hospitality, particularly Ferdinand VII of Spain, who was kept here for six years against his will. Talleyrand, the brilliant minister of foreign affairs, was buried at Valençay in 1838; a museum established here in 1953 honors him today by preserving numerous historical mementoes of the prince.

Drop in at the central tourist office at Tours (near the railway station) to pick up a folder listing visiting hours at the châteaux throughout the Loire. As a general rule, the châteaux open at 8 a.m., close for noon lunch, then reopen from 2 to 6 p.m. in summer (and till either 4:30 p.m. or 5 p.m. in winter).

Mont St-Michel

Massive walls, more than half a mile in circumference, enclose what is considered one of the greatest sightseeing attractions in Europe. At the border between Normandy and Brittany, the citadel crowns a rocky islet. Seen for miles around, the rock rises 260 feet high.

The tides around Mont St-Michel are notorious, having claimed lives. They are reputedly the highest on the continent of Europe. At particular times of the year, they rise upward to 50 feet. It is dangerous to wander across the sands around the mount. Many have been trapped in quicksands.

A causeway links the granite hilltop to the mainland. A Benedictine monastery was founded on this spot in 966 by Richard I, Duke of Normandy. It was destroyed by fire in 1203, but subsequently rebuilt. One of the most important Gothic masterpieces in Europe, the "Merveille" (Marvel), is enclosed by ramparts. The abbey church dates from the 11th century, and is noted for its flamboyant Gothic choir, as well as a Romanesque nave and transept.

The abbey stays open year round, and you must take a guided tour to see it. However, tours leave every 15 minutes and last less than an hour.

Those journeying here from Paris by train have to get off at Pontorson. This is the nearest station to "The Mont," although it is six miles away. Bus connections take you to the abbey.

While in Mont St-Michel, it's customary to order one of the legendary omelets at **La Mère Poulard,** which you'll see on your right as you begin your long climb to the abbey.

Reims and Verdun

This means a journey to the memory of two World Wars. Reims, 100 miles northeast of Paris, has one of mankind's greatest Gothic cathedrals. Dating from the 13th century, it was almost reduced to rubble by shellfire in 1914–1918, then painstakingly rebuilt with funds from a Rockefeller grant. It also contains the schoolhouse in which the Germans surrendered on May 7, 1945.

Nearby Verdun marks France's bloodiest battle epic. The old fortress town created the motto "They shall not pass!" They didn't . . . but the price was terrible, and the relics of that 1916 stand make somber viewing.

But the country all around is the champagne region, where you can sample the most splendid of all wines right at the source.

Dinard and St-Malo

These enchanting resort towns in Brittany, on the northwest coast, face each other across an estuary. St-Malo, an ancient pirates' stronghold and walled fishing village, is the more colorful; Dinard, with a gambling casino, sheltered beach, golf courses, and tennis courts, the more playful. Since they're only a boat hop apart, you can enjoy both in one trip. The scenery all around is superb.

Brittany is fascinatingly "alien," the native Breton a Celtic language more akin to Gaelic than to French. The entire peninsula has 600 miles of coast, with chains of beaches, rustic fishing ports, and some of the greatest seafood you'll ever taste.

Languedoc and Provence

The Rhône River forms the dividing line between Languedoc in the west and Provence in the east. Both portions are equally drenched in sunshine, sprinkled with vineyards and olive groves, and dotted with fascinating towns. The main difference is that Languedoc has an intriguing Spanish air and is somewhat less fashionable and expensive than Provence.

Two of its most charming cities are **Nîmes** and **Montpellier,** only 31 miles apart. Nîmes contains the most impressive Roman remains in France, including an Arena and the Temple of Diana. Montpellier is the center of southern wine production and lies in a scenic setting of unsurpassed beauty.

Provence, on the east side of the Rhône River, can be divided into two units from the vacation viewpoint. The portion closer to the Rhône is studded with fascinating towns—large and tiny —each of which provides a holiday setting.

There's **Avignon,** surrounded by ancient ramparts and the seat of the popes during the 14th century. **Arles** cast a spell over Van Gogh and inspired some of his greatest paintings. And **Marseille,** the second-largest city in France, is one of the world's major seaports and the most colorful, turbulent, and exotic place in the country.

The French Riviera

Now we come to France's sunny south, her holiday region par excellence. Known to the world as the **Côte d'Azur,** this is a short stretch of curving coastline near the Italian border. Much to the delight of holiday makers from all parts of the globe, it's a land drenched in sunshine, sprinkled with vineyards and olive groves, and dotted with some of the world's most fascinating tourist meccas.

The season doesn't start till June and lasts only till September, although many shrewd travelers prefer the months of May and October. During those out-of-favor periods, the crowds often drop by more than 70%, the prices by about 20%. The Riviera can give you then exactly what the travel posters promise.

Although making it impossible for swimming, the winter temperature is higher than in the rest of France, mainly because of the Alpine chain that protects the Côte d'Azur from those cold continental winds. Hence, many towns, such as Menton, have long enjoyed a thriving colony of expatriate visitors, drawn to such rich Mediterranean vegetation as the mimosa, the rose-laurel, jasmine, carnation, rose, the creeping and crawling bougainvillea, the eucalyptus fluttering in the sea breezes, and the inevitable orange and lemon trees studding the hillside. Nice, by the way, claims only three days of frost, the average January temperature hovering around 48 degrees Fahrenheit. In October, the average temperature at Nice is about 77 degrees Fahrenheit.

Perhaps the most compelling endorsement of the Riviera has been the number of artists drawn to its shores and hillside villas. At Cagnes, Renoir praised the "light effects" of the region. Bonnard stayed at Le Cannet. Nice was selected by Matisse as the spot in which to spend the remaining years of his life (you can visit his remarkable Chapel of Saint Dominique at Vence). For the fishermen of Villefranche, Cocteau decorated a chapel. Picasso left an art legacy from one end of the Riviera to the other. Even on one of the rainy days that occasionally occur, you can enjoy an "art-hopping" tour, seeing some of the most interesting contemporary work in Europe, such as the Léger Museum at Biot.

A trio of roads or corniches connects Nice with the Italian frontier, and stretches a distance of 20 miles. The Middle Corniche, finished at the outbreak of World War II, was created specifically for tourists, although they didn't see fit to use it extensively until many years had passed. Motorists taking this route, even rushed motorists, should stop off at the "eagle's nest" village of Eze, resting on a peak more than 1312 feet above sea level. Originally, Napoleon ordered the construction of the

Grand Corniche to replace the old Roman Aurelian Way. The Shoreline Corniche is in many ways the most interesting. You don't get the lofty spectacular views afforded by the two other motor roads, but you do receive a firsthand preview of the string of resorts dotting the coastline, including Saint-Jean-Cap-Ferrat, where W. Somerset Maugham lived for so many years.

Selecting your resort might be your most difficult decision, as there are at least 26 of them, spread out along a distance of 70 miles from Menton to Saint-Raphaël, their degree of joie de vivre varying widely. Nearly all of them have one thing in common—an excellent range of hotel facilities. The Côte d'Azur is one of the most heavily built-up hotel districts in the world, with some 150 establishments in the three- or four-star categories, some 850 hotels in the more moderately priced, yet still comfortable, two- or three-star brackets. From the most elegantly furnished "palace" to the more modest converted once-private villa that now receives paying guests, you'll nearly always find an accommodation to fit your tastes and your pocketbook.

Of course, one of the reasons visitors come to the Riviera is to dine.

Do try some of the specialties, especially the salade Niçoise, which can mean anything to every other chef, but essentially includes fresh vine-ripened tomatoes, small radishes—either red or black—green peppers, and often potatoes, and green beans. The thick, saffron-flavored fish soup of the Mediterranean, the bouillabaisse, is eagerly ordered by diners all over the Riviera, as is the ratatouille (a mixture of small eggplants, tomatoes, miniature squash, and red peppers simmered in olive oil).

NICE: Nice is the largest city, the official capital of the Riviera. Spread out along the Bay of Angels, it borders its seafront with the Promenade des Anglais, which was constructed in the 1820s to meet the demands of the considerable English colony that spent its winters on the French Mediterranean. Its open-air vegetable and flower markets draw the camera fans, and its Old Town of narrow streets and budget restaurants suggests what the resort used to be like before the days of the present widespread building boom.

In accommodations, it offers more than 300 hotels, some of which are the most economical along the entire stretch of the Riviera. Perhaps the best time to visit is during the period of the Nice Carnival, highlighted by the "Battle of the Flowers" and the flower-draped floats with the fabled beauties of the Riviera. The festivities are climaxed by the burning of King Carnival on his pyre. Those without private transportation may want to anchor into the capital, which boasts the largest number of excursion possibilities—such as the high-altitude Alpine resorts —of any other oasis on the Côte d'Azur. However, the devotee of pure sandy beaches will not like Nice, as its coast is strewn with pebbles. Incidentally, in the old aristocratic quarter of Cimiez, you can visit the Musée Matisse, an 18th-century mansion set in an archeological garden of ancient Nice, and containing more than 40 drawings and canvases by the late artist. Also in Cimiez, the state has built a museum to house works by Chagall. The Russian-born artist donated the collection to the French people in 1966 and 1972. The museum opened in June 1973 on the occasion of Chagall's 86th birthday.

CANNES: Although Nice is the official queen, Cannes is the unofficial social capital, having acquired fame in 1834 with the arrival of Lord Brougham. Its bars are sophisticated, its cars snazzy, its yachts colossal, and its prices just as high or higher than anyplace else along the coastline. Its population of starlets per square yard of beach is more plentiful and pulchritudinous than anywhere else; and its Boulevard de la Croisette is called the chicest in the world.

On the Bay of the Gulf of La Napoule, Cannes is a major port of call for great ocean-going liners. Its spring Film Festival draws movie stars in Europe and America. Two casinos operate, one in summer, the other in winter. Cannes is also the embarkation port for the Lérins Islands (St-Marguerite and St-Honorat, the former said to have sheltered the prisoner known as "The Man in the Iron Mask").

MONACO: The Principality of Monaco, that little kingdom of Prince Rainier and Princess Grace, is actually a sovereign state in miniature—and it's been one for six centuries. But you don't need to clear customs or have your passport stamped to enter, as its frontier is "invisible." Its social life is among the most fashionable in Europe, centering around the fabled Casino and the activities of the International Sporting Club. The Casino is life blood for the Monégasques. In the old days, you might spot King Farouk there, his stomach stuffed with half a dozen game hens, blandly losing thousands of dollars.

Although small, Monaco condenses its scenery and sights beautifully. Its actual man-made sights are minor, of course, but include, in summer only, the State Apartments of the Prince's Palace, as well as an important Oceanographic Museum founded by Prince Albert in 1910. In addition, the little principality is the home of the Monaco Grand Prix and the Monte-Carlo Rally.

Some of the most luxurious boutiques and some of the most elegant villas in all of Europe are to be found at Monaco. Actually, the whole thing is rather story-bookish—complete with the film star queen and the lack of an income tax. In all, it's the Riviera's Shangri-La, suffused with that ever-present hope of breaking the bank at Monte Carlo.

ST. TROPEZ: It's small—but so was the Bardot bikini that made it celebrated. Even before the advent of the blonde bombshell, the resort was known to such widely diverse female writers as Colette and Anaïs Nin. Don't be surprised if, while dining on the waterfront, you witness a yacht arriving to discharge an elegantly attired married couple and the "girlfriend" they share. St. Tropez is very sophisticated.

If you're under 30, fairly well heeled, and are so devastatingly attractive your admirers chase you across at least two continents, then this little resort is for you. In fact, you're probably already well known there. If you're none of the above, then you still might make the grade by pretending to have at least two movie credits to your name.

Once this old Provençal port was the haunt of artists. The works or paintings they left behind are exhibited today in a little museum, the Chapel of the Annunciation, near the waterfront. In summer, St. Tropez is jampacked, but that's why you go.

Chamonix–Mont Blanc

At an altitude of 3422 feet, Chamonix, opening onto Mont Blanc, is the historic capital of Alpine skiing. Chamonix lies huddled in a valley, almost at the junction of France, Italy, and Switzerland. Dedicated skiers all over the world know of its ten-mile Vallée Blanche run, considered one of the most rugged in Europe, certainly the longest. Daredevils also flock here for the mountain climbing and the hang-gliding.

A charming, old-fashioned mountain town, Chamonix has a most thrilling backdrop—Mont Blanc, Europe's highest mountain, rising to a peak of 15,780 feet.

With the opening of the seven-mile miracle, Mont Blanc Tunnel, Chamonix became a major stage on one of the busiest highways in Europe. The tunnel provides the easiest way to go through the mountains to Italy, by literally going under those mountains. Motorists now stop at Chamonix even if they aren't interested in winter skiing or summer mountain climbing.

Because of its exceptional equipment, Chamonix is one of the major resorts of Europe, attracting a sophisticated international crowd. The Casino de Chamonix is the hub of its nightlife activity.

Strasbourg

Capital of Alsace, Strasbourg is one of France's greatest cities. It is also the capital of pâté de foie gras. It was in Strasbourg that Rouget de Lisle first sang the "Marseillaise." In June of every year, the artistic life of Strasbourg reaches its zenith at the International Music Festival held at the Château des Rohan and the cathedral.

Strasbourg is not only a great university city, the seat of the Council of Europe, but one of France's most important ports, lying two miles west of the Rhine. Visits by motor launch and a number of Rhine excursions are offered from there. Go to the tourist office at the Place Gutenberg for the most up-to-date data on these excursions, whose schedules vary, depending on the season and the number of passengers interested.

Despite war damage, much remains of Old Strasbourg. It still has covered bridges and the old towers of its former fortifications, and many 15th-and 17th-century dwellings with painted wooden fronts and carved beams.

The Strasbourg Cathedral, which inspired the poetry of Goethe, was built on the site of a Romanesque church of 1015. Today it stands proudly, one of the largest churches of Christianity, and one of the most outstanding examples of German Gothic, representing a harmonious transition from the Romanesque. Construction on it began in 1176.

Nancy

In the northeastern corner of France, about 200 miles from Paris, Nancy was the capital of old Lorraine. On the Meurthe River, it is serenely beautiful, with a historic tradition, a cuisine, and an architecture all its own. Nancy has a kind of triple face—the medieval alleys and towers around the old Ducal Palace where Charles VII received Joan of Arc, the golden gates and frivolous fountains of the rococo period, and the constantly spreading modern sections with their university and booming industry.

Its heartbeat, of course, is the Place Stanislas, where you may want to head first. It was named for Stanislaus Leszczynska, the last of the dukes of Lorraine, the ex-king of Poland, and the father-in-law of Louis XV. The most imposing building on the square is the Hôtel de Ville. On the eastern side of the square, the Musée des Beaux-Arts contains one of Manet's most remarkable portraits.

The Arc de Triomphe, constructed in 1754–1756 by Stanislas to honor Louis XV, brings you to the long Place de la Carrière, a beautiful, tree-lined promenade, leading to the Palais du Gouvernement, built in 1760.

DOMRÉMY-LA-PUCELLE: A pilgrimage center attracting flocks of visitors from all over the world, Domrémy is a simple hamlet that would be overlooked except for one event. Joan of Arc was born there in 1412. There she saw the visions and heard the voices that led her to play out her historic role as the heroine of France. The Lorraine village lies 6½ miles from Neufchâteau, 35½ miles from Nancy.

A residence traditionally considered the Arc family house, near the church, is known as the "Maison Natale de Jeanne d'Arc," and can be visited. It is a simple stone cottage with a *chambre natale* that is as bleak as the January morning in which the maid was born. Beside the house is a small museum relating the epic of Joan of Arc on film.

Only the tower of the church remains where Joan was baptized. However, above the village, on a slope of the Bois-Chenu, the Basilique du Bois-Chenu was commenced in 1881 and consecrated in 1926. The tree that in spring was "lovely as a lily," and was believed to be haunted by "faery ladies," doesn't exist anymore.

Grenoble

The ancient capital of Dauphiné, this city is a major target for those exploring the heart of the French Alps. As the commercial, intellectual, and tourist center of the Alps, it is a logical stopping-off point for motorists traveling between the Riviera and Geneva. It is a sports capital in both winter and summer, and attracts many foreign students, since its university has the largest summer-sessions program in Europe. The university occupies a modern campus on the outskirts of the city, and many buildings erected for the 1968 Olympic games have been put to creative uses.

For orientation, you might head for the Place Grenette, which is a lively square made all the more so with beautiful Alpine flowers in late spring and summer. Everybody at some point in a busy day seems to stop off at this traffic-free mall, enjoying a drink or a cup of espresso. Pastel-colored sidewalk chairs are placed around table medallions. This square enjoys many associations with Standhal, who was born Henri Beyle at Grenoble in 1783 and went on to write such masterpieces as *The Red and the Black* and *The Charterhouse of Parma*.

Having soaked up some atmosphere, we'd suggest a ride on the Téléférique de la Bastille. These high-swinging cable cars swing out over the Isère River. From the belvedere where you land, you'll have a panoramic view of the city and the surrounding mountains. If you want to walk, you can return on foot. Signs point the way to the Parc de la Bastille, the Parc Guy-Pape, leading, eventually, to the Jardin des Dauphins.

Or if you prefer, from the Belvédère de Grenoble, you can take the Télésiège Bastille-Mont Jalla for an even loftier view of the environs. To board the car in Grenoble, head for the Gare de Depart, on the Quai Stéphane-Jay, facing the Jardin de Ville.

The next major sight is the Musée de Grenoble, Place de Verdun, one of the best art galleries in provincial France. The collection, however, is hardly provincial. Its fabulous modern art includes works by Utrillo and Modigliani, along with Léger's *La Danse* or a Klee or Max Ernst, perhaps Miró's *Composition*.

Finally, Grenoble has a dazzling Maison de la Culture, which stages everything from exhibits of Impressionists to cinema showings, along with orchestral concerts, perhaps a dance troupe from Tunisia.

The Heartlands

In your race south to Biarritz or through the Rhône Valley to the Riviera, you'll penetrate the heartlands of France, which remain unknown to the average North American visitor, except the most discerning who has ventured into this region. They have often returned with tales of ancient cities, lovely valleys, and of a provincial cuisine that makes one dream of going back to savor the delicacies and specialties.

With its grottoes and cave paintings, its châteaux and manor houses (many of which you can stay and dine in), and its rolling countryside, it is perhaps the most unspoiled and untainted part of France—your chance to see and be part of a life all too quickly fading.

This is a large, varied territory, containing the capitals of the old provinces—Clermont-Ferrand, capital of Auvergne; Limoges, capital of Limousin; Périgueux, capital of Périgord; and Cahors, capital of Quercy.

From the spa at Vichy to the volcanic *puys* of Auvergne, there is much to interest the visitor, and much to learn of the art of good living.

We'll follow with a few thumbnail sketches:

BOURGES: Once the capital of the Aquitaine, Bourges lies in the geographical heart of France, 95 miles northwest of Vichy, 175 miles northwest from Lyon. It can easily be visited from Orléans, at the end of your eastern trek through the Loire Valley. The commercial and industrial center of Berry, this regional capital is still off the beaten path for much tourism, even though it has a rich medieval past still very much in evidence today. Its history goes back far beyond the Middle Ages. Caesar called it one of the most beautiful places in Gaul. Joan of Arc spent the winter of 1429–1430 here.

On the summit of a hill, dominating the town, the Cathédrale de St-Étienne is one of the most beautiful Gothic cathedrals of France. It was begun at the end of the 12th century and completed half a century later, although subsequent additions were made. Flanked by two asymmetrical towers, it has five magnificent doorways, including one depicting episodes in the life of St. Stephen, to whom the cathedral is dedicated. In harmonious splendor, with a high vaulted roof, the cathedral has five aisles and is remarkably long, 407 feet deep, one of the largest Gothic cathedrals in the country. Mostly the Bourges cathedral is distinguished by its stained-glass windows, among the finest in France.

VICHY: This world-famous spa on the north edge of Auvergne—noted for its sparkling waters—looks much as it did some 80 years ago when the princes and industrial barons filled its rococo casino. From 1861 Napoleon III was a frequent visitor, doing much to add to the spa's fame throughout Europe. However, by the 1980s the clients and their tastes have changed. In recent years Vichy has begun a major step in sprucing up its hotels and modernizing its baths. In that, it has been successful. It caters not only to the elderly, but is a modern city for health and relaxation, aided in no small part by the Perrier craze that has swept not only Europe, but North America.

The Perrier Company has a contract to bottle Vichy water for sale elsewhere, and it also runs the city's major attractions. The chief spa of France, Vichy lies on the Allier River, 227 miles from Paris and 108 miles west-northwest of Lyon. In World War II, Vichy was the seat of the collaborationist government under Marshal Pétain.

Gardens separate the town from the Allier. The spa waters are said to alleviate liver and stomach ailments. Vichy is a sports and recreation center, with a casino, theaters, regattas, horse racing, and golf.

A promenade with covered walks, the Parc des Sources, is the center of the spa's fashionable life. At night it is brilliantly illuminated. Le Grand Casino, the Hall des Sources, the Galerie Napoléon, and the Grand Établissement Thermal (the largest treatment center of its kind in Europe) are found here. The baths can be visited.

CLERMONT-FERRAND: The ancient capital of Auvergne, this old double city in south-central France has looked down on a long parade of history. On the small Tiretaine River, it lies 112 miles west of Lyon, and was created in 1731 by a merger of two towns, Clermont and Montferrand. It is surrounded by hills, and in the distance is one of the great attractions of France, Puy-de-Dôme (you may want to take an excursion to this volcanic mountain later).

To begin your tour, head for the center of Clermont, the bustling Place de Jaude, where you can sample a glass of regional wine at a café—under the shade of a catalpa tree—before taking in the rue du 11 Novembre, branching off from the main plaza. This street leads to the rue des Gras, the most colorful and interesting in Clermont.

Built of dark volcanic stone, the Cathedral of Notre-Dame is one of the great Gothic churches of central France, dating primarily from the 13th and 14th centuries, although it witnessed later additions in the 19th century. After leaving the cathedral you can explore Vieux Clermont, a small surrounding sector which contains many old houses of the 16th to the 18th centuries, notably the Maison de Savaron.

One of the finest examples of the Auvergnat Romanesque style of architecture is Église Notre-Dame-du-Port, dating from the 11th and 12th centuries and rising in the northeastern part of town.

About 1¼ miles northeast of town is the shrunken and somnolent Montferrand, once socially elegant and wealthy. It contains many ancient houses with beautiful courtyards, including one dedicated to an elephant, another to Adam and Eve. Many of these Gothic and Renaissance houses are in excellent states of preservation.

LIMOGES: The ancient capital of Limousin, Limoges is a town in west-central France famous for its exquisite porcelain and enamel works, the latter a medieval industry revived in the 19th century. Rising on the right bank of the Vienne, the town historically has had two parts, the Cité, its narrow streets and old maisons occupying the lower slope, and the town proper at the summit.

If you'd like to see an enameller or a porcelain factory, go to the local office of the Syndicat d'Initiative (tourist office) on the Boulevard de Fleurus which will supply you with a list of workshops to visit.

The Musée National Adrien-Dubouché displays a beautiful collection of Limoges china. The museum is second in France only to Sèvres in its porcelain collection. Its galleries trace the entire history of chinaware, including not only that in Europe, but in Japan and China as well. The location is at the park, Place du Champ-de-Foire.

PÉRIGUEUX: Gastronomes speak of it as a "land of foie gras and truffles." Throughout France you'll see dishes appearing on menus with the appendage of "à la Perigourdine." That means a garnish of truffles, the tastiest fungus nature ever provided. Foie gras is sometimes added as well.

Capital of the province of Périgord, Périgueux stands on the Isle River, about 70 miles east-northeast of Bordeaux and some 63 miles south and slightly west of Limoges. In addition to its food products, the region is known for its Roman ruins and medieval churches.

The city is divided into three separate sections—the old Roman town or Cité, the medieval town on the slope of the hill, and, to the west, the modern town.

In the medieval quarter, known as Le Puy St-Front, the Cathédrale de St-Front was built from 1125 to 1150, the last of the Aquitanian domed churches. Dedicated to St. Fronto, a local bishop, it is one of the largest churches in southwest France.

ROCAMADOUR: The Middle Ages seem to live on here. After all, Rocamadour reached the zenith of its fame and prosperity in the 13th century. Try to make an effort to see it, even if it is out of your way—34 miles from Brive, 39 miles from Cahors. The setting is striking, one of the most unusual in Europe. Towers, old buildings, and oratories rise in stages up the side of a cliff on the right slope of the usually dry gorge of Alzou. The gravity-defying village, with its single street (lined with souvenir shops), is boldly constructed. It is seen at its best when approached from the road coming in from the tiny village of L'Hospitalet. Once in Rocamadour, you can take a flight of steps from the lower town to the churches halfway up the cliff. The less agile would be advised to take the elevator instead.

The entrance to the village is through the Porte de Figuier ("fig tree gateway"), through which many of the most illustrious Europeans of the 13th century passed. One of the oldest places of pilgrimage in France, Rocamadour became famous as a cult center of the Black Madonna. The village was supposedly founded by Zacchaeus who had entertained Christ at Jericho. He is said to have come to Rocamadour with a small black wooden statue of the Madonna (some authorities have suggested that this statue was actually carved in the ninth century A.D.).

At the Place de la Carreta, the entrance is found to the Grand Escalier (stairway), leading to the ecclesiastical center at the top. It is a climb of 216 steps. Even today, pilgrims make the difficult journey on their knees.

CAHORS: The ancient capital of Quercy, Cahors was a thriving university city in the Middle Ages, and many antiquities of its illustrious past life still remain. But Cahors is known today mainly for its almost-legendary red wine which is made principally from the Malbec grape grown in vineyards around this old city, 55 miles north of Toulouse in central France. Firm but not harsh, Cahors is considered one of the most deeply colored of fine French red wines.

The town lies on a rocky peninsula almost entirely surrounded by a loop of the Lot River. It grew up near a sacred spring which, incidentally, still supplies Cahors with water. At the source of the spring, the Fontaine des Chartreux stands by the side of the Pont Valentré, a bridge with a trio of towers, a magnificent example of medieval defensive design, erected between 1308 and 1380, although much restored in the 19th century. The pont, the first medieval fortified bridge in France, is the most colorful site in Cahors, with its crenellated parapets, its battlements, and its seven pointed arches.

Dominating the old town, the Cathédrale St-Étienne was built in 1119, but reconstructed in part between 1285 and 1500. It appears like a fortress, and was the first cathedral in the country to have cupolas, giving it a Romanesque-Byzantine appearance.

Cahors is a starting point for excursions to the Célé and Lot Valleys, which is a long, colorful journey that many French people are fond of taking in the summer, a round trip of about 125 miles, lasting some two days if you leave plenty of time for sightseeing. The tourist office in Cahors provides maps giving itineraries.

Le Pont des Arts

NOW, SAVE MONEY ON ALL YOUR TRAVELS!
Join Arthur Frommer's $15-A-Day Travel Club

Saving money while traveling is never a simple matter, which is why, almost 20 years ago, the **$15-a-Day Travel Club** was formed. Actually, the idea came from readers of the Arthur Frommer Publications who felt that such an organization could bring financial benefits, continuing travel information, and a sense of community to economy-minded travelers all over the world.

In keeping with the money-saving concept, the membership fee is low—$14 (U.S. residents) or $16 (Canadian, Mexican, and foreign residents)—and is immediately exceeded by the value of your benefits which include:

(1) An annual subscription to an 8-page tabloid newspaper *The Wonderful World of Budget Travel* which keeps you up-to-date on fast-breaking developments in low-cost travel in all parts of the world—bringing you the kind of information you'd have to pay over $25 a year to obtain elsewhere. This consumer-conscious publication also provides special services to readers:

Traveler's Directory—a list of members all over the world who are willing to provide hospitality to other members as they pass through their home cities.

Share-a-Trip—requests from members for travel companions who can share costs and help avoid the burdensome single supplement.

Readers Ask . . . Readers Reply—travel questions from members to which other members reply with authentic firsthand information.

(2) The latest edition of any TWO of the books listed on the following page.

(3) A copy of *Arthur Frommer's Guide to New York*.

(4) Your personal membership card which entitles you to purchase through the Club all Arthur Frommer Publications for a third to a half off their regular retail prices during the term of your membership.

So why not join this hardy band of international budgeteers NOW and participate in its exchange of information and hospitality? Simply send U.S. $14 (U.S. residents) or $16 (Canadian, Mexican, and other foreign residents) along with your name and address to: $15-A-Day Travel Club, Inc., 1230 Avenue of the Americas, New York, NY 10020. Remember to specify which *two* of the books in section (2) above you wish to receive in your initial package of members' benefits. Or tear out this page, check off any two books on the opposite side and send it to us with your membership fee.